REVOLUTION

Volume 23

THE PORTUGUESE ARMED FORCES AND THE REVOLUTION

THE PORTUGUESE ARMED FORCES AND THE REVOLUTION

DOUGLAS PORCH

LONDON AND NEW YORK

First published in 1977 by Croom Helm Ltd

This edition first published in 2022
by Routledge
4 Park Square, Milton Park, Abingdon, Oxon OX14 4RN

and by Routledge
605 Third Avenue, New York, NY 10158

Routledge is an imprint of the Taylor & Francis Group, an informa business

© 1977 Douglas Porch

All rights reserved. No part of this book may be reprinted or reproduced or utilised in any form or by any electronic, mechanical, or other means, now known or hereafter invented, including photocopying and recording, or in any information storage or retrieval system, without permission in writing from the publishers.

Trademark notice: Product or corporate names may be trademarks or registered trademarks, and are used only for identification and explanation without intent to infringe.

British Library Cataloguing in Publication Data
A catalogue record for this book is available from the British Library

ISBN: 978-1-032-12623-4 (Set)
ISBN: 978-1-003-26095-0 (Set) (ebk)
ISBN: 978-1-032-12825-2 (Volume 23) (hbk)
ISBN: 978-1-032-12827-6 (Volume 23) (pbk)
ISBN: 978-1-003-22637-6 (Volume 23) (ebk)

DOI: 10.4324/9781003226376

Publisher's Note
The publisher has gone to great lengths to ensure the quality of this reprint but points out that some imperfections in the original copies may be apparent.

Disclaimer
The publisher has made every effort to trace copyright holders and would welcome correspondence from those they have been unable to trace.

THE PORTUGUESE ARMED FORCES AND THE REVOLUTION

DOUGLAS PORCH

CROOM HELM LONDON
THE HOOVER INSTITUTION PRESS
Stanford, California, USA

© 1977 Douglas Porch
Croom Helm Ltd, 2-10
2-10 St John's Road, London SW11

British Library Cataloguing in Publication Data:

Porch, Douglas
    The Portuguese armed forces and the revolution.
    1. Portugal – History – 1974 – 2. Portugal –
    Politics and government – 1974 – 3. Portugal –
    Armed Forces – Political activity
    I. Title
    946.9'042   DP680
    ISBN 0-85664-391-2

Hoover Institution Publication 188

Printed in Great Britain
by Redwood Burn Ltd, Trowbridge and Esher

CONTENTS

Preface

1 The Politics of the Portuguese Army 1910–1974	9
2 Colonies and Coups: Portugal's Colonial Wars	28
3 Professional Officers and 'Temporary Gentlemen'	61
4 Spínola's Summer	90
5 The Struggle for Power	124
6 11 March	154
7 The Resistance	191
8 25 November	222
Appendix I Telegram to Porto Combatants' Congress	239
Appendix II The Armed Forces and the Nation	240
Appendix III The MFA Programme, April 1974	244
Appendix IV The MFA: Liberation Movement June 1975	248
Appendix V Governments	259
Appendix VI Naval Academy: Professions of Fathers of Cadets, 1975	263
Bibliography	266
Index	271

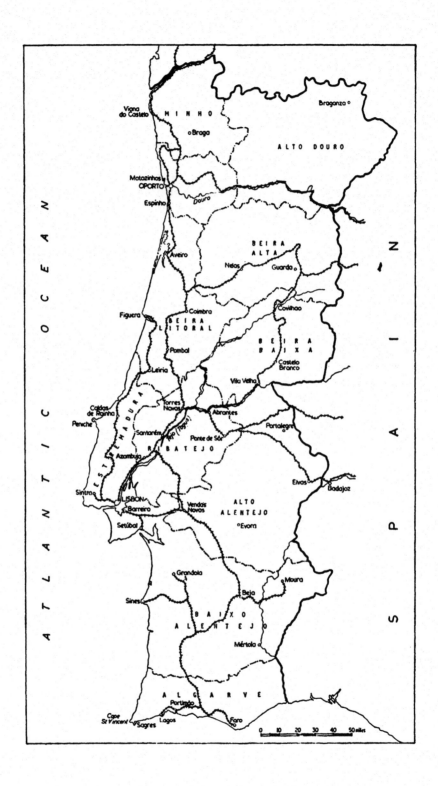

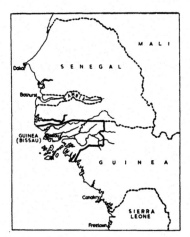

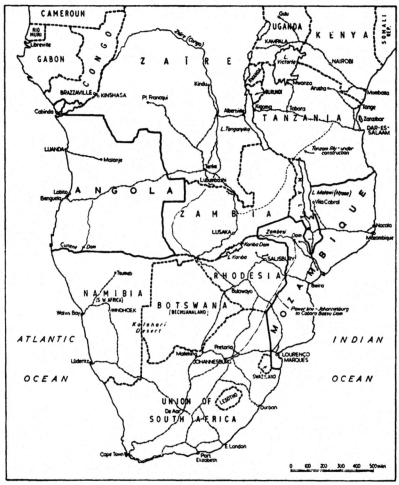

Southern Africa

PREFACE

Portugal, runs the popular stereotype, has been one of Europe's backwaters for almost three centuries. Little supposedly has happened there to attract the world's attention since Wellington's troops marched out of Torres Vedras in 1808. Its Iberian neighbour Spain has captured the lion's share of scholarly interest and political passion following each of its periodic civil wars. When the press bulletins announced on 25 April 1974, that the fifty-year-old government of Prime Ministers Salazar and Caetano had been overthrown by a military *coup*, few, admittedly, had to consult a map to find Lisbon. Most of us had been on holiday in the Algarve, read a Second World War spy adventure set in Lisbon's narrow streets, or spent an evening knocking back glasses of port on some Oxbridge high table. But we did not know how it happened, and so close to home.

This book is a study of the origins of the civil-military crisis in Portugal. Viewed in the context of Portuguese history and the experience of armies in other countries, particularly that of the French army in Algeria, the Portuguese *coup* loses much of its shock value for the West. However, the Portuguese army alone among European armies forced to fight the war of the flea' revolted against colonialism. The Portuguese revolution which followed provides a unique laboratory for the study of an army in crisis, the strains which the attempt by officers to direct the political life of the country after April 1974 placed on military organization, the traditional career patterns and attitudes of soldiers, and on discipline. It is concerned with the role of officers in government and the day-to-day problems which political upheaval created in every barracks. This is a study both of the army in politics and of politics in the army, which I have attempted to place in the broader context of the events of the revolution.

During the course of my research, I was able to interview a number of Portuguese officers in all three services, all of whom requested that their names be kept out of print. I have respected this wish. I owe them a great deal of thanks for their patience and invaluable help. The conclusions I have drawn in the book are, of course, my own.

I also owe my thanks for advice and encouragement to a number of people in the United States, Britain and Portugal, but especially to Dr. Lewis Gann, António de Figueiredo, Carl Hanson, John Vincent-Smith and Gillian Flint.

1 THE POLITICS OF THE PORTUGUESE ARMY
1910–1974

Since Clemenceau suggested over fifty years ago that war was much too important to be left to generals, soldiers on several continents seem set on proving that politics should not be left to politicians. In the Arab world, black Africa and Latin America, the gun-toting politician appears well entrenched, while uniformed general-presidents are not unknown in Asia. Nor is Europe a complete stranger to military meddling in high places. Frequent recourse to the 'whiff of grape shot' to quell popular disturbances and the disproportionate influence of military chiefs, especially in wartime, has sometimes led governments to lean heavily on their military arm. Wilhelmine Germany is perhaps the best example of a modern European government fallen under the spell of its service chiefs. Bismarck's efforts to bridle the elder Moltke, his chief of staff, eventually came unstuck in a jamboree of military parades and politics. Thus, von Tirpitz was allowed to plan his navy unmindful of international consequences, von Schlieffen to draw up his grand offensive unhindered by 'political' considerations, the younger Moltke to give guarantees to Austrian Chief of Staff Conrad in 1914, and finally Ludendorff and Hindenburg to rule Germany behind the thinnest trappings of civilian power during the last two years of the war. Few governments after 1939, least of all Hitler's, allowed this phenomenon to repeat itself.

Since 1945, decolonisation has placed the greatest strain upon civil-military relations in Europe. Great Britain mercifully wrote off her Empire without a fight. Belgium needed only the slightest arm-twisting to pack up and go home. But the continent's two other substantial colonial powers, France and Portugal, opted to learn their lessons the hard way.

Some political commentators, the historians Kenneth Maxwell and Márcio Alves among them, view the stubborn refusal of Salazar and Caetano to call it a day in the colonies as the logical corollary of Portugal's economic dependence on Africa. As America's claims in Vietnam about assuring the boundaries of the 'free world' and halting 'international bolshevism' dead in its tracks were seen by many as a smokescreen to cover economic imperialism, so Portuguese talk about a historic and civilizing mission in Africa is brushed aside as the cynical

10   *The Politics of the Portuguese Army, 1910-1974*

propaganda of a doddering dictatorship. Kenneth Maxwell writes:

> Portugal was the last European power in Africa to cling tenaciously
> to the panoply of formal dominion and this was no accident. For a
> long time Portugal very successfully disguised the nature of her
> presence behind a skilful amalgam of historical mythmaking, claims
> of multiracialism, and good public relations. The reality was
> something different. . .Economic weakness at home made
> intransigence in Africa inevitable. It was precisely through the
> exercise of sovereignty that Portugal was able to obtain any
> advantages at all from its 'civilizing mission'. And these advantages
> were very considerable: cheap raw materials, large earnings from
> invisibles, the transfer of export earnings, gold and diamonds,
> protected markets for her wines and cotton textiles.

The Brazilian Marcio Alves commented:

> To hold on to the Empire was fundamental for Portuguese fascism.
> Economically, the African territories — and especially rich Angola —
> were so important to Portuguese capitalism that Caetano took over
> from Salazar on the condition that they would be defended.[1]

If Portugal's stand in Africa is put down to pure profit motive, then
much of what happened in Portuguese Africa in the last century
becomes inexplicable. In the early thirties, Jorge Ameal distilled three
basic characteristics from Portuguese colonial ideology. First he took
the 'geographic element', expressing the sentiment that although
Portugal was a tiny country, her flag flew over what was then the
world's third largest empire. For over a decade, it was fashionable
among Lisbon writers and politicians to refer to the 'Third Empire',
while a favourite colonial quip had it that 'Angola is a great country
with a small colony in Europe.' The second element Ameal defined as
the heroic one: 'The ancestral memory of an astonishing gallery of
discoverers and builders. . .The Portuguese, like no other people, made
their enterprises of exploitation and conquest a transcendent campaign,
a sharing of material values.'[2]

The last element was the material one, in many ways the weakest of
the three. Portuguese Africa was staked out originally in the sixteenth
century as a few wood and water stations on the way to the Goan spice
bazaar. With the decline of the pepper trade and the opening of Brazil,
Bissau, Luanda and Beira vied with Belize as the world's most forgotten

The Politics of the Portuguese Army, 1910–1974

outposts of empire. Portuguese interest in Africa only revived in 1885, when the Berlin Conference announced that Germany and Britain were casting greedy eyes on the lightly held and virtually unexplored Portuguese enclaves. A series of military campaigns was launched to conquer the interior of Angola, Mozambique and Guinea, continuing fitfully until 1915.

The colonies did not live up to their rich promises in the First Republic (1910-26). Messy colonial administration, corruption and lack of capital and initiative were all blamed. But the fact remains that the profit motive was at best latent in this hurried turn-of-the-century expansion. Just as the French conquest of Algeria and the Western Sudan had been the result not of businessmen out to get rich but of military imperialism – the desire of officers to keep on going[3] – so this push into the hinterland by the Portuguese was largely a military show mounted for reasons of prestige and maintained in part as a way to keep the bloated military establishment gainfully occupied. Dubious bush victories were shamelessly exaggerated at home and once a region was subdued the conquering officers turned administrators. Progressive colonial governors like Norton de Matos realized that the extensive military presence in the colonies was one of the greatest stumbling blocks to development there.[4]

> The specific nature of the Portuguese African colonies at the turn of the 20th century is unmistakable. The normal colonies of the 19th century were the outcome of industrial expansion of the metropolitan power. . .The Portuguese colonies were wholly different in origin. In essence, they were the stagnant survivals of 16th century slave and trading posts, suddenly extended into the hinterland under the threat of rival European annexation. . .Thus, the stimulus to conquest did not come from any industrial élan: it was not internal and natural, but external and artificial.[5]

While the British and Belgians used the colonies to feed raw materials to industry for re-export as manufactured products, Portugal, with the exception perhaps of cotton for the textile industry, exported colonial bureaucrats and in return got, as one Royal Commissioner in Mozambique saw it: '. . .endless officers, bulky reports, countless laws, many decrees, a hundred unworkable regulations. Words, words, words.'[6]

For the first three decades of the twentieth century, the African colonies were a losing economic proposition. Luanda was described as

12 The Politics of the Portuguese Army, 1910–1974

'beautiful and bankrupt', and despite temporary upsurges in the colonial economy, Angola and Mozambique ran a trade deficit of 10 to 12 per cent most years. Guinea simply stagnated. In 1933, the economist Elémer Böhn lamented the economic state of Portuguese Africa and concluded that the Portuguese remained there 'only for reasons of tradition and prestige'.[7] In 1930 the Republican statesman Cunha Leal reported that the Finance Minister, Dr Salazar, thought 'The colonies were a cancer and a nightmare. . .I let drop the following phrase: "I must conclude, therefore, that if Angola were to be taken away from us, that would be a great service rendered to us." To which Salazar replied with an indefinable gesture, "I wouldn't go as far as that".'[8] One senior government official in the mid-1930s estimated that the African colonies had cost Portugal more than 150 million pounds since 1850 in budgetary deficits, administrative expenses and the cost of Portuguese intervention in the First World War, brought about by fears that her possessions would be carved up at the peace table if she held aloof.[9]

Portugal's tenacious defence of her colonies after 1961 cannot be understood on purely economic grounds any more than her willingness to fight Germany for them in 1916. Adriano Moreira, Salazar's Minister for the Overseas Provinces, refused to put Portuguese colonialism in the same bag with the economically motivated British and Belgians when he spoke of 'Our universalist mission which [Portuguese man] has been carrying on and which can never be mistaken for colonisation in terms of mere material interests and racial segregation.'[10] This is not to say that the profit motive was totally absent from Portuguese colonial calculations. Under Salazar's careful management, Africa began to turn a small profit and by 1961, with the aid of foreign investment, accounted for approximately one third of Portugal's total national income (although Portuguese statistics often fall short of reliability).[11] But the importance of these figures had become blunted after 1961 due to two important developments: the disruptive effects of the African war on the economy in terms of lost production, especially in agriculture, manpower shortages and enormous defence expenditure which accounted for over 7 per cent of the GNP and 40 per cent of the annual budget, placing Portugal in a warfare state category with Israel. Secondly, in economic terms, Portugal was becoming increasingly Eurocentric. Between 1960 and 1969, the percentage of Portugal's exports to her overseas territories fell from 43 to 25 per cent. By 1973, exports there counted for only 10 per cent of her trade compared with 45 per cent to the EEC. Only 10 per cent

The Politics of the Portuguese Army, 1910–1974   13

of her imports came from the territories while 45 per cent were from Europe.[12] While the home country continued to reap benefits from certain parasitic practices like shipping monopolies, currency exchange and the export of cheap black labour to South Africa's gold mines, it is certain that the major contributors of hard cash in the last decade have been tourists and the massive diaspora which has turned Paris into Portugal's second city: an estimated million and a half Portuguese have left home to work in French and German factories and send part of their pay packet home each month.

While the overseas territories had declined in economic importance to Portugal, those with substantial investment there, both foreign and native, began to question the wisdom of the war. They resented the enormous sums squandered on the defence and administration of the territories and the free goods and services the government required them to supply to the forces.[13] Indeed, if looking for patterns of decolonization, there appears to be an inverse relationship between large-scale economic penetration of a colony and the willingness of the colonial power to fight it out with the local maquisards. The two 'classical' imperial countries, Britain and Belgium, came to terms with the post-war world with a minimum of hesitation. It was in those countries where large economic interests did not provide a firm base for colonial exploitation – France and Portugal – that the decolonization experience was most bitter. The dreadful war the French fought in Indochina made no sense in economic terms. Algeria was hardly the lynchpin of the French economy. A colonial hardliner like Caetano was the first to admit that it would be more lucrative and more convenient 'to abandon the colonies'.[14] The death grip of both countries on their colonial wards cannot be explained in decimal points.

The failure of 'economists' to fully realise their psychological importance to Portugal has obscured the real colonial dilemma of Portuguese governments since the nineteenth century. As modern industrial nations manufacture Concordes and moonshots for reasons not of economic gain but of national prestige, so Portugal delved into the exploits of her past to paper over the poverty of her present. The 'Third Empire' provided a backdrop against which Portuguese political leaders could posture on the world stage. Without it, their perpetual political crises would, like those of some South American banana republic, have earned no more than a few lines in a back page of the *Times*. 'Africa is more than a land to exploit', Marcelo Caetano declared in the 1930s, '. . .Africa is for us a moral justification and a *raison d'être* as a power. Without it, we would be a small nation; with

14   The Politics of the Portuguese Army, 1910–1974

it, we are a great country.'[15]

Cultural chauvinism, which runs high in every Latin country, probably tops the league table in the Iberian peninsula. The Portuguese are acutely aware that their once great prestige has bottomed out in world opinion and the obsession of the Portuguese élite with their cultural heritage has been one of the main stumbling blocks to economic and political development there. The dynamic men of generations past have too often been more concerned with Portugal's 'cultural problem' than with constructing a modern political economy. The main Republican cavil against the monarchy at the turn of the century was that monarchists were more concerned with railways, trade and banking than with the 'spiritual development of the country'.[16]

For the 'New State', as for France's Fourth Republic, the colonies were a political necessity. Their loss would have revealed just how far each country had sunk in world estimation, increasing their political marginalization internationally and consequently their weakness at home. Statements associating the colonies with the historic glories of these two culturally sensitive Latin countries, eager to spread their respective civilizations and languages, cannot be dismissed simply as a thin cover for colonial economic exploitation on a grand scale or as trite *Alliance française* propaganda. The pragmatic Anglo-Saxons and the culturally divided Belgians decided that they had had a good innings, but had reached the time to cut and run. De Gaulle and the rump of the Free French eventually spared their country an agonizing cultural readjustment by administering the necessary 10ccs of grandeur in the nick of time. But unlike de Gaulle, Salazar was in no position to offer his people the spectacle of a leader backed by a *force de frappe* carving out an area of political influence between the two superpowers. Instead, the past became the ticket to political survival in the present. To Portugal fell the self-appointed historic mission of civilizing that portion of the African population which had fallen into her hands. Portugal was not Portugal without greatness, and Salazar and Caetano would not let go until the gun was actually pointed at their heads. The British historian of the Portuguese Empire, C.R. Boxer, wrote:

> It is a fairly accurate generalization that the mass of the people in most countries consider themselves to be inherently superior to those of any other. The Portuguese, who pioneered the expansion of Europe and their successors during three centuries certainly possessed this conviction in full measure — and perhaps to a greater degree than did any other nation, in the opinion of some foreign

observers. . .The result was a nationalism of exceptional durability and toughness. This exalted nationalism helps to explain why the Portuguese held on to so much of their precious sea-borne empire for so long and why they are so reluctant to relinquish any part of it nowadays, whether economically viable (Angola, Mozambique) or otherwise (Goa, Guinea).[17]

Article 2 of Salazar's 1930 Colonial Act gave, 'To the organic essence of the Portuguese nation the historical mission of possessing and colonizing overseas dominions, as well as civilising the native populations encompassed by them.'[18] 'Non-civilised' Africans were to be brought within the pale of Portuguese culture. Local traditions, social organization and law were to be maintained until all blacks could be 'assimilated' — that is taught to read and write Portuguese and converted to Christianity. They would then be granted the full rights of Portuguese citizenship, already given the inhabitants of the Cape Verde Islands, India and Macau. In practice, this policy was less than successful. Lack of schools and the often arbitrary granting of *assimilado* status meant that by 1950 only 30,000 blacks in Angola and 4,000 in Mozambique had stepped up to civilisation. Conversely, thousands of literate blacks, realizing that *assimilado* status carried few tangible economic and social benefits but on the contrary a tax hike, turned down this rather dubious honour.[19]

For the vast majority of blacks who lived by the sweat of their brow, Portuguese civilization meant virtual forced labour. Although the labour code strictly forbade unpaid labour for the state, compulsory labour and the procurement by state officials of workers for private entrepreneurs, for many years, these provisions were winked at to the point that the enforcers' eyes remained almost permanently shut.[20] Female and child labour were commonly used for heavy road work. Unemployment was equated with indolence and unemployed blacks often found themselves sweating for low wages on a state project or hived off to a local planter or contractor to keep them out of mischief. Mozambique's principal export was men to the Transvaal gold mines, up to 100,000 annually, for a procurer's fee and a slice of the sea-borne traffic to Johannesburg. These mining jobs were much sought after by Africans who faced only limited prospects of employment at home and the FRELIMO government continued these arrangements after independence. However, left-wing journalist Perry Anderson criticized this economic organization, virtually unchanged since the seventeenth century, not only as 'an astonishing anachronism', but also as

16   The Politics of the Portuguese Army, 1910–1974

uneconomical because it militated against the creation of a consumer market which would have benefited the homeland.[21]

Increased international condemnation of post-1945 colonialism pushed the government into a few cosmetic reforms. The words 'colonial' and 'colony' were eliminated from the constitution in the early 1950s to sidestep United Nations censure. Africa now became 'Portugal Overseas', and Angola, Mozambique and Guinea were given equal status as provinces with the Alentejo and Trás-os-Montes. In 1961, *assimilado* status was abolished and all blacks in the three 'provinces' became citizens. The outbreak of the war in that year also resulted in stricter enforcement of the labour codes to woo the African population.[22]

The 'civilizing' mission and the economic development of the colonies were given a leg-up by encouraging white settlement. Portuguese emigration traditionally benefited Brazil, but Salazar redirected it toward Angola and Mozambique after the war. The dictator's critics claim that this was a cynical ploy to cream off his excess working population, thus cutting short cries for industrial and land reform, as well as an attempt to transform the underdeveloped colonies into viable markets for home manufacture.[23] Angola's white population shot up from 44,000 in 1940 to roughly 200,000 by 1960, while Mozambique doubled its 1940 white population of 48,000 in 20 years. Angola's estimated 350,000 whites in 1974 comprised 5 per cent of the population, while whites counted for slightly more than 1 per cent in Mozambique.[24] This post-war white wave was not a great success either culturally or economically. The newcomers, a mainly 'fugitive' emigration of poor farmers, were a trifle short on 'civilisation'. Economically, their arrival served only to increase the gulf between blacks and whites and to exacerbate racial tensions. In the 1950s, the government transported entire villages to central Angola, giving each family thirty acres and forbidding employment of African farm workers. But the transport costs were prohibitive, the farming standards of some new arrivals primitive, and in many cases they simply drifted to Luanda or Nova Lisboa to displace Africans holding manual and semi-skilled jobs, or to swell the growing ranks of white unemployed.[25]

The presence in Angola of a large settler population cannot be underestimated as a factor which militated against a withdrawal, as had the one million white *pieds noirs* in Algeria. Many emigrants settled down in Angola's central farming region or in the northern coffee-growing lands near the Congo frontier and their reluctance to give up their homesteads was a major factor in prolonging the war.

The Politics of the Portuguese Army, 1910–1974   17

Congo-educated Holden Roberto, whose *União das Populacões de Angola* (UPA), later to become the FNLA, initiated the Angolan revolt in 1961 by attacking over the Congo border, realized too late that he was not dealing with capitalistic Belgians ready to scurry home almost with the first rifle shot, but with tough Latin farmers, too poor to go home and ready to defend themselves.[26]

In both France and Portugal the army decided to topple the government after a long and bitter struggle against colonial insurgents. Here, however, the parallels begin to diverge. The French army's grand entrance into politics was surprising because it represented a break with its traditional role as *la grande muette* – 'the silent giant'. Until 1958, even the most imaginative anti-militarist republican was hard-pressed to cite an instance when the army had overstepped the bounds of strict legality. To insulate itself against the periodic upheaval of revolutionary change in France, the army tacitly acknowledged the sovereignty of the legal government while claiming loyalty to the nation. When Marshal Saint-Arnaud flushed out the National Assembly in 1851, thereby slamming the doors on the Second Republic, he made clear that he was simply executing the orders of his commander-in-chief President Louis-Napoleon Bonaparte. This policy began to show cracks with the fall of France in 1940. When forced to choose between the doddering old marshal who represented legality in Vichy and an upstart brigadier who called for honour in London, most officers chose the former. After 1945, many of these men found themselves jobless. The tradition of loyalty to the government so long held in the army had been knocked sideways – de Gaulle had succeeded because he refused to follow orders.

But while the French army at home had been kept under the iron thumb of the government, in the colonies it had enjoyed a large degree of independence. Paris found it difficult if not impossible to prevent headstrong and ambitious generals like Bugeaud or Lyautey from pushing out the frontiers of empire or imposing pet administrative projects. While the British army was organized around a system of linked battalions which rotated between home and colonial service, many French officers spent their entire careers in the colonies, especially after the creation of a separate colonial force in 1898. To the feeling among many of these officers that Paris was remote, ill-informed on colonial matters and too left-wing, was added the dangerous expansion of colonial mercenary corps like the Foreign Legion after 1945 from the remnants of the Wehrmacht and other bits and pieces of out-of-work soldiery. That these men owed their loyalty

18 *The Politics of the Portuguese Army, 1910–1974*

not to France but to an élite group of officers proved fatal to the Fourth Republic and under a less skilful and determined politician than de Gaulle might have been so too in the young Fifth Republic.

After slogging through two bloody colonial wars in Indochina and Algeria discontent in the victory-starved French army boiled over. But while the Algerian settlers' revolt enjoyed the friendliest relations with the French army, which was enough to sink the badly listing Fourth Republic, there was never any serious question of the army stepping up to power in France. De Gaulle, like Napoleon, was respected not as the leader of the army but as the only man who could put France's house in order. He was popular not because he hailed the arrival of the tanks at the Elysée Palace, but because he was the only man able to drive the generals and colonels back to barracks. Subsequent attempts by some sections of the army to influence domestic politics against the will of the nation in the 1961 day of the barricades, followed by terrorist bombings of the clandestine OAS, staffed by renegade officers and NCOs, were derisory, if bloodstained, failures.

In lively contrast to the French army, Portuguese officers were as loquacious in political matters as their French counterparts were mute. Throughout the republican period especially, officers popped in and out of cabinets and garrisons revolted on the side of one political faction or another with dizzy regularity. The army mirrored the unstable republic which the large majority of army officers and virtually all of the navy supported. The Portuguese republic topped the list for parliamentary instability. With 45 different governments in 16 years, Portuguese cabinets lasted only four months on average. The republic was unable to bring its armed forces to heel, yet the army lacked the internal cohesion to force a programme on the government. In 1912, conservative General Pimenta de Castro staged a *coup d'état* and handed seven of the nine ministerial portfolios to military men. In May 1915, a rebellion in some army and navy units reinstated the more left-leaning Democrats. In December 1917, with most of the army either on the Western Front or fighting Germans in Africa, some Lisbon regiments revolted under the leadership of a former envoy to Germany, Major Sidónio Pais, who promptly set up a *de facto* military dictatorship and christened it *República Nova*. Pais was assassinated a year later, and immediately pro-monarchist military juntas sprang up in both the North and the South. Loyalist Lisbon regiments teamed up with the navy to crush each revolt, assuring the republic a lingering death.

The Politics of the Portuguese Army, 1910–1974   19

From 1918 until the military *coup de grace* of 1926, military influence in the government steadily increased. In this period, 12 of 26 cabinets, fully 46 per cent, were presided over by military men. Before Pais, only 15 per cent had been so governed. War veterans also became very prominent in Parliament. But the presence in high places of so many soldiers only seemed to increase the republic's petty squabbles and inability to put its economic house in order. The army was dragged into the ideological disputes of the day, and whatever solidarity still existed among those in uniform splintered into political factionalism.

Portuguese politics had been caught up in the ideological undertow of the age. Not surprisingly, the main currents came from abroad and from the right. While the left toyed with Proudhonian socialism and sought to impose a Portuguese-flavoured Third Republic, conservatives looked to recreate the France of Louis XV at home by adapting French philosopher Charles Maurras' theories of integral nationalism to the Portuguese situation. *Integralismo Lusitano* first appeared in print in 1914 and caught fire among army officers and students at the conservative Coimbra University essentially by offering monarchism with a modern face. Traditionalist in outlook, it denounced most post-1789 political doctrines including popular sovereignty and liberalism and all non-Roman religious faiths, especially Judaism and Protestantism. Its adherents preached the virtues of a society based on religion, authority and nationalism as a bulwark against left-wing internationalism.[27] But like its French counterpart, the *Action Française*, *Integralismo Lusitano* was not geared to parliamentary opposition or to the seizure of power, but rather served as an intellectual pressure group.[28] Unlike fascism, integralism was traditionalist and not remotely socialist. But the romanticism of violence among its more youthful following and the spectacle of social stability offered by Mussolini's Italy and Primo de Rivera's Spain meant that by 1926, fascism had fired the imagination of many intellectuals, not least army officers.[29] Disenchantment was increased by the 1923 entry of the left-wing *Seara Nova* group into the government. Two army revolts were crushed in 1925. Finally, on 28 May 1926, General Gomes da Costa revolted in the northern town of Braga and marched on Lisbon to end the republic.

The conspiracy was not a fascist *coup*, but an uncomfortable marriage of republican and integralist officers who sank their differences long enough to end the 'corruption and degradation' of the parliamentary republic. They gained support among the mass of officers by promising to rectify the lengthening list of economic and professional

20 The Politics of the Portuguese Army, 1910–1974

grievances. Most soldiers wanted a return to 'constitutional normalcy', not a new order.[30] Officers, like civil servants, had seen their purchasing power slashed to one-half of what it had been in 1910. They complained that bad training, poor armament and obsolete equipment had sapped morale and consequently discipline. The army, they grieved, needed a root and branch reform which would, among other things, eliminate the national militia brought in by victorious republicans in 1911. The government had swelled the forces far beyond the country's defence needs. Peacetime military strength had tripled since the declaration of the republic, absorbing 40 per cent of the national budget, and transforming the army into an elaborate system of outdoor relief for the middle-class unemployed.[31]

The emphasis on professional grievances was not the only feature which the 28 May *coup* shared with its successor 48 years later. The impetus for the plots against both régimes came from junior- and middle-ranking officers who sought leadership from select superiors known to desire a change. Even the similarity in the names of the generals who eventually assumed the leadership mantle was uncanny: in 1974 Costa Gomes inherited the job of Gomes da Costa. The young officers of 1926, like their modern counterparts, were convinced that the army must set the example for Portuguese society. Their 'revolution', therefore, became an élitist enterprise reserved for professional officers, unlike the 1925 Lisbon revolt which drew in sergeants and soldiers. Basing their operation on the Braga and Coimbra garrisons, they set up a *junta revolucionária* in almost every regiment from January 1926.[32] The heterogeneous political philosophies of the conspirators, their lack of unity, almost total absence of political experience and technical skills needed to implement reform, as well as attempts to cash in on the *coup* by political groups too small to gain power at the polls, meant that the death of the republic did not end republican influence in the government, nor military unrest. The new government under navy Commander Joaquim Mendes Cabeçadas was dominated by republican officers, but fascist-orientated groups in the army made life difficult — too difficult. On 9 July, another army *coup* directed by pro-monarchist General Sinel de Cordes ousted President Gomes da Costa and replaced him with General Oscar Carmona. Under the dual direction of the two generals, military indiscipline was compounded by financial irresponsibility. The country slid noisily towards the New State. Violent army and navy revolts rocked the government in 1927 and 1928. In 1928, Salazar was named finance minister in the cabinet of Colonel Vicente de Freitas. By the time a final military revolt was

The Politics of the Portuguese Army, 1910–1974

crushed in 1931, Salazar had become firmly established as the only man who could save Portugal from economic ruin. He soon convinced enough politicians that he was also the only man who could save her from political anarchy. Amid widespread purges of teachers, civil servants and army officers hostile to the régime, Salazar was named prime minister in July 1932.

The foundations of the fascist state were established over the next few years. All political parties, secret societies and trade unions were disbanded. Salazar installed himself as chief of the National Union, now the only legal party. The Statute of National Labour which decreed that government-controlled syndicates were to replace the old trade unions and working men's associations had whole paragraphs lifted from Mussolini's Italian Charter of Labour. Other features of the corporatiste society also owed much to *Il Duce*. As the Spanish Civil War heated up, the régime, desperate for a Franco victory, took on other trappings of a fascist state. A *Mocedade Portuguesa* (Portuguese Youth) modelled on the Hitler youth was organised in schools and, in his own bloodless version of the 'night of the long knives', Salazar converted the troublesome 'blue shirts' into the Portuguese Legion at a stroke. However, both the Portuguese Youth and the Portuguese Legion were quietly played down after 1945. As for the corporatiste organization of the new state, it betrayed a misunderstanding of modern industry and a contempt for labour which would have shamed German national socialists.[33] In economic organization, as in colonial policy, the traditionalist dictator attempted to turn the clock back to the sixteenth century by more or less reviving a guild system. And of course Salazar's racial propaganda clashed violently with Third Reich racism by extolling the virtues of Portugal's multiracial melting pot and pointing with pride to the large number of *mestiços* in the colonies as proof of Portuguese willingness to pursue their 'civilising mission' even after dark.

Salazar's take-over did not end military dissent. An alleged pro-monarchist plot was unearthed among army officers in 1934, and in 1936 a Potemkin-like revolt blew up on two battleships anchored in Lisbon harbour. But reforms designed to raise military prestige together with the smack of firm government dissuaded soldiers from trying their luck at political roulette. The restoration of discipline and the advent of world war encouraged a return to more professional considerations in the forces. The régime seemed to have captured the allegiance of the majority of the nation, including some intellectuals who saw the New State as a combination of fascism and Lusitanian

22   *The Politics of the Portuguese Army, 1910–1974*

integralism. The political vacuum of the republic had been the largest temptation to men on horseback. With Salazar's hands firmly on the reins of government, the soldiers returned to the barracks. This is not to say that the Dictator's nights were not troubled by anxiety over military mischief; the deep-rooted liberal traditions of the forces could not be pulled up by directives forbidding officers to join the communist party nor by a government propaganda barrage stressing the necessity for an 'apolitical' army. Salazar interfered little in the ideology of the forces, preferring to leave to the paramilitary Portuguese Legion and the misnamed Republican National Guard the task of defending the régime. The result, once the trauma of political and economic instability had passed, was a lingering residue of indignation among many officers over the authoritarian nature of the New State and increasing embarrassment about the ridiculous figure Portugal cut abroad as she wobbled into the post-war world. This situation was explosive, and precisely because Salazar had done his job of political stabilization too well. In a country with a strong political consciousness engrained among the middle classes, Salazar had shut off virtually all outlets of discontent. The ban on political parties and trade unions had closed popular steam valves and made the government incapable of expanding and contracting with political pressures. Many even mildly outspoken teachers or civil servants found their careers tragically shattered and, severed from the all-important public payroll, spent their lives running small shops in provincial backwaters. Courageous liberal professionals were harassed into silence by the PIDE or, like socialist leader Mário Soares, forced into periods of jail or exile. But Salazar wielded his repressive weapons with subtle skill. The Salazar régime practised what American political scientist H. Martins calls an 'economy of terror' – a controlled but persistent repression which fragmented and neutralized the opposition.[34] The notorious Tarrafal camp in the Cape Verde islands, reserved primarily for PCP militants, was shut down in the mid-1950s. Caxias prison, outside of Lisbon, became the régime's new bastille and revolutionaries who stormed it in 1974 must have been as disappointed as *sans culottes* when it disgorged barely 100 prisoners, many of whose political connections were suspect.

The result of Salazar's policies was that the armed forces remained the only place where a man could keep his own counsel albeit discreetly. The liberal traditions of the opposition were kept alive by Admiral Pinheiro de Azevedo and others who taught at the military and naval academies. Political conversions in the officers' mess were

The Politics of the Portuguese Army 1910–1974

relatively free and although one officer noted that after such discussions 'sometimes you thought to yourself. "perhaps I shouldn't have said that"',[35] their increasing frequency and openness as war-weariness increased was an important factor in spreading the disease. Political writers have claimed that PIDE agents were excluded from the army.[36] Although it is probable that the number of officers in the pay of the secret police was limited, some NCOs and a number of military employees were almost certainly paid by the line for reports on their superiors. 'We knew that in every ship or school, there were two or three petty officers or porters in the pay of the PIDE', one captain said, 'but this was never proved.' The relative immunity of the forces to government meddling can be attributed to the much maligned 'fascist' high command, which ensured that officers and NCOs involved with clandestine political groups received no more than a scolding from their commanding officer. Caetano found to his amazement that a high command supposedly in the government's pocket refused to break military conspiracy, even one which promised to cost them their jobs.[37] The Caetano dictatorship could not maintain itself in power partly because the means of coercion at its command were so weak.

Antonio de Figueiredo notes that by 1945, the army had become a 'disciplined political institution',[38] a statement whose force is somewhat diminished by the long list of military revolts which eventually culminated in April 1974. General Humberto Delgado, opposition candidate for president in 1958, claimed that the government was underpinned by an army which paradoxically detested it.[39] Salazar's policies virtually guaranteed that effective opposition could come only from the forces. The army tolerated rather than supported the government, whose muscle came from the PIDE and the Portuguese Legion. The success record of regimental revolts organized by young officers, on the decline since 28 May 1926, hit its nadir after an April 1947 attempt by a major and ten subalterns to raise the sixth cavalry regiment fizzled in Porto. The leader, Major Fernando Queiroga, complained that officer corps solidarity had been broken by Salazarist attempts to create an 'official army', and decried an incident in which an army commander allowed the PIDE to arrest and torture a group of NCOs.[40] The political opposition, hamstrung by the petty disputes and personality conflicts of the old republican élite, was even less effective. After a united opposition front cracked in 1949, the régime settled back into its Indian summer. The high command remained the only group which had yet to stick in its protest oar.

24 The Politics of the Portuguese Army, 1910–1974

The presidency traditionally had been the preserve of the armed forces, a largely honorific post occupied for years by the increasingly senile General Carmona. In 1942, Carmona was returned without opposition, but in 1949 General Norton de Matos, ex-war minister and twice governor of Angola under the republic, stepped in to challenge as the combined opposition candidate of the *Movimento de Unidade Democrática*. In a vigorous campaign, he denounced Salazarist repression and censorship and promised to restore democracy to Portugal. Many predicted a close-run election but de Matos withdrew after guarantees of a free vote were not forthcoming. Carmona, who through a haze of senility and good dinners belatedly had soured on the Prime Minister, died in April 1951. The moderate opposition put up old Admiral Quintão Meireles, who called for a return to the 'good old days' before 1926, before he too predictably withdrew to leave the field to Salazar's candidate, General Craveiro Lopes. Once in office however, Lopes proved troublesome. He formed an opposition knot with Defence Minister General Júlio Moniz, Colonel Serpa Soares, commandant of the cavalry school at Santarém, north of Lisbon, and others. Together they hoped to pack the top ranks of the forces with anti-Salazar officers as a prelude to a palace revolution. Progress was slow, however, and success patchy.[41] The conspiracy was overtaken by the 1958 presidential elections.

Air Force General Delgado's decision to stand with the opposition surprised many. A keen Salazar supporter and Portugal's representative at NATO, he was regarded as one of the best of a new generation of dynamic pro-régime technocrats. His lengthy tours in North America and Western Europe, however, had impressed upon him the backwardness of his home country. His campaign, which drew mass support in Lisbon and Porto, did not fail to make a ripple in the forces: 'We followed the elections very closely', said one officer, then a naval cadet. 'My father had been dismissed from his job as a music teacher in the early years of the régime after some political troubles. I felt that this election was my family's revenge.'[42] Salazar's National Union abandoned the unreliable General Lopes for Admiral Tomás. Despite Delgado's claims that 'there is no government that can take this election away from me; I have the people and Europe behind me',[43] he went down by 758,998 votes to 236,528 in what was almost certainly a rigged result. It is unlikely, however, that he could have carried even a fair contest given an electorate carefully restricted to the property owners. When Delgado's appeal to the Supreme Court was snubbed, he sent a barrage of letters, first to Admiral Tomás asking him to step

The Politics of the Portuguese Army. 1910–1974   25

down, and then to four reform-minded generals including General
Moniz calling on them to revolt. His increasingly conspiratorial
behaviour lost him much public sympathy. He went from exile to the
headline-grabbing hijack of a Portuguese liner, the *Santa Maria,* and
eventually to death in 1965 at the hands of the PIDE in a Spanish
churchyard.[44]

With a high command conspiracy on the back burner, a handful of
middle-ranking conspirators including Captain Vasco Gonçalves, future
Prime Minister of the Second Republic, formed the Independent
Military Movement in February 1959. Its platform, signed by nine
officers, called for an end to dictatorship, a provisional government to
dissolve the National Assembly and political police and draw up a new
constitution, guarantees of the fundamental political liberties, freedom
for political prisoners and the election of a new government reflecting
the true will of the people.[45] Their revolt, planned for 12 March,
flopped when some of the conspirators pulled out at the last minute.

The 12 March conspiracy is seen as the last of the revolts dating
from the republican period and 'motivated by principles more ethical
than revolutionary, unprepared for violent acts'. The conspirators had
no idea of what sort of government they wanted and were not remotely
socialist: 'Perhaps this explains, in part, the withdrawal of the PC. . .
although all revolutions are moral, moral force is not enough to throw
off oppression.'[46]

The Portuguese 'revolution' of 1974 startled the world not only by
its suddenness, but also by the left-wing orientation of its presidium of
middle-ranking officers. 'We knew something was going to happen',
said one American diplomat. 'What surprised us was the direction it
took.'[47] Placed in the context of Portuguese history and the experience
of other power-seeking armies, however, the latest Portuguese explosion
is divested of much of its originality. The 1974 *coup* had the same
underpinning of moral indignation as that of 1959, was equally vague
about the sort of government it proposed and its socialist orientation
emerged only with time. Nor was a year and a half of revolution marked
by particularly 'violent acts'. Officers involved in the 12th of March
were equally concerned with the grinding poverty of a substantial
portion of the Portuguese people, and in Vasco Gonçalves they had a
direct link with the future. The opportunist PCP probably pulled out,
not because the officers of 12 March wanted a Western-style
democracy, but because the conspiracy had not the remotest chance of
success. The basic difference between the two conspiracies lay with the
success of the latter. The 1959 *coup* collapsed when several key officers

26   The Politics of the Portuguese Army, 1910–1974

got cold feet. In 1974, to the amazement of the *coup* coordinator, Major Otelo de Carvalho, no one chickened out.[48] This suggests that there was an added ingredient to bring the latent moral indignation in the officer corps to boiling point, and that ingredient, as on 28 May 1926, was the growing professional grievances of the army. These were a direct result of the colonial wars which brought discontent in the army to the surface and gave it unity and direction enough to push Portuguese officers once again into the political arena.

Notes

1. K. Maxwell, 'The Thorns of the Portuguese Revolution', *Foreign Affairs,* January 1976, p.251; Márcio Alves, *Les Soldats socialistes du Portugal,* Paris, 1975, p.34.
2. James Duffy, *Portuguese Africa,* London, 1959, p.270.
3. See C.-A. Julien, *Histoire de l'Algerie contemporaine,* Paris, 1964, and A.S. Kanya-Forstner, *Conquest of the Western Sudan: a Study in French Military Imperialism,* Cambridge, 1969.
4. Duffy, op.cit., p.226.
5. Anderson, 'Portugal and the End of Ultra Colonialism', *New Left Review,* London, 1962, No.15, p.102.
6. Duffy, op.cit., p.241.
7. Ibid., pp.264-5.
8. António de Figueiredo, *Portugal: Fifty Years of Dictatorship,* London, 1975, p.72.
9. Ibid., p.73.
10. Anderson, op.cit., No.16, p.113.
11. Ibid., No.17, p.108.
12. A.R. Bandeira, 'Military Intervention in Portuguese Politics', unpublished paper, York University, Toronto, August 1975, p.49.
13. Ibid.
14. A. Rodrigues, C. Borga and M. Cardoso, *O Movimento dos Capitães e o 25 de Abril,* Lisbon 1974, p.87.
15. Anderson, op.cit., No.16, p.116.
16. A.H. de Oliveira Marques, *History of Portugal,* vol.II, London, 1972, p.140.
17. C.R. Boxer, *The Portuguese Sea-borne Empire, 1415-1825,* London, 1969, pp.377-8.
18. Marques, op.cit., p.227.
19. Ibid., pp.228-9.
20. Figueiredo, op.cit., p.80.
21. Anderson, op.cit., No.16, p.99.
22. Marques, op.cit., p.232.
23. Figueiredo, op.cit., p.76.
24. Anderson, op.cit., pp.101-2, and A. Humbarachi and N. Muchnik, *Portugal's African Wars,* London, 1974, pp.16, 24.
25. Anderson, op.cit., No.16, pp.102-3.
26. D. Wheeler and R. Pelissier, *Angola,* London, 1971, p.177.
27. Marques, op.cit., pp.177-8.
28. H. Martins, 'Portugal', in S.J. Woolf (ed.), *European Fascism,* London, 1968, p.309.

The Politics of the Portuguese Army, 1910–1974

29. Marques, op.cit., p.179.
30. Ibid.,
31. D. Wheeler, 'Situation Obscure – The 28th of May Movement and the Fall of the Parliamentary Republic', Workshop on Modern Portugal, October 1972, University of New Hampshire, Durham, pp.5-6.
32. Ibid., p.8.
33. Figueiredo, op.cit., p.70.
34. Martins, op.cit., pp.328-9.
35. Interview.
36. Insight, *The Year of the Captains*, London, 1975, p.18.
37. Caetano, *O Depoimento*, Rio de Janeiro, 1974, p.176.
38. Figueiredo, op.cit., p.118.
39. Rodrigues *et al.*, op.cit., p.118.
40. Figueiredo, op.cit., pp.118-9 calls Queiroga a lieutenant, Rodrigues, p.153, a major.
41. Rodrigues, op.cit., pp.154-5.
42. Interview.
43. Bandeira, op.cit., p.23.
44. Figueiredo, op.cit., pp.200-3.
45. Rodrigues, op.cit., pp.168-9.
46. Ibid., pp.178-81.
47. Maxwell, 'Portugal under Pressure', *New York Review of Books*, 29 May 1975, p.24.
48. Carvalho interviews in *Expresso*, 27 July 1974, and *Revista do Povo*, 1 December 1974.

2 COLONIES AND COUPS: PORTUGAL'S COLONIAL WARS

Colonies are a double-edged sword. In the nineteenth century, they served the same function as do many Third World ambassadorships today: a more or less comfortable exile for politically restive officers. French North Africa became a repository for soldiers whose ambitions, politics or, in Moroccan Governor-General Lyautey's case loves, could not be contained within the hexagon. Saint-Simonists and republican officers like Cavignac were encouraged to let off steam in the colonies and this, according to the American historian J.S. Ambler, accounts in great part for the relative stability of French civil-military relations for well over a century.[1] 'What a shame I did not come here ten years earlier', the future Marshal Lyautey wrote to his sister from Tonkin in 1894. 'What careers there are to be established and led here! Here there are none of these little lieutenants, post and reconnaissance commanders, who do not develop more initiative, will, endurance and personality in six months than does an officer in France in his entire career.'[2]

While it is certain that native-bashing was usually enough to content most potentially troublesome officers, it is also true that the colonies did on occasion become a springboard from which ambitious officers launched a power bid. Captain Cavignac, bounced to Algeria in 1832 for his left-wing political views, reappeared in June 1848 as the only man who could save France from anarchy. His bid for the presidency of the Second Republic was only just headed off by the quixotic Louis-Napoleon Bonaparte, whose name held enough magic to swing the mass of French voters. Thirty-eight year old Lieutenant Saint-Arnaud, his career apparently stalled, joined a newly mustered Foreign Legion battalion embarking for North Africa in 1836. In 1848 he returned a general, and if lacking personal ambition, was eager to manoeuvre with Louis-Napoleon on the fringes of legality to transform the Second Republic into the Second Empire. Marshal MacMahon, the first official president of the Third Republic, was a colonial soldier and the flamboyant General Boulanger first attracted a following as Governor of Tunis where he encouraged much publicized duels between French and Italian officers. As late as 1942, Admiral Darlan spoke for France from the Governor-General's residence in Algiers.

Portugal too had its military men whose road to political prominence

Colonies and Coups: Portugal's Colonial Wars 29

passed through the colonies, the most famous being Generals Mousinho de Albuquerque and Norton de Matos. Top posts in the colonial administration traditionally went to the forces, and, as the republic began to totter, several soldiers like Major Paiva Couceiro, African hero and ex-governor of Mozambique who headed a northern military rebellion in 1919, rushed to cash in on reputations staked out in the colonies. Caetano too found that the ambitions of colonial officers did not stop at the equator. Ultra General Kaúlza de Arriaga Mozambique commander from 1970, led an active intrigue on the right, while General Spínola's colonial expertise and performance in Guinea won him the job as Caetano's successor in 1974.

The isolation of the colonial army abroad also militated against political stability. Officers who spent long periods in distant garrisons soon developed parochial attachments. At best this meant a resentment of meddlesome politicians and bureaucrats in Paris or Lisbon whose ignorance of colonial problems was often profound. But officers soon lost touch with the society which had spawned them, greeted the latest domestic political developments with incomprehension and during rare home leaves felt like trespassers in a foreign land. The homeland reciprocated by treating the colonial soldier as a curious type whose attitudes, manners and even language stepped out from thirty or forty years in the past. The estrangement of the two communities explains in part why, when the crunch of decolonization came, the gulf between home and overseas was too vast to be bridged by politicians. Those sent to defend the colonies felt that they were being sacrificed and abandoned by the nation, which reciprocated with charges that the soldiers were fuelled on concepts of heroism and patriotism which belonged more properly to the nineteenth century than the modern age. French and American[3] soldiers returning from Vietnam and Portuguese soldiers from Africa were stunned to find that the struggle to keep the flag flying abroad, the horror, the close brushes with death which they had endured for months and even years were greeted with indifference, if not downright hostility, at home. French soldiers were scandalized by communist demonstrations around hospital trains of troops wounded in Indochina and by Red Cross donors who demanded that their blood not go to French wounded. Nor were they happy when in 1948 the government bowed to left-wing pressure and refused to register citations earned in Indochina in the *Journal Officiel.*[4] The increasing volume of anti-war propaganda took its toll on American morale: 'I did three tours in Vietnam', one American major said. 'The first time I wanted to earn medals. The second time I wanted to do my

30 Colonies and Coups: Portugal's Colonial Wars

job. The third time, I just wanted to get out alive.'[5] Regular soldiers began to feel that the American public did not understand the true nature of the enemy, the demands of modern war or the political implications of a communist victory. Increasing exasperation over what they regarded as a politically hamstrung war effort told in demands to 'get in and win the war, or get out'. 'People say we lost in Vietnam', one career sergeant said. 'Everybody knows that America could have whipped a runny-nose country like North Vietnam. But the politicians wouldn't let us.'[6]

The colonial isolation of the Portuguese army helps to explain both the April 1974 *coup* and much of the subsequent political disorder brought about by young officers whose colonial experience did not equip them to deal with or even to understand the realities of Portuguese politics. The indignation which swept Portugal following the 1961 Indian invasion of Portuguese Goa allowed Salazar to consolidate support for the African wars which began the same year. But as the wars dragged on, most of the country lost interest, leaving professional officers to fight on with unenthusiastic conscripts and anti-war subalterns. The General Staff swept aside suggestions that most regular cadres be allowed to reside permanently in the colonies, preferring a system of two years' service in Africa followed by a few months rotation home. This system was the worst possible, for it gave officers no personal stake in the colonies and kept them away from Portugal and their families, and too often from virtually all human contact. Unlike the Algerian FLN, Portugal's guerrilla enemies avoided the towns forcing Portuguese officers to sit for twenty-four boring months in remote outposts in bush and jungle increasingly frustrated by their inability to inflict a final crushing blow on an enemy established in inviolate sanctuaries in Zaire, Tanzania and Zambia. Many officers below the rank of colonel were mentally and physically exhausted after spending the vast portion of their careers in the debilitating climates and tough combat of Goa and Africa. 'With increasing frequency, the officer who returned from overseas found at home argumentative and anti-militarist sons who hardly recognised him and he deeply regretted not having been on hand to guide them', Caetano admitted. 'There were some real dramas.'[7]

Cut off from their families, officers felt increasingly estranged from the country. The indifference of most Portuguese to the wars was matched only by the growing anti-war sentiment among those expected to do much of the fighting. The 1962 Lisbon student demonstrations had a definite anti-war flavour, as did those of 1973.

Colonies and Coups: Portugal's Colonial Wars 31

Student discontent was hardly appeased by the 1967 decree increasing national service to four years. As the army more than doubled its 1961 strength, its appetite for officers increased far beyond the Military Academy's production capacity. It was forced to draw virtually all of its subalterns from lycée and university graduates whose commitment to the war was somewhat short of enthusiastic.

The role of conscript, or *miliciano,* officers in politicizing the officer corps has been hotly debated. Caetano blamed them for infecting the regular officers with left-wing ideas picked up in the classrooms: 'Because of this constant infusion of university graduates, the armed forces absorbed the ideas which agitated the younger generation and circulated in the schools', he wrote. And these ideas, as I have noted, opposed the existing social order and the legitimacy of Portugal overseas. In the officers' messes, thick with conversation and discussion, the milicianos carried out their indoctrination.[8] Socialist party chief Mário Soares supported this view: 'Each spring for the last seven or eight years, Portuguese universities were the scene of student demonstrations against oppression. Each year between four and six hundred students were asserted and sent into the army as punishment. Many of these young radicals afterwards became lieutenants, captains and majors.'[9] Márcio Alves, however, argues that the milicianos' political role was minimal because, apart from the odd left-wing faculty like economics, Portuguese universities, frequented by the affluent middle classes, are notoriously conservative: 'Political indifference, and, even more, political ignorance are the characteristic traits of most Portuguese students today, more than a year after the fall of fascism', he writes. The MFA was originally formed in opposition to the conscript officers, and no MFA leader credited their influence on the movement.[10]

The importance of the milicianos does not lie in the political doctrines which they did, or did not, plant in the minds of army officers. The attitudes of the milicianos increased the sense of isolation and estrangement felt by professionals. Apart from a handful of colonial-born milicianos, most conscript lieutenants and captains were opposed to the war, and were prepared to say so in the mess, only sometimes placing their opposition in the wider context of the political issues facing Portugal. 'Anti-war sentiment was strong, but it took no real political form', said a Lisbon University lecturer.[11] Milicianos and reservists resented being pulled away from their families and careers, many at a relatively advanced age, to risk their lives for two years in the jungle. From this discontent came their political objections. Debates

32   Colonies and Coups: Portugal's Colonial Wars

and discussions about the war between younger regulars and their temporary colleagues soon became a feature of military life. Professional officers realized that they were stuck with a series of wars which Portuguese society, especially those whom it leased to the army, did not support.

Portugal's anti-war atmosphere was forcefully underlined by a rocketing desertion rate — between 1961 and 1974, an estimated 110,000 conscripts failed to report for military service.[12] Caetano claimed that the political significance of these figures was grossly exaggerated by the opposition. Most 'deserters', he said, were workers of military age who formed part of the 'gravely pathological' manpower drain toward France and who simply did not bother to return when their number was called. He argued that politically motivated desertion was limited almost exclusively to the middle classes: 'In contrast to what anti-Portuguese propaganda so often claimed, the number of youths who emigrated to avoid military service was relatively small', he wrote, and although it increased in the last years, it did so more among the bourgeoisie and the rich, than among the people.'[13] It was precisely this middle-class character of anti-militarism and desertion which increased the sense of isolation among professional officers. In Africa they shared barracks and mess tables year after year with resentful middle-class milicianos. Their brief visits home were marked by increasing hostility on the part of their friends and younger members of their middle-class milieu to the war. This feeling of abandonment, of being made the 'scapegoat' for an unpopular war, is clearly visible in the pre-*coup* manifestos of the MFA:

> If, before 1961, the prestige of the armed forces was not openly, or very violently, attacked, it is because the régime's internal crises had not reached an excessively critical stage [read 'The Armed Forces Movement and the Nation' of March 1974]. Beginning, however, with the loss of India and above all as the African wars dragged on, the armed forces discovered their real separation from the nation — a discovery not without surprise for many soldiers who for the first time saw things clearly. The armed forces are humiliated, stripped of prestige and presented to the nation as those most responsible for the disaster.[14]

Nor could officers seek solace in the colonies. The Portuguese army and the African colonists enjoyed the worst relations between a colonial army and a white community on record. British officers lent dignity and

Colonies and Coups: Portugal's Colonial Wars 33

prestige to Indian colonial society, and while some friction existed between the French army and the white *pieds noirs*, whole battalions found that drinks in Algerian garrison towns were on the house after successful actions.[15] In Africa, colonists frequently cast doubt on the martial spirit, not to mention the courage, of their military protectors. They resented the army's increasing reliance on black troops – part of Caetano's 'Africanization' of the war – which made up over half of Portugal's army overseas.

Table 1: Portuguese Troop Strength[16]

Guinea		Angola		Mozambique		Portugal
Black	White	Black	White	Black	White	
24,800	6,200	37,800	25,000	19,800	24,200	60,000

'The army sold us out', said one white Mozambican. 'They fought well at first, but then it was rubbish. From about 1970, officers began to say that this was not their country, it was not their war. I would estimate that 75 per cent of the officers felt this way.'[17]

Like the French army in Algeria, Portuguese officers found that civic action programmes designed to raise the low African living standards and give them a stake in Portuguese Africa met bitter opposition from local whites. Not only did they cavil about construction work lost to local contractors, but they complained that the army was upsetting traditional race relations: 'If the Africans had complaints, they would come to the army to complain about the officials', one officer in Angola said. 'The officials did not like this. They were used to an easy life.'[18] White officers commanding black troops were often totally out of sympathy with the white community. In some cases the forces actually intervened to prevent bloody white retaliation on the local black community, following guerrilla attacks.[19] White hostility to the local garrisons made itself felt even in the most petty aspects of everyday life: 'Whenever I or my wife went to the shop', one air force officer in Angola said, 'you could hear people say: "when the army arrives, prices shoot up".'[20] A January 1974 attack on the officers' mess in Beira, Mozambique, by whites incensed by the army's failure to protect them against guerrilla murders was the last

34 Colonies and Coups: Portugal's Colonial Wars

straw. For many officers it served as a raw illustration of their isolation: 'The recent events in Beira, Mozambique, once more confirm this reality for everyone', read an MFA circular which condemned this 'insult to the army' in the bitterest terms.[21]

A 1970 confidential report which Amílcar Cabral attributed to the psychological warfare section of the Portuguese general staff probably provides an accurate summary of the army's increasing isolation:

> The proliferation of anti-government organisations and the agitation that they create leads to an unsuitable psychological climate which, by affecting the activities of students, affects the country, which seems troubled and does not know what to do to lead its children back to the right path. . .In the metropolis generally, the population continues to show little interest in the war overseas and ignores the efforts being made by the armed forces. The student masses remain vulnerable to pacifist propaganda.
>
> The working masses, ignoring great national problems, let themselves be easily led by the propaganda — orientated towards demanding better wages and living conditions. The most advanced groups continue to be hot-beds of subversion and the groups which are springing up have proved highly effective.
>
> Overseas, in general, the native populations tend towards subversion, especially when they are strong or when geographical conditions make actions by our troops difficult or impossible. The indigenous populations on the periphery of the largest urban centres, generally detribalised, continue to be very susceptible to enemy propaganda. The European population continues to demonstrate overt support for the war, but only co-operates against subversion when its material interests are directly endangered. The psychological situation is precarious, in the metropolis as well as overseas.[22]

Declining morale soon began to make itself felt by a small but unsettling desertion rate among regular cadres. In many cases the annual disappearance of two or three comrades could be explained away. A small number of sailors and petty officers jumped ship each year in South Africa, Australia or Canada and although they sometimes asked for political asylum, economic motivations were strongly suspected. As the war crept on, a number of good officers began to slip away. Fifteen engineering cadets, regarded as the cream of the Military Academy, walked across the frontier in 1973 after completing their four-year course. Other officers failed to return from holidays abroad. One naval

Colonies and Coups: Portugal's Colonial Wars 35

officer pointed out:

> One or two lieutenants deserted each year. But there was always
> some doubt if they took this decision for political reasons. In most
> cases we suspected debt or alcoholism. But later on, several
> desertions created a certain impression, especially that of a
> Lieutenant J.-G. who was the son of a general. He was one of our
> best officers. One of the top cadets at the Naval Academy also left.[23]

If colonies can be won, they can also be lost. Defeat is a third way in
which colonies may infect the homeland with political instability. A
thrashed army builds up resentments which often boomerang on the
government. After the loss of South America in the early 1820s, both
the Spanish and the Portuguese army sowed dissension at home. The
French army was imported to quash insurgent Spanish generals, but
in Portugal, where discontent over Brazilian independence ran high,
military intervention in politics resembled a dry run for the First
Republic. The mutual recriminations between the government and
the soldiers which followed the 1918 defeat Ludendorff inflicted on
the Portuguese expeditionary force in Flanders helped the republic on
its way to total collapse. Apart from the odd African tribal disturbance,
the Portuguese army steered clear of war between 1918 and 1961.
Portuguese 'volunteers' turned up on the nationalist side in the Spanish
Civil War and even on Germany's eastern front, but the army machine
was not oiled and tested for over forty years. When the crunch came
in 1961, the inevitable result set the government and the high command
at each others' throats once again.

After Salazar spurned Prime Minister Nehru's repeated requests that
Portugal hand over its Goan enclave, India launched an invasion which
overwhelmed the tiny Portuguese garrison in a matter of hours. 'I will
not permit a truce or Portuguese prisoners', Salazar had wired to the
Governor General Vassalo e Silva on the eve of the invasion. 'No
surrender of ships. Soldiers and sailors either victorious or dead. . .God
will not let this officer be the last governor of the State of India.'[24] The
results were somewhat different: 'There were 3,000 troops in Goa when
the Indians launched the air, sea and land invasion with 30,000', left-
wing Captain Valera Gomes noted. 'Salazar ordered our troops to fight
"to the last man". They didn't have a single anti-aircraft gun. The
officers on the spot refused to obey Salazar.'[25] The Governor General,
the military commander, his chief of staff, one naval captain, six majors,
four captains, a sub-lieutenant and a sergeant were cashiered by the

36   Colonies and Coups: Portugal's Colonial Wars

council of ministers for cowardice. Four captains, four miliciano lieutenants and a lieutenant-commander were suspended for six months.[26] Officers felt that they had been 'unjustly punished' for the Goan débâcle.[27] 'The disaster of Goa was an emotional shock that brought to the surface the repulsion and concern which the healthy majority of the armed forces felt for a long time toward the designs and methods of the New State', Valera Gomes wrote.[28]

While the army put all the blame for the defeat on the government, protesting against the impossible odds, the government felt, not without some justification, that military resistance had fallen far short of honourable. 'To be quite honest, no one really thought that they would invade', one officer present in Goa confessed. 'I have never seen such panic.'[29] And despite reproaches levelled at the Salazar government by officers over the Goan 'insult', the revolution did nothing to rehabilitate the disgraced officers.[30] Salazar's motive for insisting on the defence of an indefensible colony has never been clearly established. Canadian political scientist A.R. Bandeira argues that the sacrifice of Goa was an elaborate public relations stunt calculated to rally national support for the African wars. Government propaganda called on Portugal to remember its '1,018 martyrs murdered in Goa', and although the actual casualty figure was nearer 30, mostly from a destroyer which ran aground, this produced the required hysteria. Several old soldiers re-enlisted amid great publicity, and national support for the African empire solidified.[31] But if this was the result Salazar had hoped for, it backfired, for Goa simply increased the misgivings of many of the forces, including the high command, about the feasibility or even desirability of colonial defence.

The truth is probably less subtle. Like a true miser, Salazar refused to part with one inch of his territory overseas. '. . .Goa was not militarily defensible against the Indian army', wrote Marcelo Caetano, 'but it had a garrison, which would take a formal act of war to conquer, and which would honour, with a symbolic resistance, the national flag. We hoped that the duration of this resistance would permit us to whip up international opinion and call a meeting of the United Nations Security Council. But there was no resistance worthy of the name. And the officers who allowed themselves to be taken prisoner without a fight never got over the shock'.[32] For the vast majority of officers who preferred to leave heroic last stands to Cambronne and Custer, Goa bore the ominous message that the government was prepared to manipulate and sacrifice them in hopeless missions and to court-martial virtually all survivors. 'The fact is that officers who were in India at the time of the

Colonies and Coups: Portugal's Colonial Wars 37

Indian invasion never ceased to reflect a certain attitude', Caetano complained. 'And many of them took it with them to the African provinces.'[33] But who could blame them if, as defeat loomed larger, many officers feared that Guinea would make Goa look like a Sunday school picnic. 'The example of India is a precedent which haunts the future we fear', former commander-in-chief of Guinea, General António de Spínola, wrote in 1974. 'No one thought possible what, in fact, was inevitable, but this did not prevent a tragedy. The attention of the nation was immediately turned on the circumstantial aspect of military operations by accusing the armed forces of not fighting heroically, while in reality our defeat was only a question of days.'[34] One of the officers arrested in March 1974 after the abortive revolt of the fifth infantry regiment at Caldas da Rainha explained that 'the example of India' and the feeling that Guinea too was a trap pushed them to revolt.[35] The MFA blamed the government for not realizing the implications for the country and the army of its political hard line in Africa.[36]

Psychologically the African wars began for Portugal at the worst possible moment. In March 1961, sixteen African countries won their formal independence. France was the latest of a series of once powerful colonial nations to haul down its flag in Africa. The obvious preference of world-class politicians like de Gaulle and Kennedy for African independence was a strong argument for a graceful Portuguese exit, and one which the US was prepared to back up at the United Nations. 'The integration of the Portuguese armed forces inside NATO had led to strong American influence on the general staff', Perry Anderson wrote. '"Atlantic" norms and tactics began to impinge on the archaic world of the Portuguese military caste. Thus, when the USA publicly disavowed Portugal in the Security Council, the shock for the NATO-orientated officers must have been acute.'[37] The shock to the 'archaic world of the Portuguese military caste' was probably less severe than Perry Anderson imagined. To the army's ingrained distaste for Salazar, to the trauma of Goa, to the embarrassing publicity surrounding the *Santa-Maria* affair, was added the realization that the army was desperately under strength. When Holden Roberto's FNLA launched its attack in March 1961, the Portuguese had barely 3,000 troops in Angola.[38] Defence Minister General Moniz told Salazar that a sustained Portuguese campaign against decolonization would create for the army's 'a suicide mission in which we could not succeed'. His opinion was shared by Army Minister Colonel Almeida Fernandes and Army Under-Secretary Colonel Costa Gomes and other top officers who already had

38 Colonies and Coups: Portugal's Colonial Wars

argued in an August 1960 meeting of the Supreme Defence Council *(Conselho Superior da Defesa Nacional)* against right-wing Air Force Secretary Kaúlza de Arriaga's contingency plans for colonial defence.[39] This time, however, General Moniz did not limit his comments to military affairs. He blasted the régime's 'wasteful political values' and absence of 'moral foundation'. He told the Dictator that 'a profound change of people, methods and organisation' must precede the restoration of human rights and fundamental social and economic reforms.[40] Most generals had decided that Salazar must go and apparently were prepared to tell him so. However, arcane cunning once again prevailed over the winds of change. Salazar sacked Moniz and Fernandes, transferred Costa Gomes and other dissident officers and the 'generals' plot' collapsed in a heap. In 1962 following an unsuccessful armed attack on the barracks at Beja in the Alentejo led by artillery Captain Valera Gomes, the cabinet was again reshuffled to axe Army Minister General Mário da Silva, Overseas Minister Moreira, and several of his under-secretaries, and Angolan Governor General Deslandes, indicating that many at the top had severe misgivings about Portugal's colonial commitment.[41]

Like Hitler, Salazar ignored the advice of his generals at his own peril. The Portuguese military machine, rusty after forty years of peace, was cranked up to provide armies for a war on three fronts. By increasing the portion of the national budget spent on defence from 25 per cent in 1960 to 42.4 per cent in 1968,[42] the troop strength more than doubled from around 60,000 to over 200,000 men.[43] Yet the wasteful and antiquated organization of the forces largely sabotaged the war effort, creating resentment among combat officers which eventually cost Caetano his job: 'We did not have an organisation adequate to direct the army in operations', he admitted.[44] The haphazard and piecemeal organisation of Portuguese defence meant that the army was ill-equipped to cope with a long war, for bureaucratic intransigence, service rivalries and peace had sidetracked reform. The forces for decades had been a puzzle of squabbling fiefdoms and overlapping authorities, with separate metropolitan and colonial armies and the navy under the jurisdiction of the colonial ministry. Under the influence of NATO, a first stab at a unified defence structure resulted in the creation of a defence minister in 1950 whose job was to coordinate the policies and programmes of the ministries of the army, navy and, after 1952, the air force. Caetano wrote:

But this in no way resembled a ministry, its services limited to a

Colonies and Coups: Portugal's Colonial Wars

secretariat directly dependent on the Chief of the General Staff of the armed forces. . .in practice, the relations between the defence ministers and the ministers with military portfolios were always difficult, as those who wanted to justify their existence intervened in matters they believed vital to defence, while the [military ministers] retained their independence.[45]

The defence minister was also meant to speak for the forces in the Supreme Defence Council which included the prime minister, the ministers of the interior, finance, foreign affairs, the colonies and the chief of the armed forces general staff. The military ministers could also be brought in at the prime minister's discretion. However, the Supreme Defence Council failed to draw up a coordinated defence policy. Under Salazar it rarely met: 'Dr Salazar did not like committees, always deploring the amount of time he wasted in meetings of any sort', Caetano noted. 'He preferred meetings restricted to those who had something to say or a mission to accomplish. . .Perhaps he was right.'[46] Defence ministers were left to their own devices in seeking cooperation from civilian ministries, which too often had little time or sympathy for defence problems.[47] After 1962, Salazar largely directed colonial defence himself, with patchy results.

Caetano revived the Supreme Defence Council in 1968: 'Dr Salazar alone took on the job of conducting colonial defence. He could manage it because he had the necessary prestige. But this was not the case for me.'[48] He also tried to put some muscle in the defence ministry by demoting the three military ministers to under-secretaries: 'It was increasingly apparent that military operations needed a close inter-arm co-operation, and this collaboration must be facilitated in peacetime by the unity of political direction and by the existence of a combined general staff.'[49] The army and the air force accepted this arrangement reluctantly.

The navy remained. This body was extremely jealous of its autonomy and reacted vigorously to the idea of being deprived of its own ministry. The naval ministry also contained the merchant marine and fisheries administrations, so that its reduction to a pure military secretariat of state implied a sad amputation for officers who had always had responsibilities in the civil sector. This being the case, they refused to consent to the desired unity. For this reason, I found it preferable to leave the military ministers control of their provinces, instead of relegating them to the painful situation of subalterns of

40 *Colonies and Coups: Portugal's Colonial Wars*

the defence minister.[50]

The spectacle of the navy successfully defying its commander-in-chief provided a forceful demonstration of military power which did not go unnoticed.

Centralized direction of the war effort was further undermined by the frequent appointment of brigadiers and even colonels like Fernandes to ministerial rank. These men seldom had the authority over their more senior colleagues in the general staff to make themselves obeyed. Nor could the general staff, which should have been the brain of the armed forces, provide an effective blueprint for colonial operations. Service rivalries, jurisdictional disputes between Lisbon generals and colonial governors and appalling organization combined to sabotage central war planning. While the army retained a large degree of autonomy under successive Portuguese governments, fears of strong army leadership meant that politicians refused to create a rank above that of major general. Like many features of Portuguese political life, this piece of antiquated organization was lifted bodily from pre-1914 France, with the result that regional commanders, colonial governors, the inspector general, the chief of the general staff, the military ministers when generals, the defence minister and even the president of the republic all held the same rank. Portugal boasted the only European army where the various hierarchical strata were occupied by generals of equal rank. With seniority rather than stars between them, generals often chose to squabble rather than to obey.

The situation in the colonies was equally chaotic. Commanders-in-chief had no staffs, only a small military cabinet with which they attempted to coordinate operations with navy and air force commanders jealous of their autonomy. 'The army disliked the navy, and this was reciprocated', noted one miliciano serving in Guinea. 'Spínola had absolutely no time for the navy. During one of his absences from Guinea, his second-in-command, an admiral, decided to mount an operation using marines. It was a complete fiasco. When Spínola heard about it he was furious. I remember the angry telegrams coming from Lisbon.'[51] Only in July 1969 were governor generals authorized their own staffs, command of the naval and air force units within the colonies, and control of logistics and supply. 'It took some time to put into operation', Caetano said of his reform, 'and perhaps was only effective in Mozambique.'[52]

This Lisbon war machine was also coughing badly. The army and combined general staffs especially suffered from the lack of a firm

Colonies and Coups: Portugal's Colonial Wars

hand, largely due to the presence in the defence ministry of generals only too willing to respect the eccentricities of armed forces organization. In 1970 for the first time, a civilian, Silva Cunha, was picked to put the forces' house in order – barely a year before the régime was overthrown.[53]

Poor staff work was in great part due to the existence in the Portuguese army of a separate staff corps. In military organization, the staff corps is a museum piece: most armies abandoned them in the mid-nineteenth century, but staff corps in Portugal and Venezuela soldiered on. Military theorists since the elder Moltke generally preferred officers to alternate between troop service and staff duty rather than to cream off a few clever young officers for permanent desk jobs. The case was considered proved in 1870 when the French staff corps, stuffed with men who had never heard a shot fired in anger, performed abysmally enough to merit its dissolution. Anti-staff prejudice runs high in all armies, especially in wartime; in Portugal, it reached a fever pitch. Caetano noted:

> The staff corps had a reputation for being excessively theoretical, responsible for the delays in operations and errors committed in them, and for unjustifiable privileges. The army general staff. . .was full of officers who accumulated other jobs, above all teaching, to such an extent that only in the evenings did offices function as they should. Preparation of projects there took an immense amount of time, much to my consternation and that of the overseas commanders.[54]

One of Silva Cunha's first acts was to decree that all staff officers report to work at 9 a.m. rather than their habitual 2 p.m.[55]

Combat officers begrudged their staff colleagues' air conditioned offices in Lisbon and Luanda, were riled by the lateness and inaccuracy of their operations plans and resented their higher pay and faster promotion. Recruited by competitive examination among captains, staff officers were virtually guaranteed a senior rank. While only 5 per cent of regular artillery officers, 7 per cent of infantry officers, 9 per cent of engineering officers and 11 per cent of cavalry officers reached the rank of colonel, fully 30 per cent of staff corps officers did so.[56] Their knowledge of army organization gave them an edge at the Institute of Higher Military Studies, from which colonels were selected for higher rank. Brigadier Bettencourt Rodrigues, promoted out of the staff corps to command the eastern region of Angola, was rated among

42 Colonies and Coups: Portugal's Colonial Wars

the best senior officers. Although it is impossible to gauge what percentage of brigadiers and generals came through the staff corps, they almost certainly counted for more than their 4 per cent of the regular officer corps. Nor was the army organization helped by the corrupt promotion system which pushed the wrong officers to the top. The belief that the high command was incompetent was widespread among younger professionals condemned to support the burden of their seniors' errors. After the 25 April *coup*, virtually all the 90 brigadiers and generals were axed, branded as incompetent and shameless lackeys of an immoral régime. Captain Otelo de Carvalho told journalists:

> Before the 25th April, the generals were chosen and promoted by the council of ministers which guaranteed that they would do as they were told. And a general who 'acted well' knew that he would find, at the end of his military career, a high civil service post, very lucrative, paying tens of thousands of escudos. This purchase of generals guaranteed the security and continuity of the government and eliminated those who did not offer such guarantees. How was it possible to credit generals thus sold out with protecting the prestige of the armed forces or the good of the people? From this, it is clear that with rare exceptions the most lucid and intelligent men were retired as colonels.[57]

The MFA promised to 'put an end to the government's interference in the appointment of general officers, whose selection should pass over to military jurisdiction'.[58]

The 'directorship craze' was cited as direct proof that generals had sold out to the establishment. Many top generals and admirals served simultaneously on the boards of large companies — Kaúlza de Arriaga sat with the directors of Petrangol and the Espírito Santo enterprises, Admiral Tenreiro owned one of Portugal's largest fishing fleets, Admiral Sarmento Rodrigues was president of the Torralta group, General Sottomayor's connections with his family's interests were obvious, and Spínola sat on the board of the Metalúrgica Nacional, to name only a few. The generals thus served the interests of fascism and big money, leaving their subordinates to fight on forgotten in the jungle. 'Since most of the junior officers were not slotted into the co-optive mechanisms of the system, the close association of the generals with political and economic power favoured an irreconcilable schism within the armed forces', Bandeira concluded.[59]

Colonies and Coups: Portugal's Colonial Wars 43

The competence of the high command was certainly questionable. Under Salazar, the council of ministers filled top posts from lists presented by the selection committee of top generals and admirals in each arm. Caetano handed this job over to the Supreme Defence Council, which named officers

> in full liberty. The circumstances demanded the selection for the vacancies of officers when possible young, vigorous, intellectually capable, professionally competent, ready to carry out any mission. In theory all the candidates of the army, having been filtered through the Institute of Higher Military Studies, which selected colonels for promotion to brigadier, would meet these criteria. In practice, it was somewhat different. Each time it was necessary to name a general for some difficult assignment, we culled out from the list those A. who were ill, B. were not intelligent. C. were not suited for the job, D. who were good, but for one reason or another could not be transferred. . .It was hell to find someone who could do the job reasonably well.[60]

Caetano placed the blame for the poor selection of generals on the shoulders of the army, rather than on the fascist régime's concern for political orthodoxy above professionalism. Most Portuguese generals, whose average age of 61 in 1972 compares with that of the notoriously crusty and inefficient French high command in 1914, had clawed their way slowly up the peacetime promotion ladder. They formed a gerontocracy at the top of the army which was too old, too ill or simply not 'modern' enough to fight a guerrilla war. Caetano pointed out:

> In truth, the officers on the promotion committees could not resist the criterion of seniority in ranking candidates. This was understandable. It would be unfortunate to pass over officers with a clean, at times, distinguished career, who through no fault of their own found that after a period of intensive service their promotion came a little slowly. And the Supreme Defence Council would not agree to alter this criterion, although it was tempered by the choice of more modern officers whose merits were generally recognised.[61]

While politics and political intrigue were not absent from the selection process, seniority emerged as the more important factor. When the

44   Colonies and Coups: Portugal's Colonial Wars

régime had to choose between politics and competence, it usually chose the latter. The forces had a tradition of political immunity which was respected, within limits, even by Salazar. Generals Moniz, Lopes, Spínola and Costa Gomes were only a few of the top officers known to enjoy less than warm relations with the dictatorship. As for the charge that the 'directorship craze' illustrates the régime's 'purchase' of the high command, two things must be noted. Firstly, the Salazar régime was never particularly sympathetic to big business. Rather than a political coalition in favour of industrial capitalism like Batista's Cuba, the New State was an anachronism on a grand scale. For decades it resisted capitalist development in Portugal, jealously guarding the traditional values of a poor, landed society. Big money was allowed to flow into Portugal only in the mid-1960s, when the demands of the war made the creation of some sort of tax base mandatory. Political observers have traced a web of interests binding a capitalist-conservative coalition to colonial defence. Kenneth Maxwell wrote:

> The Portuguese empire was thus underpinned by economic linkages that combined an almost mercantilist restrictiveness with complex networks representing the interests of Western European, North American, and South African capital. Though it was never apparent on the surface, the pressures to hold on to Portuguese Africa and to protect European capital in Portugal itself were closely interconnected. . .They were simply doing what came naturally, defending their interests and helping their friends.[62]

But the first concern of the leaders of large multinationals of the sort which had substantial interests in Portuguese Africa was the survival of their organizations.[63] With both weaponry and world opinion running strongly in favour of African independence, most businessmen preferred to make their peace with the future. Portuguese officials put the guerrilla failure to strike at the vulnerable oil installations in Cabinda and Diamang near the Zaire border down to secret company pay-offs. The Marxist MPLA's invitation to Gulf Oil to resume drilling in Cabinda only weeks after the end of the Angolan civil war simply confirmed that agreements between gnomes and guerrillas are far from impossible. It was these large monied interests led by Portuguese industrialists António Champalimaud and Manuel Vinhas which were among the first to voice serious doubts about the wisdom of the wars; Jorge de Mello's giant CUF (Companhia União Fabril) group with large holdings in Guinea financed the 1974 publication of Spínola's book

Colonies and Coups: Portugal's Colonial Wars 45

criticizing the government's colonial policies.[64] Big business-high command connections, then, weakened rather than strengthened the political links between the generals and the government. Secondly, the 'directorship craze' was simply a high command version of a traditional Portuguese practice of holding simultaneous civil employment. A senior officer's pay was desperately low by European standards. Portuguese colonels, brigadiers and generals were paid 40 to 50 per cent less than their counterparts in the British and French armies. The colonel of an infantry regiment stationed in Portugal earned 10,200 escudos per month. A British colonel earned the equivalent of 19,770 escudos and a French colonel 18,317 per month. Pay differences for the higher ranks were even more marked. A Portuguese general could expect to earn only 14,500 escudos while his British equivalent would be paid more than twice that amount. Not surprisingly, well-connected senior Portuguese officers made up their pay deficit by sitting in company boardrooms. Middle ranking officers complained most bitterly about their low income, but it was their pay which compared more favourably with that of other European armies. A Portuguese major earned 7,800 escudos per month which rose to 11,250 escudos in a combat zone. Captains were paid 7,000 escudos in Portugal and 10,000 under fire. A British captain earned roughly the equivalent of 8,458 escudos per month and a French captain 10,900. However, slow promotion meant that a middle ranking Portuguese officer would be older on average than officers of equivalent rank in Britain or France, and therefore relatively less well paid. Also, the prohibitively high cost of living in Angola and Mozambique put Portuguese officers constantly out of pocket. Economic development at home opened up new avenues of employment for middle class Portuguese. Hence, the relative position of army offices in the social hierarchy declined. Lower down, Portuguese NCOs at home earned half of that paid to their counterparts in Britain and France, and in the colonies faced the same cost of living increases as their superiors. Soldiers were fed and clothed and in combat zones given enough money to pay for about one night a month in town.

In peacetime, soldiers topped up their pockets by moonlighting. NCOs did manual or artisan jobs in off-duty hours or resorted to the supply sergeant's fiddles. Combat officers could dip into the 'saco azul' that is draw rations for soldiers sent home on extended leave. Staff and administration officers found spare-time teaching or clerical posts while those with technical expertise could pick up extra cash as advisers or, like engineer Colonel Vasco Gonçalves who owned a construction firm,

46   Colonies and Coups: Portugal's Colonial Wars

Table 2: British Army: Monthly Pay in Escudos, 1970[*]

Rank	
General	36,889
Lieutenant General	30,976
Major General	27,408
Brigadier	22,110
Colonel	19,770
Lieutenant Colonel	15,488
Major	12,484
Captain	8,458
Lieutenant	5,806
Second-Lieutenant	4,433
Warrant Officer	6,954
Staff Sergeant	6,312
Sergeant	5,628
Corporal (daily pay)	157.45
Lance Corporal (daily pay)	134.00
Private (daily pay)	*23.95

French Army: Monthly Pay in Escudos, 1970

Brigadier	26,000
Colonel	18,317
Lieutenant Colonel	15,756
Major	12,146
Captain	10,900
Lieutenant	9,106
Second-Lieutenant	6,266
Officer candidate (aspirante)	6,320
Adjutant-Chief	5,850
Adjutant	5,630
Sergeant Major	5,360
First Sergeant	5,065
Sergeant	4,820
Corporal	4,525

*British army pay scales taken from *Whitaker,* London, 1970, pp.477, 479.
French army pay scales have been calculated from the *Journal Officiel,* arrêtes
of 18 September 1968 for officers and February 1970 for other ranks. Obviously,
each officer's pay reflects his family status, seniority, qualifications and
assignment. These figures represent an average monthly salary in each army.

Colonies and Coups: Portugal's Colonial Wars 47

in the booming building industry. When war broke out, this practice
had unfortunate consequences: military efficiency plummeted because
despite the now increased work load, officers could not afford to drop
their·extra jobs: military affairs took a back seat to extracurricular
activities, especially among staff officers.[65] Stuck in the bush, combat
officers found their chances of earning extra money virtually nil.
Resentment increased against rear-echelon colleagues, often suspected
of flogging material destined for the war zones. The situation was
aggravated by rampant inflation. In the last years of the régime, tourist
money and remittances from Portuguese in France augmented the
money supply and drove prices up by 21 per cent a year.[66] Those on
fixed incomes, including officers, were forced to pull in their horns.
Caetano wrote:

> I realized that inflation favoured political unrest and social
> agitation. . .For the classes with fixed incomes (and this included the
> military) the spectacle of easy fortunes earned in speculation. . .
> together with shortages in shops of certain basic products due in
> many cases to their withdrawal pending the next price rise,
> constituted a scandal. And with the conceptual ingenuity of the
> common man, the government was not allowed to escape
> responsibility.[67]

The situation was even worse in the colonies where a protected import
market and exchange rates beneficial to Portugal drove prices through
the roof. An officer's pay not only bought little, but compared badly
with salaries earned by those doing menial jobs. Touched in their pride,
the mood of combat officers turned nasty. Captain Sousa e Castro, one
of the original MFA members, complained:

> The army is always blamed for anything which goes wrong in this
> country. We were blamed for everything when we were in Africa.
> For 13 years the soldiers — I am speaking of the cadres — were
> belittled and exploited in the war. Personally, I can say that as a
> sub-lieutenant in the combat zone I earned 4,500 escudos, less than
> a porter at the Imperial Cinema in Luanda. As a captain commanding
> a company in Mozambique I earned less than a barber in Nampula,
> 10,000 a month. And I went months on end without seeing my
> family or my friends. I and my soldiers, we all went to war. Now we
> soldiers are attacked because in Africa we obtained the most material.
> This is false. Everyone knows that when an army fights, even a

Table 3: Monthly Salaries of Portuguese Army Officers, 30 June 1970

	Basic Salary — Metropole and Provinces	Complementary Pay			
		Guiné, Angola and Moçambique	Cape Verde and S. Tomé and Principe	Macau	Timor
General	14,500$00	5,700$00	4,700$00	5,100$00	5,700$00
Brigadier	13,000$00	5,200$00	4,300$00	4,700$00	5,200$00
Colonel	(1) 11,000$00	4,450$00	3,700$00	4,000$00	4,450$00
	(2) 10,500$00	4,300$00	3,600$00	3,900$00	4,300$00
	(3) 10,200$00	4,200$00	3,500$00	3,800$00	4,200$00
Lieutenant Colonel	(1) 9,400$00	3,900$00	3,250$00	3,550$00	3,900$00
	(2) 8,900$00	3,750$00	3,150$00	3,400$00	3,750$00
	(3) 8,600$00	3,650$00	3,050$00	3,300$00	3,650$00
Major	(1) 8,500$00	3,650$00	3,050$00	3,300$00	3,650$00
	(2) 8,100$00	3,550$00	2,950$00	3,200$00	3,550$00
	(3) 7,800$00	3,450$00	2,850$00	3,100$00	3 450$00
Captain	(1) 7,600$00	3,250$00	2,700$00	2,900$00	3,250$00
	(2) 7,300$00	3,100$00	2,600$00	2,800$00	3,100$00
	(3) 7,000$00	3,000$00	2,500$00	2,700$00	3,000$00
Lieutenant	(2) 5,200$00	2,550$00	2,150$00	2,300$00	2,850$00
	(3) 4,900$00	2,500$00	2,050$00	2,200$00	2,850$00

Table 3 *(contd.)*

		Basic Salary — Metropole and Provinces	Complementary Pay			
			Guiné, Angola and Moçambique	Cape Verde and S. Tomé and Principe	Macau	Timor
2nd Lieutenant	(2)	4,100$00	2,500$00	1,800$00	1,950$00	2,400$00
	(3)	3,800$00	2,500$00	1,750$00	1,850$00	2,400$00
Officer Candidate	(a)	3,500$00	2,500$00	1,750$00	1,850$00	2,400$00
	(b)	2,600$00	2,500$00	1,750$00	1,850$00	2,400$00

(1)   General Staff Corps and Complementary General Staff Course.
(2)   General Staff Course, Engineer and Artillery Courses.
(3)   Remainder of Arms and Services.
(a)   Regular Officers and Reserve Officers after completing their compulsory military service.
(b)   Reserve officers while doing their military service.

Figures furnished by the American Embassy, Lisbon.

Table 4: Monthly Salaries of Army Sergeants, 30 June 1970

| | Basic Salary — Metropole and Provinces | Complementary Pay | | | |
		Guiné, Angola and Moçambique	Cape Verde and S. Tomé and Principe	Macau	Timor
Sergeant major	3,500$00	2,000$00	1,650$00	1,800$00	2,000$00
1st Sergeant	3,200$00	1,900$00	1,600$00	1,700$00	1 900$00
2nd Sergeant	2,900$00	1,800$00	1,500$00	1,600$00	1,800$00
Corporal	2,600$00	1,800$00	1,500$00	1,600$00	1,800$00

Monthly Salaries of Naval Petty Officers, 30 June 1970

Sergeant major	3,500$00	2,000$00	1,650$00	1,800$00	2,000$00
1st Sergeant	3,200$00	1,900$00	1,600$00	1,700$00	1,900$00
2nd Sergeant	2,900$00	1,800$00	1,500$00	1,600$00	1,800$00
Sub-sergeant	2,600$00	1,800$00	1,500$00	1,600$00	1,800$00

Monthly Salaries of Air Force Sergeants, 30 June 1970

Sergeant major	3,500$00	2,000$00	1,650$00		
1st Sergeant	3,200$00	1,900$00	1,600$00		
2nd Sergeant	2,900$00	1,800$00	1,500$00		
Corporal	2,600$00	1,800$00	1,500$00		

Figures furnished by the American Embassy, Lisbon.

Table 5: Daily Salaries of Army Corporals and Privates, 30 June 1970

	Ranks & Reenlistment Periods		Base Pay					Complementary Pay				
			Portugal	Guiné Angola Moçambique	Cape Verde S. Tomé Principe	Macau	Timor	Reenlist-ment	Guiné Angola Moçambique	Cape Verde S. Tomé Principe	Macau	Timor
Corporals and Privates from Portugal	1st Corporal	(-)	3$00	-0-	-0-	-0-	-0-	-0-	29$00	15$00	24$00	24$00
		(1)	3$00	-0-	-0-	-0-	-0-	29$00	29$00	20$00	24$00	29$00
		(2)	3$00	-0-	-0-	-0-	-0-	36$00	31$00	22$00	25$00	31$00
		(3)	3$00	-0-	-0-	-0-	-0-	43$00	33$00	24$00	27$00	33$00
		(4)	3$00	-0-	-0-	-0-	-0-	50$00	35$00	26$00	29$00	35$00
	2nd Corporal (PFC)	(-)	2$00	-0-	-0-	-0-	-0-	-0-	23$00	12$00	21$00	18$00
		(1)	2$00	-0-	-0-	-0-	-0-	22$00	25$00	16$00	21$00	20$00
		(2)	2$00	-0-	-0-	-0-	-0-	29$00	27$00	18$00	23$00	24$00
		(3)	2$00	-0-	-0-	-0-	-0-	36$00	29$00	20$00	25$00	28$00
		(4)	2$00	-0-	-0-	-0-	-0-	43$00	31$00	22$00	27$00	30$00
	Private	(-)	1$00	-0-	-0-	-0-	-0-	-0-	23$00	9$00	18$00	16$50
		(1)	1$00	-0-	-0-	-0-	-0-	22$00	24$00	15$00	21$00	19$00
		(2)	1$00	-0-	-0-	-0-	-0-	29$00	26$00	17$00	23$00	24$00
		(3)	1$00	-0-	-0-	-0-	-0-	36$00	28$00	19$00	25$00	27$00
		(4)	1$00	-0-	-0-	-0-	-0-	43$00	30$00	21$00	27$00	29$00

Table 5 *(contd.)*

	Ranks & Reenlistment Periods		Portugal	Base Pay				Reenlist-ment	Complementary Pay			
				Guiné Angola Moçambique	Cape Verde S. Tomé Principe	Macau	Timor		Guiné Angola Moçambique	Cape Verde S. Tomé Principe	Macau	Timor
		(-)	-0-	32$00	18$00	27$00	27$00	-0-	-0-	-0-	-0-	-0-
		(1)	-0-	32$00	23$00	27$00	32$00	29$00	-0-	-0-	-0-	-0-
	1st Corporal	(2)	-0-	34$00	25$00	28$00	34$00	36$00	-0-	-0-	-0-	-0-
		(3)	-0-	36$00	27$00	30$00	36$00	43$00	-0-	-0-	-0-	-0-
		(4)	-0-	38$00	29$00	32$00	38$00	50$00	-0-	-0-	-0-	-0-
Corporals and Privates from Overseas		(-)	-0-	25$00	14$00	23$00	20$00	-0-	-0-	-0-	-0-	-0-
		(1)	-0-	27$00	18$00	23$00	22$00	22$00	-0-	-0-	-0-	-0-
	2nd Corporal (PFC)	(2)	-0-	29$00	20$00	25$00	26$00	29$00	-0-	-0-	-0-	-0-
		(3)	-0-	31$00	22$00	27$00	30$00	36$00	-0-	-0-	-0-	-0-
		(4)	-0-	33$00	24$00	29$00	32$00	43$00	-0-	-0-	-0-	-0-
		(-)	-0-	24$00	10$00	19$00	17$50	-0-	-0-	-0-	-0-	-0-
		(1)	-0-	25$00	16$00	22$00	20$00	22$00	-0-	-0-	-0-	-0-
1st Class	Private	(2)	-0-	27$00	18$00	24$00	25$00	29$00	-0-	-0-	-0-	-0-
		(3)	-0-	29$00	20$00	26$00	28$00	36$00	-0-	-0-	-0-	-0-
		(4)	-0-	31$00	22$00	28$00	30$00	43$00	-0-	-0-	-0-	-0-
	Recruit		-0-	4.50	4.50	4.50	4.50	-0-	-0-	-0-	-0-	-0-

Figures furnished by the American Embassy, Lisbon.

Colonies and Coups: Portugal's Colonial Wars 53

guerrilla war, it must have a logistical back-up and means of communication. Stores, hospitals, magazines, garages etc. have to remain in the rear, in the cities. . .soldiers who ran them lived in the best conditions. But this must not be confused with the army which fought in Africa. The combat arms were the sacrificial arms. This is not an exaggeration. When people argue. . .that the army made the revolution of 25 April to evade the war, all I can say is that the soldiers are damned if they do and damned if they don't.[68]

In Guinea, the idea that the army was forced to carry the can for an unimaginative government gained universal acceptance as defeat began to look certain. The war in Angola was going well due to the presence of a large white population and three separate tribal-based liberation movements which faced enormous logistical difficulties and spent almost as much time killing each other as fighting the Portuguese. The army even hit back at resistance sanctuaries in Zambia through the *Flechas* – guerrilla deserters organized by the Portuguese who infiltrated and disrupted independence forces. The army in Mozambique had more or less contained the FRELIMO in the North away from the populated areas; in Guinea, however, after only a few years of combat, the army had its back to the wall. Under the capable leadership of a Portuguese-educated Cape Verdean, Amílcar Cabral, the PAIGC liberation movement launched its first attacks in 1962. Westmoreland-style sweeps by the Portuguese through the swampy, river-laced terrain had little effect against guerrillas generously supported by Senegal and Conakry. By 1967, the army had been forced back on the towns where Guinea's 2,000 whites, mostly colonial administrators, were concentrated.[69] In 1968, Brigadier Spínola, in Lisbon after a fact-finding tour in Guinea, reported to the Supreme Defence Council that the war was lost. He criticized the strategy of Governor General Arnaldo Schultz which neglected civic action programmes vital in winning over the population and lashed military chiefs who covered up the magnitude of the Portuguese reverses. Portugal's only hope lay in regaining enough ground to negotiate an honourable settlement with the guerrillas to retain some links with the lost colony. Caetano returned Spínola to Guinea with a *carte blanche* to apply his ideas.[70]

Whatever his subsequent failings as a politician, General Spínola's Guinea command stands as a monument to inspired military leadership. Like a twentieth-century poor man's Bismarck, he set out to reforge Portugal overseas through 'blood and smiles'. In four years he managed both to restore the military confidence of an army whose morale stood

54   *Colonies and Coups: Portugal's Colonial Wars*

at rock bottom and to institute an extensive programme of civic action and African participation in the government, administration and the war effort. Already regarded by most of the high command as a spoiled child, he made new enemies on his arrival by relieving many incompetent officers and banishing others to the bush. Hopping about the country by helicopter, he breathed new life into the war effort, inspiring tremendous loyalty among officers unused to seeing generals, competent or otherwise, near danger. He built up a battalion of black commandos led by two white officers but otherwise totally staffed by black officers and NCOs, with plans for an eventual black takeover of senior positions. Officers who served under him were impressed by his ability. One miliciano who served under the General noted:

> Guinea was full of spies, spies on both sides. We captured one chap named Rafael Barbosa. After three months in prison, Spínola decided to rehabilitate him. He worked for both sides. One day he showed up in Spínola's office with three bombs in a briefcase. He told the General that the PAIGC had asked him to place them in Bissau, what they called 'selective terrorism'. He told the General that he did not want to kill innocent people, so he was turning the bombs over. Spínola said, 'Fine, I will take them. Now let me have the other two.' He knew that Barbosa had been given five to plant.[71]

In 1970 Spínola launched a campaign to win the 'hearts and minds' of the black population by erasing injustices which he believed drove them into the arms of the PAIGC. Aiming to 'build a better Guinea', ninety million escudos were spent to construct over 15,000 houses, 164 schools, 40 infirmaries, 163 fire stations and 86 fountains. Twenty per cent of teachers and 95 per cent of doctors in Guinea were furnished by the army. Soldiers also advised Africans on agriculture and improved roads and air fields. Hand in hand with economic improvement, Spínola set out to democratize Guinean government by placing blacks in the administration, ensuring that they received fair treatment in the courts and through a system of 'People's Congresses': 'The government wants criticisms to be freely expressed', Spínola told them. 'Only in this way can we correct faults and govern for the good of all.' Officers sat down with representatives of tribal and religious groups to discuss grievances. A system of ethnic-based congresses was devised, culminating in a general congress in Bissau. Spínola also set up a legislative council presided over by himself with fourteen elected members, three of them by universal suffrage. The official statement read:

Colonies and Coups: Portugal's Colonial Wars   55

The People's Congresses. . .aim to form strong instruments of mass psychological mobilization around government policy and are particularly important as a means of dialogue between the government and the people in order to decide on the fundamental objectives we propose to realise. Only through an open and constructive dialogue can the government effectively enlighten and in turn be enlightened, exercising an influence on the population to obtain active participation in the tasks of defence and progress.[72]

The importance of 'psychological action' in Guinea in raising the political consciousness of officers cannot be overstated, although it has often been misinterpreted. Alves, Maxwell and others credit the PAIGC with the tactics and techniques aped by Portuguese 'psychological action' teams, as well as the Marxist stamp of the MFA drawn largely from Guinea-based officers. Officers like Carvalho, 'head of psychological warfare in Guinea', turned against 'liberalism' through the study of PAIGC propaganda and were converted to the idea that only firm action on a Marxist model could attain the necessary transformation of Portuguese society.[73] 'The practical Marxism of PAIGC, FRELIMO and MPLA had a remarkable impact on the young "petty bourgeois" officers of the Portuguese army in Africa, for whom Amílcar Cabral's notion of a petty bourgeois "revolutionary vanguard" had more than usual appeal',[74] Maxwell writes. Captain Duran Clemente, one of the officers involved in the left-wing *coup* attempt of 25 November 1975, claimed that PAIGC propaganda had a 'pedagogical effect' on officers. Alves also concluded that the officers' examination of their opponents meant that the liberation movements 'educated the Portuguese army for socialism at the same time as they prepared their peoples for liberation'.[75]

Spínola's adoption of 'psychological warfare', although a necessary counterpart to the political indoctrination techniques of the guerrillas, was not an imitation of PAIGC methods but was rather drawn from the experience of other armies, especially the French, who had been fighting guerrilla wars before the PAIGC was born. By 1968, psychological action had become a long-established constituent of counter-insurgency strategy, used also by the Americans in Vietnam. Its object was not to provide an alternative tyranny, but to demonstrate the virtues of a liberal constitutional society in stark contrast to the rigidly organized and dictatorial liberation movements. It was characterized by a well-intentioned idealism and a desire for social justice which marked the MFA rank and file. There is no more reason

56 Colonies and Coups: Portugal's Colonial Wars

to suppose that enemy propaganda provided the road to Damascus for 'petty bourgeois' Portuguese officers than it had for 'petty bourgeois' French and American officers in Algeria and Vietnam. Nor can the extreme left-wing views of a number of naval officers who spent the war ferrying supplies between Lisbon and Luanda be put down to guerrilla contact. Despite the superficial Marxist veneer a few officers gave to the MFA and its avowed ambition after 11 March 1975, to become a Portuguese liberation movement, in fact the MFA never concocted anything resembling a coherent political philosophy. Its actions were stamped by a woolly idealism more akin to boy scouting than Marxist internationalism. The Marxist orientation of a few top officers was not the result of the study of PAIGC literature, but came from other sources. Carvalho was not the head of psychological action in Guinea, but an affable PR man whose job was to show visiting journalists the best side of the Portuguese civic action projects. His subsequent ideas do not reflect the clear analysis of Cabral and other revolutionary ideologists, but the vague, if passionate, reformist spirit brought to the surface by Spínola in Guinea. A psychological-action officer who worked closely in Guinea with Carvalho and Carlos Fabião, future army chief noted for his progressive ideas on 'revolutionary discipline', stated that neither 'were particularly left-wing while in the colonies'. While civic action programmes did make some officers more conscious of social inequalities, their left-wing politics were a product of Portugal's revolutionary situation following the April 25, 1974 *coup*, not of their bush contact with guerrillas.

Guinea was important because it gave officers a mission and a leader, giving direction to the war and at the same time placing them squarely to the left of their government. The political opinions of their charismatic, anti-establishment general and the liberalizing orientation of his strategy was not lost on those who served under Spínola. To the admiration of his military qualities, his intolerance of military incompetence and his sense of justice was added relief and joy at finding a leader who openly expressed what until now had been only muted criticism of the régime. Spínola's sarcastic comments on the 1972 'election' of Admiral Tomás as president sent a ripple of pleasure through the barracks.[76] His openly expressed conviction that the war must be brought to a negotiated settlement gained even wider approval. 'Spínola was very anti-régime', one of his staff officers noted. 'The letters which he wrote to Lisbon both officially and privately, stressed that there could be no military solution to the conflict. We discussed it openly among ourselves. We all agreed with General Spínola.

Colonies and Coups: Portugal's Colonial Wars 57

This attitude spread through all the troops. We felt that a political solution was necessary, but that we must fight in the meantime.'[77]

By 1971, the Portuguese had regained enough terrain to be able to hold their own at the negotiating table. Pushed by President Senghor of Senegal who was keen to limit the future influence of Conakry in his southern neighbour, Caetano gave the nod for exploratory talks to begin in 1971 with the Senegalese as mediators. In mid-1972, Caetano approved a meeting between Spínola and the Senegalese President which took place in a small village in Southern Senegal. Senghor suggested a ceasefire followed by direct meetings between the General and Cabral with eventual joint Portuguese-PAIGC participation in the Guinea government as the goal. Caetano slammed on the brakes. He reminded the general that 'no matter how great his prestige was in Guinea', Cabral was not a simple bandit but an experienced politician with considerable UN support. Spínola, he feared, would be outclassed at the conference table while the guerrillas, under the cover of a ceasefire, 'would keep their freedom of subversive manoeuvre. . .'. He was also certain that the PAIGC would insist on controlling the Cape Verde islands, so putting under 'the domination of the socialist world a key position in the Atlantic Ocean'.[78] Caetano then let drop that he had never been serious about negotiations in the first place:

Even if negotiations over Guinea were successful, one could not forget that we held Angola and we held Mozambique, with hundreds of thousands of whites and millions of loyal blacks whom we could not sacrifice lightly. The difficulty of the Guinea problem was this: it was part of a larger global problem that had to be considered and acted upon as a whole while upholding the legal and political principles which accompanied it.

Caetano recorded the following conversation with the stunned Spínola:

. . .For a global defence of overseas [provinces] it is preferable to leave Guinea with an honourable military defeat rather than to negotiate with the terrorists, opening the door to other negotiations.
— But your Excellency would prefer a military defeat in Guinea, exclaimed the General, scandalized.
— Armies are made to fight and must fight to win, but it is not power which wins. If the Portuguese army is beaten in Guinea after having fought to the limit of its possibilities, this defeat would allow us to initiate legal-political steps to continue the defence of the rest

58 Colonies and Coups: Portugal's Colonial Wars

of the overseas provinces. . .The General returned to Bissau profoundly shocked and without concealing his anguish.[79]

Caetano concluded that he had even pondered making Spinola overseas minister but reconsidered after he realized that the General saw colonial problems 'through a Bissau gunport'.[80] More than anything, Caetano's clear preference for glorious defeat over negotiated settlement pushed Spinola into opposition. Writing more than a year after his exile, Caetano proved that, like an unreconstructed French aristocrat, he had learned nothing and forgotten nothing. Why should the army allow itself to be bloodied beyond recognition so that the Prime Minister could crow into television cameras 'L'armée portugaise meurt, elle ne se rend pas'?

With the collapse of negotiations, the Portuguese position in Guinea rapidly began to deteriorate. Spínola's tour ended in early 1973, about the time that a book bomb believed sent by the PIDE blew up in Cabral's face, killing him instantly. Attitudes on both sides hardened. The end of the Vietnam war meant that the stream of arms flowing through Hanoi could be diverted to Guinea, giving the PAIGC sophisticated ground-to-air missiles which kept the air force planes in their hangars and deprived the army of its overhead cover. The loss of five planes in a few days had a devastating effect on morale: 'I remember the day an officer walked into the mess and announced that one of our planes had been shot down by a missile', a miliciano said. 'It was terrible. . .We knew then that we were headed for defeat.'[81] At the same time, international pressure on the merchants of death intensified the arms problems which Portugal had experienced throughout the war. Caetano created a Director General of Armaments in the defence ministry to coordinate the production of homemade arms. But the absence of both quantity and quality compounded by army resentment over private industry moving in on the preserve of its own ordinance foundries doomed this to limited success.[82]

The introduction of sophisticated weapons, including some Mig sorties out of Conakry against Portuguese positions, tipped the precarious psychological and military balance in the insurgents' favour. Spínola's dynamic leadership had served only to paper over serious cracks in the Portuguese war effort. Guinea became a tinderbox after the departure of Spínola. By prolonging an unwinnable war, thereby encouraging division and discontent in the forces, Caetano was not 'courting an honourable military defeat' but rather a *coup d'état*. Both Spínola and the young MFA spoke of the 'ever present spectre of Goa'—

Colonies and Coups: Portugal's Colonial Wars

Caetano could not have his Dien Bien Phu and keep his job too. The Rebelo decrees provided the spark which ignited the revolution.

Notes

1. Ambler, *The French Army in Politics, 1945-62*, Ohio State University Press, 1966, p.49.
2. Ibid., p.46.
3. I include the American army here not because it is a colonial army but because its Vietnam war experience produced the same feelings of isolation among its professionals as were common in France and Portugal.
4. Ambler, op.cit., p.104.
5. Interview.
6. Interview.
7. Caetano, *O Depoimento*, op.cit., Rio de Janeiro, 1974, p.75.
8. Ibid., p.176.
9. Charles Foubert, *Portugal, les années d'espoir*, Paris, 1975, p.34.
10. Alves, Mario, *Les Soldats socialistes du Portugal*, op.cit., Paris, 1975, p.14.
11. Interview.
12. Bandeira, A.R., 'Military Intervention in Portuguese Politics', op.cit., unpublished paper, York University, Toronto , August 1975, p.51.
13. Caetano, op.cit., p.100.
14. Quoted in Rodrigues, *O Movimento dos Capitães*, op.cit., Lisbon, 1974, p.97.
15. See Pierre Sergent, *Je ne regrette rien*, Paris, 1972.
16. *Revista Militar*, No.11, November 1974, pp.571-2.
17. Interview.
18. Interview.
19. See D. Wheeler, 'The Portuguese Army in Angola', *Journal of Modern African Studies*, vol.7, No.3, 1969, pp.425-39.
20. Interview.
21. Rodrigues, op.cit., p. 98 and pp.286-7.
22. Quoted in Humbarachi, op.cit., pp.40-1.
23. Interview.
24. Bandeira, op.cit., p.28.
25. Ibid., p.29.
26. *República*, 19 September 1974.
27. Interview.
28. Bandeira, op.cit., p.29.
29. Interview.
30. *República*, 19 September 1974.
31. Bandeira, op.cit., pp.28-9.
32. Caetano, op.cit., p.174.
33. Ibid., p.174.
34. Spínola, *Le Portugal et son avenir*, Paris, 1974, p.224.
35. Rodrigues, op.cit., p.80.
36. See MFA manifesto, 'The Army and the Nation' in Rodriques, op.cit., pp.97-8.
37. Anderson, Perry, 'Portugal and the End of Ultra Colonialism', *The New Left Review*, op.cit., No.17, p.109.
38. Wheeler, 'The Portuguese army in Angola', *Journal of Modern African Studies*, October 1969.

60 *Colonies and Coups: Portugal's Colonial Wars*

39. Rodrigues, op.cit., p.186.
40. Ibid., pp.183-4.
41. Anderson, op.cit., No.17, p.112.
42. João Luis de Costa André, 'Prospectiva do Financiamento das Despesas da Defesa', *Revista Militar,* January 1971, p.26.
43. Bandeira, op.cit., p.33.
44. Caetano, op.cit., p.172.
45. Ibid., p.166.
46. Ibid., p.165.
47. Kaúlza de Arriaga, 'A Defesa Nacional Portuguesa nos Ultimos 40 Anos e o Futuro', *Revista Militar,* vol.18, Nos.11-12, November-December 1966, pp.551-2.
48. Caetano, op.cit., p.165.
49. Ibid., p.166.
50. Ibid., pp.166-7.
51. Interview.
52. Caetano, op.cit., p.171.
53. Ibid., p.172.
54. Ibid., pp.168, 172.
55. Ibid., p.172.
56. Based on figures taken from Ministério do Exército, *Lista Geral de Antiguidades dos Officiais do Exército (Quadro Permanente),* Lisbon, 1972.
57. Rodrigues, op.cit., pp.108-9.
58. Bandeira, p.41; see also Maxwell, 'The Hidden Revolt in Portugal', *New York Review of Books,* 17 April 1975, p.30.
59. Ibid., p.32.
60. Caetano, op.cit., p.167.
61. Ibid., pp.167-8.
62. Maxwell, 'Portugal under Pressure', op.cit., pp.26-7.
63. See Antony Samson, *The Sovereign State of ITT,* New York, 1973.
64. Rodrigues, op.cit., pp.263-4.
65. Caetano, op.cit., p.172.
66. Bandeira, op.cit., p.46.
67. Caetano, op.cit., pp.101-2.
68. *A Capital,* 1 February 1976.
69. See Humbarachi and Muchnik, op.cit., and W. Minter, op.cit.
70. Rodrigues, op.cit., p.238.
71. Interview.
72. Lt. Col. Mário Stoffel Martins, 'Guiné Portuguesa', *Revista Militar,* July 1974, and Official Folder typed 1972.
73. Maxwell, 'Portugal under Pressure', op.cit., p.27.
74. Ibid., 'The Hidden Revolt in Portugal', p.32.
75. Alves, op.cit., p.37; see also Rodrigues, op.cit., p.249.
76. Rodrigues, ibid., p.248.
77. Interview.
78. Caetano, op.cit., p.190.
79. Ibid., pp.191-2.
80. Ibid., p.192.
81. Interview.
82. Caetano, op.cit., p.173.

3 PROFESSIONAL OFFICERS AND 'TEMPORARY GENTLEMEN'

War can be a nourishing experience for armies. Provided the casualties are not too debilitating as in the First World War, the scope and nature of the fighting allows the imagination of generals full reign — again the First World War springs to mind — and if the country stands behind the war effort, war can allow an army to iron out organizational inefficiencies, weed out incompetents and push bright young officers to the top, and forge links between the army and the nation to focus national pride on the forces. The French army of the Revolution, with the aid of the guillotine, produced a fine stable of generals and crack units. Victorious armies emerged strengthened out of the Second World War, and the idea still lingers in Britain at least that the war instilled a spirit of sacrifice and respect for authority in the generation which fought it. One wonders, however, if little old Portuguese ladies, reading of the latest student disturbances at Lisbon University or scanning the groups of idle young men who decorate Lisbon cafés and street corners, utter the same sort of platitude on the therapeutic effects of a good war on the younger generation.

Those who followed the Portuguese army through thirteen years of war and another year and a half of revolution can only agree with the Russian grand duke who found war regrettable if only because 'it spoils armies'. If after April 1974 many claimed that soldiers were simply 'the people in uniform', before 1961 — and later for some officer categories - the forces equally could have assumed the mantle of 'the civil service in uniform'. Maintaining the same level of comfortable inefficiency as the bulk of the Portuguese bureaucracy, the army could not be expected to cope with anything more serious than a fairly modest tribal rebellion. When, after an initial suspension of disbelief, the high command realized that Doctor Salazar meant what he said about colonial defence, it uncourageously went along with him. The strain proved too much for the forces and for the country. That the Portuguese army at last rebelled is not at all surprising. One may well wonder, however, why the revolt was so long in coming.

The 25 April image of an army of revolutionary giant killers, soldier Jacks who chopped down the fascist beanstalk and sawed off the head of Iberian reaction became the one celebrated in Portugal and abroad. Poster art, one of the few industries which flourished with the

61

62   Professional Officers and 'Temporary Gentlemen'

revolution, depicted cartoon soldiers vigilantly guarding worker democracy, guaranteeing the 'MFA-POVO' alliance by force of arms. In sterner communist party versions of the same theme, menacing figures armed to the teeth frowned down on passers-by as if straight out of Stalin's Russia. MFA-inscribed, trinkets − key chains, lapel pins, posters, paper weights − hawked by street vendors became the inconography of revolution while, in the early days at least, soldiers with little to keep them busy in barracks found a warm and often alcoholic welcome in Lisbon.

Had officers realized just how unpopular the régime had become, perhaps they would have not suffered more than a decade of war before taking matters into their own hands. For they did not need General Spinola to tell them that the wars would lead Portugal to ruin. As early as 1966, Kaúlza de Arriaga had written in the *Revista Militar*, a fighting man's *Cosmopolitan* because of its general intellectual level and the fact that it is meant to be displayed on every officer's coffee table, that Portugal could not go on spending such enormous amounts on defence but must look instead to developing the economy.[1] By the early 1970s, articles on the disruptive effects of the war appeared not infrequently. Luís da Costa André, Secretary of State at the Treasury, repeated the message in January 1971. Those who countered for the government argued basically that the war was beneficial because it spread Portuguese civilization and resulted in the training of around 18,000 lorry drivers yearly.[2] Officers with a critical eye, however, noticed that within the scope of apologist arguments, the sixteenth century seemed to exist uncomfortably next to the twentieth. Yet, this knowledge failed to push officers to political action. They soldiered on in Africa until the army's situation became intolerable, then they bolted. 'We had wanted for a long time to alter the political situation', Vítor Alves told *Expresso*, 'but we did not have the conditions to unite the officers. . .'[3] These conditions were provided by the war. That the army took so long to crack was due largely to the poor quality of the guerrilla opposition. The disorganization of the army and its increasing inability to cope with the extensive colonial wars was at last forcefully brought home in Guinea with the departure of its charismatic commander. Poor utilization of units, bad training, dependence on black troops who now began to falter brought morale crashing down and exacerbated the growing tensions between professional officers and their conscript colleagues. 'Until 1973, the situation was well in hand', one professional officer said. 'The guerrillas were not well trained, but then one could say the same for our own

Professional Officers and 'Temporary Gentlemen' 63

troops. We had only a few thousand decent soldiers.'[4]

In Africa, all troops fought as infantry in tasks for which many artillery, engineer or even cavalry units were not trained. Regulars shook their heads at the perversion of professional standards, an impression reinforced by the quarterly arrival of drafts of half-trained conscripts. As the war progressed, the quality of these men steadily declined. The well-connected, like socialist party chief Mário Soares, could wrangle a medical certificate, a student deferment, or if pushed, could travel abroad until the heat was off. Many potentially good fighting men took trains north to France, leaving for the most part those who lacked the money or energy to emigrate to man the trenches. Training should have been intensified to deal with ever more poorly educated, and in many cases illiterate, soldiers. But a shortage of professional officers and NCOs threw the burden of troop preparation on to conscript cadres whose quality declined with that of the conscript classes from which they came. The men were badly trained and badly led', Caetano admitted.

> Training was given by inexperienced miliciano officers and otherwise by regulars only recently arrived from overseas who spent some months in Portugal before returning overseas, weary and in need of a complete rest. This was our great problem, the fatigue of our regular cadres.[5]

A 'cost efficiency' system of training and manpower allocation borrowed from the American army also did little for unit morale. Conscripts were trained in large camps usually by milicianos and conscript NCOs themselves just out of training, rather than by the men who would lead them into battle. Officers at the front found that the constant coming and going of soldiers and NCOs undermined regimental cohesion.

For this more 'efficient' manpower allocation system, the Portuguese, like the Americans in Vietnam, paid a stiff price – and an unnecessary one. For American historical teams set up after 1945 to study combat motivation reached the same conclusion which the British army had demonstrated for centuries in the tightly knit regimental structure of their army: namely that peer pressure is more important than formal discipline in pushing troops into combat. 'Whenever one surveys the forces of the battlefield', American General S.L.A. Marshall wrote in *Men Against Fire,*

64 *Professional Officers and 'Temporary Gentlemen'*

it is to see that fear is general among men, but to observe further that men are commonly loathe that their fear will be expressed in specific acts which their comrades will recognize as cowardice. The majority are unwilling to take extraordinary risks and do not aspire to a hero's role, but they are equally unwilling that they should be considered the least worthy among those present.

'Mutual acquaintanceship' did wonders for a unit's fighting spirit: 'When a soldier is. . .known to the men who are around him, he. . .has reason to fear losing the one thing he is likely to value more highly than life − his reputation as a man among other men.'[6] But Marshal's conclusions fell on the deaf ears of the confident corporation men like MacNamara who in the 1950s and 1960s imported cost efficient techniques worked out in General Motors' boardroom into the Defense Department and from there into NATO. Garrisons in combat zones more resembled transient barracks where commanders patched together a unit from passing troops. The result was low morale, low efficiency and high casualties.

Portuguese tactics lifted a page from the French counter-insurgency book. Stationary garrison troops commanded almost exclusively by milicianos carried out civic action programmes, patrols and gathered intelligence while élite, often black, units of commandos, paratroops or marines shifted about the country doing most of the fighting. These men were led by regular officers or keen miliciano volunteers and contrasted sharply with the often timid stationary units captained by milicianos. Stories of the combat evasive action of miliciano-led units, some almost too ludicrous to be true, were rife among regular officers. 'The aim of the soldiers was to stay in the barracks and avoid a fight', one regular officer said. 'When they were meant to patrol, they simply crawled into a bunker. They were usually led by milicianos − just doctors or lawyers in uniform.'[7] Milicianos seldom minced words when discussing their professional colleagues. A conscript lieutenant said:

In Guinea, the anti-war feeling was strong among the milicianos. Bissau was a beastly place. We had a very common saying: 'I'm fed up with this place! I'm fed up with them − meaning the regular officers! Get me out of here!' This feeling was reciprocated by the professional officers. The milicianos felt that they were being used to do the dirty work.[8]

Dad's army probably could have taken on the Portuguese with at least

Professional Officers and 'Temporary Gentlemen'

a 50-50 chance of success. 'The Portuguese do not fight well under strict discipline', a professional officer confessed. 'We are not a very martial race.'[9]

Ill-feeling between conscript 'temporary gentlemen' and regulars claiming a monopoly on professional competence is not uncommon, especially in wartime. But in the Portuguese army this unfriendly rivalry erupted into bitter discontent in June 1973 with the publication of the Rebelo decrees. Increasingly worried by the erosion of the regular cadres, both in quality and quantity, which a few years later translated into severe shortages in the middle and higher ranks, the government looked to entice milicianos 'who had proved themselves in combat' to abandon their amateur status and turn professional. This switch had been possible at some time, but after several years' service few milicianos relished the idea of beginning again in the Military Academy. Decree law 353-73 therefore created an accelerated two-semester course at the Military Academy for conscript captains.

This sort of multiple entry into a military career was common in western armies and should have been regarded as another small step towards modernization had its effects on the rather archaic promotion system in the Portuguese army not proved so disruptive. Most armed forces attempt to strike a balance between seniority and ability in the promotion stakes, giving preference perhaps to top Military Academy graduates. But Portuguese promotion was based almost exclusively on seniority: Military Academy graduates were listed according to their class rank, and, unless they proved exceptionally brave or talented, they simply shuffled slowly upward in the queue to the rank of colonel where they might be able to make a splash in the Institute of Higher Military Studies. What so enraged regulars was that newly converted milicianos were now allowed to count all their service toward seniority. 'It was not many days later that my military adjutant. . .informed me that the decree law had not been well received in the army', Caetano recorded. '. . .There are captains, he told me, who have jumped lieutenant-colonels [in seniority] . And he reminded me of the enormous importance a soldier attaches to his seniority on the ladder: "seniority is a job".'[10]

Reaction was quick and bitter, especially among career captains and majors who stood to be bumped. If 25 April was Portugal's 1789, it was also prefaced, like the Great Revolution, by its own military version of the 1787 nobles' revolt in defence of feudal privilege. Regulars claimed that the application of Defence Minister Rebelo's decree would mean the immediate promotion of one miliciano captain to lieutenant-colonel

66   *Professional Officers and 'Temporary Gentlemen'*

and 69 others to major.[11] Military Academy graduates in the middle and junior ranks would find their already long overdue promotion delayed still further. Milicianos, however, fired the first shots in the paper war of the circulars. 'Stagnation or Progress' declared in the summer of 1973:

> Since the French Revolution. . .countries have always looked to place the most clever, the most capable, those who offer guarantees of progress and evolution in important positions. There have always been — and there will continue to be in the eternal march of humanity struggling for perfection — conservatives and reactions of a minority or a silent majority. Our country is no exception. . . After fighting overseas, after enduring the bitterness of the war and the bitterness of following orders, these conscripts, many of whom have studied one, two, three, four or more years at university, and who have chosen a military career, joined the regular cadres, now find themselves thanks to decree law 353-73 placed in the military hierarchy at the point warranted by their diplomas and determined by the country's evolution. Despite the opinions of a few reactionaries, no one can cast aspersions upon our military qualifications, our medals and laurels coloured with bitterness. Few can doubt our professional competence without calling into question the universities, the Military Academy, the courses for miliciano officers and sergeants, our military chiefs and the theatres of operations where we learned our profession. Since 1961, this country, where military service is obligatory, has fought a war largely with its conscripts — officers, sergeants and soldiers — who are our technicians, engineers, doctors, lawyers, economists, architects, etc. This is a country of conscripts of whom some for various reasons have chosen to enter the professional officer corps and follow the career of arms: WE WILL NOT PERMIT STAGNATION, THE OLIGARCHY OF AN EXTREME RIGHT-WING MINORITY.[12]

In an August tract, 'Dos Espúrios aos Puros', meaning literally 'From the Sons of Whores to the Pure', later denounced by the MFA for its 'crude' language, the 'Puros' or regular officers were labelled 'champions of imbecility, vanity and egoism'. The milicianos had equivalent qualifications, experience and suffering to break the stranglehold of Military Academy graduates on the top ranks.[13]

Whatever disagreeable remarks passed in the mess between the

Professional Officers and 'Temporary Gentlemen'

warring military factions, regulars realized that the main thrust of their discontent must be aimed at the government. The most open attack on the Rebelo decree came, inevitably, out of Guinea where a sense of martyrdom and political discontent was already well developed among officers. An open letter to the government signed by 38 officers of all arms, some of whom were later to rise to prominence in the MFA, went beyond the simple cavil over seniority to labelling the law an insult to the forces. Their protest betrayed the élitist mentality which made dynamite of any attempt to tinker with the status of professional soldiers and which subsequently marked the emerging MFA:

> These officers, who believe that they are speaking for all of their comrades, ex-cadets of the old Army School and of the present Military Academy, feel wounded in their prestige, in their dignity, in their professional honour and intellectual standing by the thought that a two-semester course can in any way substitute for the four-year course which they completed at the Military Academy. Faced with the growing demands of international life, with technical progress which has influenced certain aspects of military life and with educational improvements which all countries are striving for, they feel that the Military Academy course must be intensified, expanded and made tougher, accessible only to the most interested and adept, to create an élite which will guarantee that the missions confided to the armed forces can be carried out. They feel that with this decree, the best qualified Portuguese will not be attracted to a badly paid career requiring great sacrifices and lacking intellectual prestige comparable to that of the professional schools, given the danger to the primacy of the Military Academy.
>
> They feel that as their major mission is to lead men and that as their own lives are at stake more intense preparation will be necessary to guarantee a high position recognized by a country which wants always to count on capable and prestigious armed forces whose preparation will be compatible with the authentic values of the dignity of man.
>
> These officers, therefore, cannot remain silent before this flagrant inversion of values.[14]

At this point there was nothing particularly political about the protest. True, the traditions of the officer corps as a whole were constitutionalist, liberal, to the left of the régime. Most disapproved of

68 Professional Officers and 'Temporary Gentlemen'

the wars and, in Guinea at least, looked forward to a political rather than a military solution. Many had been disappointed, not to say angered, when the government organized a June 1973 'Combatants Congress' in Porto, clearly designed as a flag-waving demonstration in support of Portugal overseas. A telegram purportedly representing the views of 400 officers dissassociated itself from the congress' purpose and conclusions.[15] But few were ready at this point to consider their own political solution; most had not yet lost faith. Caetano, after all, had a reputation, wholly undeserved as it transpired, for liberal sympathies and it was rumoured even that Spínola would soon take over the presidency from ageing Admiral Tomás. That something would be done, both to correct the immediate injustice of the decrees and to solve the longer term problem of the wars was still thought likely.

The world was startled when in April 1974 it woke up to a left-wing military revolt in continental Europe. Arab officers with an eccentric ideological combination of nationalism, Islam and collectivism had overthrown governments more or less regularly for a quarter of a century. More recently, there had been rumbles between some Latin American governments and Marxist-inspired military factions. But Portugal was largely a political blind spot where it was assumed that a semi-fascist government had an army to match. When the government was toppled by its guardians, a desperate search began for an explanation as to why 'the army' went left.

The first explanation offered for the leftward turn of the armed forces was the influx of lower-class cadets into the Military Academy. 'Recruitment patterns to the army officer corps were dramatically altered when Salazar in 1958 removed all tuition charges and offered salaries to cadets for the first time', wrote Philip Schmitter.[16] Márcio Alves also noted that the war and the abolition of tuition at the Military Academy 'considerably popularized the [social] origins of regular officers of the armed forces. One must note that almost all of the members of the Revolutionary Council became officers after 1958.'[17] The result was a distinct social cleavage between middle-ranking officers who began their careers in late 1940s and the 1950s and the younger wave of officers of more modest background who flocked to take advantage of the free education offered after 1958. The resulting generation gap was apparent to all: 'You could sense the difference between the middle and the junior officers', one middle-ranking naval officer remarked. 'The younger ones were less well educated, they had less *culture générale.*'[18]

Concern for the proletarianization of the officer corps dates from

Professional Officers and 'Temporary Gentlemen' 69

the French Revolution when emigration and the guillotine swept the French army almost clean of aristocrats and successive revolutionary governments desperate for officers to staff the burgeoning armies flung the doors open to all comers. Napoleon institutionalized the 'career opened to talents' with some notable successes, in particular that of Ney, 'le brave des braves' son of a cooper promoted to Marshal of France in 1804. After the Bourbon restoration of 1815, many feared the political tensions generated by an army staffed by lower social orders. These fears were based on two suppositions: first, that these lower-middle-class officers and NCOs were imbued with the left-wing ideals of the Revolution totally incompatible with the white flag of the *ancien régime;* second, that a lower-class army would have fewer scruples about overthrowing the government than would a well-disciplined corps drawn principally from the aristocracy. Alexis de Tocqueville held that 'democratic' armies tended to political instability because of the ambitious lower orders who supplied the cadres. While in most European armies, a man's ambitions stopped abruptly at the relative position of his social class in the military hierarchy, the marshal's baton which every French soldier proverbially carried in his knapsack made the sky the limit. An aristocratic officer's ambition was limited because his prestige stemmed from his social position rather than his military rank. Ambitious lower-class officers fired with levelling revolutionary ideas were hardly bothered about the niceties of respect for civilian authority.[19]

De Tocqueville's 'democratization equals politicization' thesis laid out over 125 years ago retains much of its freshness even today. Political scientists shake their heads knowingly each time a 'democratized' officer corps dispatches a régime in an underdeveloped country. The case of Egypt where an officer corps recruited among sons of minor civil servants booted out a decadent aristocracy topped by the corpulent King Farouk, provides perhaps the best of many examples. Morris Janowitz feared that officer 'democratization' could alter even the bland political tradition of the American army by limiting traditional restraints on ambition and weakening civil authority.[20] The increasingly lower-class character of the French officer corps after 1945 was considered an important milestone on that army's road to revolt in Algeria. Likewise, the Portuguese army after 1958 eased down the slippery slope to 'democratization' and eventual politicization.

The Naval Academy, traditionally the preserve of a social élite, provides the best illustration of the changing social character of the

70 Professional Officers and 'Temporary Gentlemen'

officer corps. The influx of cadets of more modest origin began soon after 1945 and accelerated with the outbreak of the African wars, as anti-militarism and alternative career opportunities deflected young men into other sectors. Throughout the 1940s, the aristocracy warmed most benches at the deck officers' section of the Naval Academy which contained roughly three quarters of the future officers. Crested family rings were worn by 91 per cent of the cadets who entered in the so-called 'marquis' promotion of 1944, and although this was a particularly vintage year, blue bloods continued conspicuously into the early 1950s. Thirty per cent of cadets in the class of 1947, 40 per cent in 1948, 45 per cent in 1949 and 31 per cent in 1950 came from the nobility. With the Academy's expansion in the 1950s, the aristocratic profile became lower. Thirteen per cent of the 1952 class were aristocrats, 12 per cent in 1953, 8 per cent in 1954 and only 7 per cent between 1955 and 1958. By 1975 all vestiges of social exclusivity had disappeared, with sons of printers and policemen and even dustmen and farm labourers accepting places.[21] In the absence of statistics one can assume that a similar transformation occurred at the Military Academy.

What was the effect of this 'democratization' of the Portuguese officer corps on the political outlook of officers and on their respect for civilian authority? De Tocqueville's praise for a benign military aristocracy would hardly have found an echo of agreement from Bismarck or Bethmann-Hollweg, for whom Junkers in uniform were a perpetual political headache. Had he looked more closely at the recent history of his own country, he would have discovered that ambitious soldiers were not drawn exclusively from the lower orders. Aristocratic generals were quick to desert the *ancien régime* for the prospect of a high command in the Revolutionary armies. Robespierre and the Terror were propped up by a posse of aristocratic generals like Carnot, Demouriez, Deslandes, Kléber and Lafayette, many of whom were axed for their troubles. And the Revolution eventually succumbed to a Corsican aristocrat whose ambitions were paid for with grapeshot.

Those who defend the 'democratization-politicization' thesis note that opposition to government was concentrated in the 'democratized' middle and lower ranks of the professional officer corps. But it was precisely these officers who had borne the brunt of the fighting and isolation of the colonial wars, and who had been most angered by the Rebelo decrees. In his study of the French army in Algeria, American historian J.S. Ambler pointed out that among 150 officers involved in the April 1961 putsch or subsequently arrested for OAS terrorism at least 10 per cent bore aristocratic *noms à particule* – twice the average

Professional Officers and 'Temporary Gentlemen' 71

for the army as a whole. Politically active soldiers were those most committed to *Algérie française*, irrespective of family background. In the Portuguese army too, the war-weary provided the political impetus to revolt.

Those who put the left-wing orientation of the revolutionary Portuguese officers down to their social origins overemphasize the importance of social class on the political development of the officer corps, if indeed political ideas can be equated with social class at all. After 1958, the 'democratization' of the officer corps was undoubtedly accelerated, and Alves concludes that 'almost all of the members of the Revolutionary Council became officers after 1958'. But recruitment patterns are seldom changed at a stroke. The British army abolished purchase of commissions in 1871, but social recruitment to the regular officer corps remained virtually unchanged until the First World War, and not appreciably changed until after 1945. The Portuguese Military Academy was made 'free' in 1958, but applications continued to decline until cadets were offered 3,000 escudos per month in 1969. So, the Military Academy was never 'free' until 1969, and therefore not really accessible to the truly underprivileged sons of working men except under exceptional circumstances. Even after 25 April, most of the lower classes did not go for in the forces in a big way. Nor did cadets choose military careers because of free tuition. Fees at the Academy before 1958 were low and well within reach of even modest families. Officers from modest backgrounds who went both to the Naval and Military Academies before 1958 noted that low tuition was only 'a consideration' usually brought in to reinforce a decision to follow a military career.[22]

Alves' claim that 'almost all' members of the Revolutionary Council left the academies after 1958 does not stand close scrutiny. Only some 50 per cent of 24 members of the Revolutionary Council in July 1975 had left one of the academies after 1958, and three of those had begun their studies before the academies were made 'free'.[23] Some of the most prominent and politicized members of the Revolutionary Council like Vítor Alves, Melo Antunes, Pezarat Correia and others left the Military Academy well before 1958. The 'Red Admiral' Rosa Coutinho, later to distinguish himself as a friend of the Marxist MPLA while Governor General of Angola, belonged to the Naval Academy's 1944 'marquis' promotion. Left-wing naval militants Vítor Crespo and Jorge Jesuino both left the academy in 1952. And those whom Vítor Alves cited as the most active in the MFA's conspiratorial days before the 25 April *coup* include a large majority of officers like Colonel Vasco Gonçalves, Lieutenant-Colonels Banazol, Charais, Lopes Pires, Costa Bras, Firmino

72   Professional Officers and 'Temporary Gentlemen'

Miguel and Major Hugo dos Santos who left the Military Academy in the mid-1950s and even late 1940s.[24]

1958 does not appear to have produced the great social divide between officer generations which many have claimed for it. It was an important year, however, not because the academies were made free, which in reality they were not, but because apart from engineering courses, cadets no longer had to meet the educational standards of the university. Declining demand forced both the Naval and Military Academies to abandon the university stint required of all cadets, allowing them to enrol school-leavers whose intellectual capacities had often already been stretched to the limit. The low educational standards sanctioned in 1958 slipped downward as the war progressed and the lustre of a military career dimmed. Cadets who would have raised a professorial frown with 16 out of 20 marks in examinations in the 1950s, were waved through with 10 or 11 marks a decade later.[25]

Plummeting applications to the Military Academy bore stark testimony to the declining standards. Applicants in 1969, for instance, were down 80 per cent on those for 1961.[26]

The generation gap was an important feature of the 25 April *coup*. But no one has grasped its true nature. The youngest generation of officers was not the most revolutionary. The largest group of pre-*coup*

Table 1: Military Academy Applications and Admissions

Year	Applicants	Admissions
1960	381	174
1961	559	257
1962	444	266
1963	392	180
1964	307	137
1965	283	129
1966	199	90
1967	175	90
1968	149	58
1969	112	33
1970	151	62
1971	169	103
1972	154	72
1973	155	88

Professional Officers and 'Temporary Gentlemen' 73

MFA activists had left the Military Academy well before 'democratization' had taken a dangerous turn. The *coup* appears not so much one of the younger generation against the older, but of the middle generation of officers in their thirties and early forties together with a few of their younger intellectual peers who regarded themselves as culturally and educationally superior to most of the newcomers. As with the French army in Algeria, political discontent in the Portuguese army was concentrated in the middle generation of fighting officers who most suffered from the army's declining prestige.

Of the majors and colonels whom Vítor Alves cited as active in the MFA conspiracy, almost all were over forty and one, Lieutenant-Colonel Banazol, was fifty-five. Carvalho said:

> We felt that the nation was being defrauded by a war without meaning, a war that had no connection with us. We felt that we were jeopardizing the future of the country and our own futures. It was from this point that we began to think in terms which went beyond the simple struggle against the decrees. The events of Beira on 17 January in which our comrades were insulted by the racist population of the town, enlightened us further and served to confirm my comrades in the feeling for a struggle which went beyond the decrees. From this point, the entire prestige of the forces, especially of the army, seemed to be at stake.[27]

In much the same vein, middle-ranking American officers most resented the Vietnam War because recruitment pressures had saddled them with inferior junior officers: 'We were forced to lower our sights', one lieutenant-colonel explained, 'and what did we get? Officers like Calley.'[28]

Table 2: Age of Members of the Revolutionary Council, July 1975.[29]

Age	%
over 60	4
over 50	7
over 40	25
36-40	14
30-35	32
under 30	4
no information	14

74 *Professional Officers and 'Temporary Gentlemen'*

One of the salient features of the changing patterns of Portuguese officer recruitment since 1945 is the increase of recruitment from within the military community. Many potential middle-class cadets who balked at low military prestige and poor career opportunities were replaced at the academies by soldiers' sons. Sons of military families occupied nearly 20 per cent of the places at the Naval Academy in 1975. If one includes the 'militarized' sections of the civil service as the police and the *guarda fiscal,* this rises to 25 per cent. A civilian instructor at the Military Academy also noted that a 'great number' of his students sprang from military backgrounds. Internal recruitment increased the isolation of the military community after 1961, when the army also was forced to take 20 per cent of its regular officers from among NCOs. The military background of an increasing number of officers, combined with a common education and experience further reduced the influence of social class in formulating the officers' political outlook. The war especially dissolved divisions in the forces into a shared bitterness and resentment against the government.

The importance of the 'democratization' and internalization of officer recruitment was not that it pushed the army 'closer to the people', but, on the contrary, that it made it more conscious of its separate status. The 'democratization' of the Portuguese officer corps served to make purely professional issues more important. as it had for the French army after 1815 and 1945. Low pay, slow promotion and the 'degradation of the army' were explosive issues for men whose livelihood and social prestige rode solely on their uniform. 'A policeman in the street could humiliate a captain at any time and get away with it', an officer noted. 'They gave orders to officers in uniform. We had no money, no prestige and nothing from the country.'[30]

The *coup* on 25 April aimed not only to restore the lost prestige of the army; many of the subsequent political demonstrations in the forces were but thinly disguised professional ambitions. When de Tocqueville spoke of 'democratic' armies, he was referring as much to a French army promotion system which allowed direct promotion from the ranks as to the lower-middle-class NCOs who were likely to take advantage of it. In 1830 and 1848, French NCOs not infrequently denounced their officers as white reactionaries and then moved in to fill the vacancies. The Portuguese military revolution threw up a system of elected promotion, or more accurately nomination by committee, which produced results similar to those de Tocqueville had witnessed more than a century before. Meteoric advancement was available to officers who sported the proper revolutionary credentials. Otelo de Carvalho,

Professional Officers and 'Temporary Gentlemen' 75

Vasco Lourenço, Carlos Fabião and Ramalho Eanes were but a few of the officers who jumped from the middle ranks into the military imperium literally overnight. Other, often less successful, officers were quick to hop on the revolutionary bandwagon once the political wind was plainly blowing from the East. Mário Soares denounced 'the men, both soldiers and civilians, who never even thought of revolution before 25 April and who today strut about or beat their chests and cry: "I am a revolutionary." They look ridiculous.'[31]

The Army's mission is a more important factor in explaining the growth of military populism or 'Poujadism' in the 1950s and 1960s than is social recruitment, and here a comparison with the French experience is useful. Whatever their social backgrounds, officers looking to win the 'hearts and minds' of the peoples they were fighting to save for the homeland were forced to concede that victory would only follow fundamental transformation of government and society. Such a view not only gave them a political role beyond that traditionally expected of combat officers, but also brought them into conflict with colonists and officials committed to the *status quo*. Friction between the two colonial armies and their governments built up tensions which finally broke out into open mutiny. To explain why two officer groups whose revolts stemmed from common complaints and experiences should take stands at opposite ends of the political spectrum, one must look closer into the peculiar circumstances which affected each. The two wars differed in their underlying suppositions, the way in which they were fought and in their outcome.

Fear of defeat explains in large part the tenacity with which French officers held on to Algeria. Suez had been only the latest of a string of military humiliations which began with the 1940 fall of France and ran through Indochina. The 'abandonment' of Morocco and Tunisia did little for the pride of officers who believed in the empire and had not tasted victory since 1918. In Algeria, many believed that they had met and mastered the international communist conspiracy, and were damned if the Fourth Republic would sign away at the conference table the victory which at last had been won on the battlefield.

For the Portuguese army, however, the colonial venture was from the first a non-starter. The Portuguese had no defeats to avenge. Decolonization was on the cards in 1961, and Britain, Belgium and France had pointed the way. Even officers with strong colonial sympathies, if they were honest, had to admit that the task was really beyond tiny Portugal. They accepted French counter-insurgency techniques but declined the accompanying theory of 'la guerre

76 Professional Officers and 'Temporary Gentlemen'

revolutionnaire', the belief shared by many French soldiers at the
height of the Cold War that colonial disturbances were centrally
directed from the Kremlin and the Forbidden City. Right-wing General
Faria Leite Barandão produced maps in the *Revista Militar* with arrows
pointing from the dark heart of red Russia and China toward Southern
Africa.[32] But by the mid-1960s it was patently clear that the
communist world was too deeply divided to produce a unified strategy,
and that nationalism was a more important element than communism
in colonial revolts. There was no real ideological commitment on the
army's part to defend the West, and after a few years of war, if not
before, they sternly rejected the government's claims to be doing so.
One air force colonel noted:

> In 1965, most of us already thought that Angola should become an
> independent and racially mixed country like Brazil. We saw that we
> could not win in the colonies. It was impossible to continue.
> Freedom had to come gradually because the people were not
> prepared for it. The military would be very useful in preparing the
> political solution. It was a task which we could not do in two
> months, but in six or seven years. We had to prepare the
> government and the local governments. The army had to maintain
> independence, build up the armed forces and so on.[33]

While intellectual French officers concocted a counter right-wing
ideology of 'integral nationalism', Portuguese officers labouring under
an inflexible right-wing government were content to take over existing
left-wing terminology to express their discontent.

In Angola, Mozambique and Guinea, civilian casualties were
minimized because guerrillas fighting from bush camps generally had
avoided populated areas. The absence of urban warfare which had
formed an important part of the Algerian war helped the Portuguese
army on its way leftwards. Its route was smoothed by the PIDE, which
did the dirty work of interrogation and torture which had made the
French paratroopers and their General Massu the villains of the piece
during the battle of Algiers. The stern, not to say brutal, inquisition of
suspected urban terrorists contributed to the French defeat by
alienating those, at home and in the colonies, upon whom it depended
for victory. Each time a journalist or a deputy denounced the
Gestapo-like tactics employed by some French units, the resentment
and humiliations of officers built up until eventually they topped the
danger mark. Labouring under no such onus, the Portuguese army

Professional Officers and 'Temporary Gentlemen' 77

could present itself to the nation as an untainted, if somewhat unexpected, liberator.

Lastly, the Portuguese war effort, in Guinea at least, was clearly headed for disaster on a grand scale. The French army had all but crushed the Algerian FLN, but the feeling was growing among Portuguese officers that the time to cut and run had arrived. Colonialism and imperialism were not only morally reprehensible, they were also militarily indefensible. In this atmosphere, it was easy to see how a politicized military minority could direct a strong current of professional discontent toward political ends. Those who assumed that the Portuguese army had swallowed Marxism whole missed this point. 'The Portuguese army is neither more nor less left-wing than other armies', Mario Soares contended.[34] An instructor at the Military Academy summed up the situation: 'I would say that you always have about 5 per cent of the students who are intelligent and think about things. They are always a minority. But after the war became unpopular, they began to be listened to. That was the drift.'[35] The government, by its own inflexibility, virtually guaranteed this militant minority a large and attentive audience.

The political leanings of a small handful of the MFA élite pre-dated the war and supposed guerrilla contact. Like Nasser, Sadat and Gaddaffi,[36] some left-wing Portuguese officers had been conspicuous as cadets. Classmates of both Antunes and Alves at the Military Academy noted that they had been politically active even then. Naval Lieutenant Judas 'slept with a copy of Lenin under his pillow' according to classmates at the Naval Academy. In some cases they managed to convert one or two close friends to their revolutionary views, but the mass of the forces remained uninitiated. 'I realized that things must change when I was at the Military Academy in 1954', Vítor Alves told *Expresso* on 20 September 1975:

> . . .We had long wanted to alter the political situation, but we did not have the conditions to unite the officers. . .We never were many [politicized officers]. Most officers separated their profession from politics. Among those who did not, I can name Captain Vasco Lourenço, General Otelo (de Carvalho), Major Dinís de Almeida, Major Azevedo, General Pinto Soares and several others, but not so many as there seem to be today. . .The impetus of the movement was always military and not political.

A feeble attempt to staunch growing military unrest in August 1973 by

78 Professional Officers and 'Temporary Gentlemen'

guaranteeing the promotion rights of majors simply stoked officer discontent. Bissau witnessed the first protest meeting on 28 August when over 100 officers met to vent their grievances. On 9 September, 136 officers met in Evora, and to avoid contravening restrictions on unlawful assembly and to throw curious PIDE agents off the scent were ferried to a 'picnic' outside town, organized by a group already calling itself the Armed Forces Movement.[37] At the end of a lively discussion, a document was agreed calling on the government to find 'a just solution for ex-miliciano officers who become regulars, without however compromising the interests of professional officers or the prestige of the army which serves faithfully. . .'[38] On 11 September, a group of officers led by Major Fernandes, later a close associate of General Spínola, visited Costa Gomes to discuss the poor state of army administration, pay and prestige.[39]

Pressure by Costa Gomes and protests rolling in from officers at home and in the colonies forced the Supreme Army Council to reconsider the decrees in a 26 September meeting. Rebelo, however, was adamant that the army's salvation lay with his reforms: 'are you with the government or with the captains?' he challenged, and faced with such a black-and-white choice, general dissent quickly hushed.[40] Undeterred, the Chief of Staff went immediately to the Prime Minister. Costa Gomes told Caetano that he had come to speak for the captains 'since they had no generals in the army who could speak for their aspirations'. At this point Caetano demonstrated the narrowly legalistic approach to government that dishonoured his wily predecessor. He wrote:

> I told him that the armed forces cannot exist without respect for discipline and the attitude of the captains, shown in the organization of their movement and the presentation of their demands, is clearly indisciplined. This attitude would irremediably undermine the military hierarchy: after the captains, who can deny the legitimacy of a movement of sergeants? or a soviet of soldiers? A government conscious of its responsibilities cannot recognize any movements, much less talk with them. As for myself, I have no love of power, and if the armed forces want to force their will there is only one thing to do — take over the government.

Costa Gomes protested that the captains had no such pretention but 'only wanted justice done' by the government. 'I had to explain that justice was one thing, their manner of asking for it was another',

Professional Officers and 'Temporary Gentlemen' 79

Caetano replied. 'When I was satisfied that discipline was completely re-established, I would reply. . .The demands must cease, all anti-disciplinary organizations must be dissolved. . .' Caetano claimed lamely that a cabinet reshuffle soon after which replaced Rebelo with Silva Cunha was deliberately engineered to redesign the decrees.[41] However, the damage had been done. It was evident that the one-year course was a wartime expedient', Caetano pleaded 'But given that the disease existed in the armed forces, any pretext served to detonate the explosion.'[42] When in January 1974 a pay increase was offered, officers denounced it angrily as a sop to discontent. 'The captains' movement progressed, politicized each time more under the influence of left-wing officers, set firmly on the road to a conspiracy', Caetano concluded.[43]

On 6 October, a Lisbon meeting united delegates from the colonies and metropolitan units, together with observers from the navy and air force. Against the background of the parliamentary elections which

Table 3: Pay Scales — January 1974

General (4-Stars) and Admiral	18,900$00 Escudos
General and Vice Admiral	17,200$00
Brigadier and Rear Admiral	15,500$00
Colonel and Navy Captain	13,900$00
Lt. Colonel and Commander	12,300$00
Major and Lt. Commander	11,400$00
Captain and Navy Lieutenant	10,400$00
Army Lieutenant and Navy Lt. j.g.	7,300$00
Lieutenants and Guardo-Marinha	6,000$00
2nd Lieutenant or Navy Ens	4,700$00
Sergeant-Major (adjudant)	5,700$00
First Sergeant	5,400$00
Second Sergeant	5,000$00
Sub-Sergeant	4,700$00
Corporal	4,700$00
First Corporal	3,400$00
Second Corporal	3,300$00

(The last two enlisted ranks receive periodic increases of 200S00 up to a maximum of four increases totalling 800$00.)

80   Professional Officers and 'Temporary Gentlemen'

despite official interdiction increasingly concentrated on the war, the first signs of a political awakening were visible as delegates discussed the wars, the cost of living and poor military leadership. But for the mass of officers thoughts of a *coup d'état* were as yet far off. They voted to threaten a collective resignation in the event that progress stalled on their claims.[44] On 12 October, the new defence minister agreed to create a committee to consider each officer's seniority case individually.[45] A 23 October MFA circular to all units outlined the state of play and concluded that justice would no doubt be done while at the same time hinting at the 'drastic' alternative 'which no one wants'.[46] Discontent proved contagious, however. A group of air force sergeants complained in circulars about the force's low prestige, their low pay and the inability of sergeants promoted to officer status to rise above the rank of major.[47]

Many officers were growing increasingly impatient with government foot dragging. A circular from officers in Guinea denounced the decrees and a further MFA circular of 1 November re-stressed their position. Officers meeting at the artillery school angrily asked why they should go down 'on their knees' to the government.[48] At a November meeting in Parede Lieutenant-Colonel Banazol rejected the 'paper war' and openly called for the government's overthrow.[49] Undoubtedly, Banazol's plan to take over Evora and declare a Junta could have been suicidal.[50] Vítor Alves, however, countered that they were quite keen, only that it was clear that those supporting a 'drastic solution' were still very much a minority. He told *Expresso* on 20 September 1975:

> Our attitude and motivations were above all professional and concern for the prestige of the armed forces. . .We wanted to redirect this professional motivation until we were able to create a group sufficiently strong to make political demands. The political claims were declared openly in 1973 by Lieutenant-Colonel Banazol at a meeting in Parede. . .This time the reactions were negative and I realized that there had not been enough preparation. The political motivation came to be accepted much later at the Obidos meeting.

The Obidos meeting of 10 December was crucial to the development of the MFA, for not only was a *coup* seriously discussed for the first time, but the voting procedure was altered to favour the young turks in the movement. The eighty delegates representing several hundred officers rejected a *coup*, preferring instead to limit their protests to the

Professional Officers and 'Temporary Gentlemen' 81

law. But this ostensible victory for caution was transformed into a left-wing *coup*, when militants objected to the claims of some officers to hold the proxy votes of their comrades. One paratroop officer especially raised eyebrows when he held up his hand for 129 officers. The Movement's organization was regularized, with only those present being allowed to vote. As the most active included a powerful section of left-wing officers, this threw the weight of the movement to the left. The Coordinating Committee was formalized to include representatives of the navy, air force, infantry, cavalry, artillery and various logistical services for a total of nineteen members, topped by a triumvirate of Otelo de Carvalho, Vasco Lourenço and Vítor Alves, who were to draw up the Movement's political programme.

The left-wing officers had now formally seized control of the Movement, squeezing out Fernandes and the more moderate officers. Coordinating Committee representatives were more or less coopted from among the political faithful, creating a simmering resentment in the bulk of the reformist officer corps which bubbled to the surface after 25 April 1974. Despite the vote in favour of legality, the conspirators went ahead with their preparations for the *coup*, drawing up a short list of generals – Costa Gomes, António de Spínola and Kaúlza de Arriaga – who might play the Naguib to their movement. '. . .It was in Obidos that the movement took a clear political direction', Vitor Alves told the *Expresso*. 'For only there, meeting with representatives of the branches of the armed forces did one feel that a true political consciousness existed.'

To milk the officers' natural respect for their superiors, a general had to be chosen to lend his prestige to the movement. The nomination of Kaúlza de Arriaga whose political views were somewhere to the right of the late Doctor Salazar's was a strange choice for the Coordinating Committee, explicable only if it was assumed that he would be dumped soon after the *coup*. A natural conspirator, Kaúlza jumped at the chance to lead a *coup* based on Banazol's blueprint while Caetano was visiting Spain in December. His enthusiasm, his stated intention to eliminate liberal officers like Costa Gomes and Spínola and no doubt the hidden fear that he might prove more than a match for the Coordinating Committee once in power, produced more sober second thoughts on the left. Vasco Lourenço tipped off Spínola and Costa Gomes while one of Spínola's Guinea staff officers, Major Carlos Fabião, publicly announced at the Institute of Higher Military Studies that a 'top general' was planning a *coup*. In this way, Spínola was put in touch with the brewing revolt.[51]

82   Professional Officers and 'Temporary Gentlemen'

Kaúlza took his revenge by spilling the beans on the MFA, while carefully extricating himself from any involvement in the conspiracy. No one yet has satisfactorily explained the failure of the government to nip the *coup* in the bud by placing the conspirators under lock and key. Caetano certainly was aware of officer discontent and PIDE agents shadowed every MFA 'picnic'. Yet government repression was limited to a few ineffectual transfers: Fabião was sent to Braga, Dinís de Almeida to a garrison near Porto and in January Vasco Lourenço was confined to barracks. This did little to break up conspiracy in such a small country with meeting places always within a few hours' drive, but rather served to spread the disease.

The real reason for the success of the *coup* was the refusal of the service chiefs, supposedly in the régime's pocket, to move firmly against the plotters, even when it was to cost them their jobs. Traditional service freedom from political interference, lack of any real commitment among senior officers to the Caetano government and an almost total absence of courage and energy at the top combined to sabotage repression until too late. Caetano, who saw the dark hand of international Marxism behind the conspiracy stated this clearly:

> In vain on several occasions I called the attention of the military chiefs and ministers to the need for firm information on the morale of officers and to make our point of view known. No one lifted a finger. Our intelligence services were well aware of everything the enemy did, said and thought, but did nothing to combat its arguments and ideology. . .The army had psychological action for the overseas population, but little or nothing for its own men. . .
> As for informing, the generals considered it dishonourable for officers, even commanding officers, to relate the thoughts and actions of comrades. I told them that this was wartime, it was indispensable to detect possible enemy infiltration in our ranks, especially as it could result in a deterioration of the morale of our own men. They did not take issue with this: but they held the notion of camaraderie which came from the early years of the Military College (a preparatory school for the Military Academy) where everything which passed between students must be settled between themselves. . .a juvenile house law which made a secret of the intimate life of the inmates. For this reason, the government in its last hours was ignorant of the threatening reality within the armed forces.[52]

Professional Officers and 'Temporary Gentlemen' 83

A senior staff colonel confirmed this view: 'It was common knowledge among senior officers that there was a movement among the captains, but we said nothing', he said. 'It was easier for young officers to start a movement than it was for us. Besides, they had suffered more from the colonial wars.'[53]

When Caetano did finally decide to crack down in March 1974, it was too late. Like France's Charles X in 1830, firmness translated into a rigid rejection of reform and provided officers with no option but a *fuite en avant*. The immediate object of Caetano's wrath was General Spínola. Long recognized for his jaundiced view of the régime and especially of its colonial policy, Spínola finally put it down in writing. The 22 February 1974 publication of *Portugal and the Future* dropped like a bombshell in Portuguese politics. Significantly, the manuscript was written as early as 1971, but only in 1974 was the time judged ripe for publication. 'The first draft was completed, I suppose, by 1971', one of Spínola's staff officers said. 'One day in 1972, he gave me a copy of the typescript and asked me to read it.'[54] Almost desperate for a prestigious figure who could point the way out of the colonial labyrinth, the country bought the book in lorry loads.

The effect of the book on the development of the MFA has been the subject of much controversy. The spectacle on 26 April of Spínola surrounded by the young officers of the Coordinating Committee led many to believe that *Portugal and the Future* had provided the MFA with its guiding political line. Otelo de Carvalho hotly denied this: 'The book had no influence on the course of the Armed Forces Movement', he told the *Revista do Povo* on 1 December 1974. 'That was already a developing force. There are many people who cite General Spínola's book as catalyst of the movement, but this is not true. Besides, many of us were not happy that the book was published at this time. . .The process leading to 25 April was already underway.' Rodrigues agreed that Spínola's ideas were different from those later expressed by the MFA leaders so that his role 'in the process of 25 April was not that attributed to him by the foreign press. . .'[55]

At this point in the development of discontent, however, Spínola's book was vital. Although he later fell out with the handful of politicized conspirators who had more or less definite ideas about the shape of a post-*coup* Portugal, before 25 April *Portugal and the Future* provided the MFA with its only statement of policy, certainly much more concrete than the rather pallid MFA manifesto patched together hours before the *coup*. By virtue of this book, Spínola also won the position of provisional president designate away from his hierarchical

84 *Professional Officers and 'Temporary Gentlemen'*

superior Costa Gomes, favoured by many of the more politicized officers. So before 25 April, the MFA was seen to be a 'Spínolist' movement, both in doctrine and leadership. His book drew in many apolitical officers by the prestige of its author and by placing the war in the wider context of Portugal's political and economic problems. Officers who would not have touched the MFA had they realized the true political complexion of the Coordinating Committee, could sign on confident that the conspiracy was in good hands. Those who attribute the success of the *coup* almost exclusively to Carvalho's meticulous planning ignore the fact that plans, even the best laid, need dedicated men to carry them out. For the vital cooperation, the lack of which had scuttled so many previous attempts to overthrow the government, Carvalho had largely General Spínola to thank. 'When Spínola's book appeared, backed by all of his prestige, we were certain that with this man our revolution would not come from the street', one officer remembered.[56]

The book was widely read among officers. At home, they could buy it freely off the book shelves or read *Expresso's* excerpts. In the colonies, however, where the government barred sales, copies of the book circulated clandestinely. In most colonial messes, the one or two books which those on leave smuggled in passed from hand to eager hand. 'The government tried to prevent its dissemination in the colonies', one Guinea officer noted,

> and the officers would pass copies around. One day an air force officer just arrived from Lisbon turned up in my office with a package for me. When I opened it, I found 30 copies of the book with a letter from Spínola asking me to give them to certain officers. I told the Governor General before I did this. I later found out that the PIDE were not at all happy about this and that it was entered on my file. We discovered that they kept a file on all of Spínola's staff.[57]

For the army, Spínola's message was plain: Portugal could not continue spending almost half its annual budget fighting an unwinnable war for indefensible principles. He blasted the 'old hermits' in the government isolated. . .in a halo of spiritual grandeur' who had divided the country with the prospect of 'an eternal prolongation of the war'.[58] 'We must begin by divesting ourselves of the notion that we are defending the West and the western way of life.'[59] 'The problem of the overseas territories is considered our major national problem today', he

Professional Officers and 'Temporary Gentlemen' 85

continued. 'The future of Portugal depends on an appropriate solution to the problems raised by the war which, by consuming lives, resources and talent, increasingly compromises the rhythm of development which we must have to catch up with other countries.'[60] By insisting on the continuation of the war, the government 'will finish by leading our country into revolutionary disintegration. . .destroying the national unity which it claims to defend'.[61]

The war lay at the root of Portugal's problems. By hanging on tenaciously to a few million acres of African jungle, the government had increased Portugal's international isolation which in turn had stunted its economic and social evolution. 'Internally, it has been responsible for a climate of apprehension and insecurity which has made public opinion susceptible to negative ideologies.'[62] The opposition had acted with little more responsibility by calling for a complete pullout. 'The people, in their realism and sometimes naive good sense, simply emigrate, incontestible proof that we must consider certain problems in a new light.'[63]

The full economic consequences of the war had been cushioned by money sent home by emigrants, tourism and public expenditure. But emigrant remittances would dry up once the families settled in their new countries, tourists were notoriously fickle and might flock to Greece next year, and unchecked public expenditure, especially on defence, could not continue without dire economic consequences. All of these sources of income and expenditure created inflation without building a solid foundation for economic growth.[64] 'Militarily speaking, one must recognize that a prosperous future for our nation and to its survival depends on the re-establishment of peace', Spínola concluded.[65]

Military regulations required that officer publications be approved by the appropriate superior officer. On 11 February, Costa Gomes sent Caetano a paragraph summary of Spínola's book with the recommendation that its publication would be a 'brilliant' service to the country.[66]

On the 18th, I received a copy of *Portugal and the Future* with the friendly dedication of the author [Caetano wrote]. I could not read it that day, nor the following one which was taken up by the council of ministers. Only on the 20th after a tiring day did I pick up the book after 11 o'clock at night. I did not stop reading until I reached the last page. And when I closed the book, I had understood that a military *coup d'état*, which for some months I sensed had been brewing, was now inevitable.[67]

86 *Professional Officers and 'Temporary Gentlemen'*

The very next morning he called in Spinola and Costa Gomes

> for the most serious and disagreeable conversation of my life. . .
> General Spínola's book contained a critical opening section which
> could not fail to influence the desire of the armed forces to continue
> to defend the overseas provinces, and to weigh on public opinion,
> affecting international affairs and reducing the already narrow
> margin of manoeuvre open to the government in its foreign policy. . .
> Written by the vice-chief of the general staff and approved by his
> superior. . .it opened a breech between the Prime Minister and the
> highest chiefs of the armed forces. It would be impossible to
> continue to govern with an insubordinate officer corps and
> discordant military chiefs.[68]

Caetano claimed that he wanted to keep the two generals in office 'to
avoid a pretext for a growth of indiscipline', but their unrepentant
spirit and the publication of excerpts of the book by the widely read
weekly *Expresso,* beginning on 23 February, forced his hand.

On 5 March, Caetano called on the National Assembly to rubber-
stamp his continued defence of Portuguese Africa. At almost the same
moment, a few miles away in Cascais, 204 officers were discussing the
government's overthrow. The increasing politicization of the captains
who on 5 March approved the text of 'The Movement, the Armed
Forces and the Nation', the most overtly political of the Movement's
pre-*coup* circulars published on 16 March, and who voted Spínola and
Costa Gomes into the chair, made some action imperative. On 8 March,
for MFA officers including intellectual Marxist artillery Captain Melo
Antunes, were given their marching orders overseas, while two others
were sent to cool their heels in the military fort of Trafaria. On 14
March, after one last attempt to talk Spínola and Costa Gomes around,
he gave them the sack, abolishing Spínola's job and replacing Costa
Gomes with pro-régime General Edmundo Luz Cunha. That very night
at a military reception for senior officers meant to underline military
support for the wars, Caetano told them 'the armed forces do not have
their own policies, but must carry out those of the government'.[69]

Spínola's dismissal was interpreted by officers as a door slammed in
the face of reform: 'Spínola had been the first general to say that the
solution to the wars was political and not military', one naval officer
noted. 'This had impressed many officers. When he was dismissed, we
were indignant.'[70] On 15 March police surrounded the Military
Academy where cadets were holding a protest meeting. Indignation over

Professional Officers and 'Temporary Gentlemen' 87

the dismissal of the two generals and the Belém jamboree to decorate the 'Rheumatic brigade', boiled over in the fifth infantry regiment at Caldas da Rainha. 'They [Spínola and Costa Gomes] are among the few generals who stand up for the armed forces and for a better Portugal', one subaltern explained.[71] Confusion over a Carvalho plan for a coordinated uprising of several units for a march on Lisbon left the fifth infantry to act alone. In the early hours of 16 March regular captains and lieutenants locked up their superiors, assembled the men and explained their 'mission and ideas'. The response from milicianos, sergeants and men 'surpassed anything which we had hoped for'.[72] However, their success fell somewhat short of expectations. Crammed into ten armoured personnel carriers, they were halted a few miles down the road by a group of Republican National Guards and surrendered quietly. Arrests and transfers of an estimated 200 officers involved followed, but many like Carvalho avoided detection. An MFA manifesto circular denounced 'administrative terrorism' in the transfer of officers and castigated the government's use of the PIDE-DGS in the investigations. The Caldas uprising, it claimed, was not an isolated movement but symptomatic of a growing crisis in the armed forces and the country brought about by bad government.[73] Carvalho claimed that the abortive uprising had been useful in that it underlined the necessity of a thorough and well-coordinated plan of operations. When the successful *coup* of 25 April was launched, there was none of the amateurish spontaneity which had marked its March predecessor.

Notes

1. Kaúlza de Arriaga, *Revista Militar*, vol.18, Nov.–Dec. 1966, p.591.
2. See A.F. Pinto Bessa, 'Contribuicão das Forças Armadas na Integração, Valorização e expansão da cultura Portuguesa', No.1, January 72, p.54.
3. 20 September 1975.
4. Interview.
5. Caetano, *O Depoimento*, Rio de Janeiro, 1974, p.174.
6. J. Keegan, *The Face of Battle*, London, 1976, pp.72-3.
7. Interview.
8. Interview.
9. Interview.
10. Caetano, op.cit., p.185.
11. Rodrigues, *O Movimento dos Capitães*, Lisbon, 1974, appendix documents 2 & 3.
12. Ibid., appendix document 4, pp.371-2.
13. Ibid., document 5, pp.373-8.
14. Quoted in M.R. Da Cunha, *Radiografia Militar*, Lisbon, 1975, pp.xv-xvii.

88   *Professional Officers and 'Temporary Gentlemen'*

15. See Appendix 1.
16. 'Liberation by Golpe', *Armed Forces Society*, vol.2, No.1, February 1975, p.23.
17. Alves, Marcio, *Les Soldats socialistes du Portugal*, Paris, 1975, p.13.
18. Interview.
19. See for instance, Edward Shils, 'The Military in the Political development of The New States' in J.J. Johnson (ed.), *The Role of the Military in Underdeveloped Countries*, Princeton, 1962, pp.17, 24.
20. *The Professional Soldier*, Glencoe, Ill., 1960, pp.10-11, 254.
21.

Year	Cadets	Aristocrats	
1944	11	10	91%
1945	9	6	66%
1946	11	2	18%
1947	10	3	30%
1948	10	4	40%
1949	11	5	45%
1950	13	4	31%
1951	10	2	20%
1952	22	3	13%
1953	32	4	12%
1954	24	2	8%
1955	14	1	7%
1956	9	0	0%
1957	7	1	14%
1958	30	2	6%

Figures based on *Lista da Armada*, 1974, and information furnished by naval officers.
22. Interview.
23. 12/12 and 4 no information. Based on information obtained in the *Lista da Armada, Lista do Pessoal da Força Aérea* and *Lista do Exército*.
24. *Expresso*, 20 September, 1975.
25. Insight, op.cit., p.16.
26. *Expresso*, 17 August 1974. Some confusion seems to have arisen over these figures. *Expresso* claimed that the low number of applications left many unfilled places at the Military Academy, fully 427 in 1969. However, academy officials contended that they were seldom able to absorb more than 150 cadets in a 'good year', and that figures for 'unfilled places' were incorrect.
27. *Revista do Povo*, 1 December 1974.
28. Interview.
29.

Over 60	1	36-40	4		
Over 50	2	31-35	9	no information	4
Over 40	7	under 30	1		

30. Interview.
31. Soares, op.cit., p.12.
32. 'A Nação Portuguesa no Aspecto Militar', *Revista Militar*, No.11, November 1972, pp.585-629.
33. Interview.
34. Soares, op.cit., p.76.
35. Interview.
36. See Eliezer Be'eri, *Army Officers in Arab Politics and Society*, London, 1970, p.92.
37. Movimento das Forças Armadas, hereafter referred to as MFA.
38. Rodrigues, op.cit., pp.318-19.
39. Insight, *The Year of the Captains*, London, 1975, p.35.

Professional Officers and 'Temporary Gentlemen' 89

40. Rodrigues, op.cit., pp.321-2.
41. Caetano, op.cit., pp.187-8.
42. Ibid., p.186.
43. Ibid., p.188.
44. Rodrigues, op.cit., p.323; Insight, op.cit., p.36.
45. Rodrigues, op.cit., appendix, document 12, p.401.
46. Ibid.
47. Ibid., document 10, 11, pp.390-6.
48. Ibid., p.328.
49. Ibid., pp.331-3.
50. Insight, op.cit., p.38.
51. Ibid., pp.40-1.
52. Caetano, op.cit., pp.176-7.
53. Interview.
54. Interview.
55. Rodrigues, op.cit., p.235.
56. Ibid., p.253.
57. Interview.
58. Spínola, *Portugal et l'avenir,* Paris, 1974, p.10.
59. Ibid., p.119.
60. Ibid., pp.9-10.
61. Ibid., p.13.
62. Ibid., p.22.
63. Ibid., p.23.
64. Ibid., pp.30-32.
65. Ibid., p.37.
66. Caetano, op.cit., p.195.
67. Ibid., p.196.
68. Ibid.
69. Ibid., p.202.
70. Interview.
71. Rodrigues, op.cit., p.103.
72. Ibid., p.121.
73. Ibid., pp.138-42.

4 SPINOLA'S SUMMER

Major Carvalho told *Revista do Povo* on 1 November 1974:

I began to draw up the operational plans from 24 March, after meeting with my comrades on the Coordinating Committee. I told them that the *coup d'état* would be carried out in the week of 22 April. After the uprising at Caldas, I knew the units we could count on. We subsequently took a few more into our confidence. During the week which preceded 25 April, that beginning on the 15th, I finalized plans with delegates of the plotting units, and with my communications officer. All the units had been contacted by the 23rd: all I had to do was press the button. At 15.00, I told the leader of my liaison committee that zero hour was scheduled for 03.00 on the 24th. At 18.00, I brought together my officers for final instructions. I gave each of them their call signs. The signal and the confirmation signal were two songs which would be broadcast on the radio: *E Depois do Adeus* (After Goodbye) and *Grandola Vila Morena,* to be transmitted at 10.55 and 00.25 by two different stations.

All my comrades who would participate from Minho to the Algarve had all necessary information on the night of 24 April. We counted on almost every unit in the country. It would be easier to mention those we did not count on, for they were few. There were a great many friendly units, those we thought would stay neutral — that is not move one way or another — and those which would move against us. Only five were hostile. . .

I knew the risk of meeting opposition was minimal. I carried out a psychological study after the Caldas da Rainha uprising which convinced me that no government forces would oppose us. The Republican National Guard, the state and the traffic police could not stop our progress because they felt themselves too weak *vis-à-vis* the army. A military column, its 100 or 200 men armed with G-3s [standard Portuguese army rifles], make up a force which is too strong for a section of five or six Republican National Guards.

I gave precise instructions to our comrades as to where they were likely to meet government forces. They should avoid opening fire unless pressed to the limit. The commander of each column must

Spínola's Summer 91

explain [to loyal government troops] that all resistance was futile because our forces were too strong, and demand free passage of the column. But the opposition did not show itself as expected. In any case, our troops had prior orders to shoot at no one.

Our first objectives were the radio and television stations. We wanted to seize all public news sources immediately. Secondly, Lisbon airport to prevent the flight of capital immediately following news of the *coup* was taken. The high command headquarters formed a psychologically important objective because its conquest would be a demonstration of power. We had also singled out as priorities for protection the houses of the generals chosen as members of the junta – Spínola and Costa Gomes – and the political prisons for PIDE agents could have found it convenient to exterminate prisoners whose testimony would have compromised them.

Although it cost several lives, the PIDE [headquarters] was not immediately surrounded, for I counted on what in fact happened: when our success was known, the PIDE would fall by itself. It was unnecessary to force it. If we had tried at the beginning their agents would have resisted from the early hours of the morning, for they were armed and would not have hesitated to shoot at my comrades. We wanted to feel that they needed our protection to save them from the hatred of the people.

Deprived of support and confidence, the fifty-year-old régime buckled almost without firing a shot. Tanks from the cavalry school at Santarém, fifty miles northeast of Lisbon, rolled into Libson's central Praça do Comércio unopposed. Units from Lisbon and beyond seized the Salazar Bridge across the Tagus to prevent resistance from the south. Other objectives too were taken on schedule. Loyalist army commanders who reached for their guns – and there were a few in Lisbon, Evora and the north – had second thoughts when they realized the formidable forces ranged against them. From the first daylight hours, excited crowds filled the streets congratulating the slightly bewildered soldiers and themselves on a successful operation.

Carvalho's meticulous plan placed a high priority on the arrest of several prominent members of the government around whom resistance might rally. Caetano, who had been expected to run for the government's communication headquarters at Monsanto, broke instead for the Carmo barracks of the pro-régime Republican National Guard, where he was cornered by a tank detachment and a large crowd. A complicated series of negotiations ensued between Caetano, Spínola who was at home, and the MFA operational headquarters at Pontinha, culminating in Spínola's arrival at the barracks to accept Caetano's surrender. Because

92 *Spínola's Summer*

Caetano held out until Spínola arrived 'so that power would not fall into the streets', many observers have credited him with the king maker's role on 25 April. French political scientist Alain Joxe claimed that the Coordinating Committee was caught at the post by Spínola:

> Caetano's government, under siege at the Carmo barracks which dominates the centre of Lisbon, succeeded in negotiating its resignation by publicly imposing Spínola as president on the MFA. The accord initiated by a negotiator for Spínola while an MFA tank captain had just given [Caetano] an ultimatum, was only endorsed by the MFA during the course of the negotiations. . .For Caetano, it was a question of passing power to a man in whom he had confidence, despite everything. The movement [was] taken slightly by surprise.[1]

On closer examination, however, Caetano's role in Spínola's rise to power was strictly limited to catalyzing a more or less prearranged scenario. Holed up in a back bedroom of the Carmo barracks, protected only by a handful of lightly armed police against tanks and an angry crowd, the Prime Minister was hardly negotiating from a position of strength. His immediate concern appeared to be for his own life rather than the transfer of power. He admitted to the tank commander in their first meeting that his position was quite hopeless. When asked who had organized the *coup*, and told Spínola and Costa Gomes,[2] he then attempted to contact the General. Eager that the siege should end without bloodshed, everyone agreed that Spínola should accept the surrender.

There is no evidence that the Coordinating Committee planned to take power directly on 25 April as Joxe suggests. Negotiations between Spínola and Costa Gomes and the Movement had begun some months before, and it was generally agreed by the young officers that a general or junta of top officers was absolutely vital if the country was not to be plunged into civil war. The bare bones of government, including a ruling body of generals, had been approved by the Coordinating Committee on 5 March. Spínola, because of his prestige, was the obvious choice to lead it. There was also a strong current of opinion even within the left-wing Coordinating Committee that the role of young officers in the future political life of Portugal was to be a strictly limited one.

As Caetano and a few of his entourage were smuggled from the Carmo barracks in an armoured car at about 19.30, headed for

Spínola's Summer 93

Madeira and eventual Brazilian exile, shots could be heard from the nearby PIDE barracks where 200 secret police hemmed in by a hostile crowd formed a last desperate pocket of resistance. An early attempt to rush the building left five dead and more wounded on the pavement. In the evening, an agent who stepped outside to spray a machine gun burst into the crowd was seized and executed on the spot by soldiers. At 03.00 on the morning of 26 April, the PIDE ran up a white flag. The dictatorship was dead.

At 01.30 on the morning of 26 April, sleepy Portuguese saw General Spínola introduce the ruling 'Junta of National Salvation' on television. Its seven members – Generals Spínola, Costa Gomes and Silvério Marques representing the army, Galvão de Melo and Diego Neto the air force, and Admirals Pinheiro de Azevedo and Rosa Coutinho for the navy – were selected to inspire confidence in a *coup* whose political complexion and leadership were largely unknown, even to the officers who executed it. In a brief statement, Spínola promised to guarantee basic human rights and freedom of expression, the election of a constitutional assembly and a president and declared finally that Portugal would respect all existing treaty obligations. The MFA's programme contained little to shock the nation. Since its 5 March approval by the Coordinating Committee, it had been chopped and changed by Spínola and Costa Gomes until its final version was hurriedly typed up only hours before the *coup*. A brief preamble stated that the officers' revolt had been prompted by the government's inability to define an overseas policy, and pledged the officers to carry out reforms 'in the interest of the overwhelming majority of the Portuguese people'.

Under the MFA programme, the Junta of National Salvation designated one of its members as provisional president, and he in turn named a provisional government responsible to him. A Council of State was stitched together from the seven members of the junta, seven representatives of the armed forces, and seven civilians appointed by the President. Lastly, the courts were to be maintained. The programme pledged the election of a national assembly within a year, after which time the armed forces would withdraw to the barracks, 'restricted to their specific mission in defence of national sovereignty'.

The very success of the *coup* seemed to push the MFA into the shadows. In the first days of May, the General seemed to have locked up a government intent on returning the country to normalcy, and few would have tipped him to finish second after a five-month power struggle behind a platoon of junior officers. His trips through the

94 *Spínola's Summer*

corridors of power in Lisbon and Guinea gave him a long lead in experience. The range of his support was no less impressive. The direct successor of Caetano, he was regarded as the safest possible leader supporters of the *ancien régime* (and they were not insignificant) could have hoped for. His impeccable revolutionary and military credentials gave him enormous prestige in the army and in the country, and he was backed by an administration which appeared eager to lend their full support to restore order in Portugal.

The MFA, in contrast, seemed small and divided. The most optimistic estimated its numbers at around 800, almost certainly an exaggeration. More realistic estimates placed the number of MFA activists at around 300, roughly 7 per cent of the army officer corps.[3] Within this group, only a fraction paraded left-wing sympathies; the vast majority of officers active in the *coup* were content to place the future of the revolution in the hands of their superior. The success of this dedicated core of revolutionaries in overturning Spínola has never been satisfactorily explained. Mário Soares noted that, from the first, Spínola moved 'to break the MFA. . .and dissolve the Coordinating Committee, the head of the movement, which watched him closely. He also wanted to reinforce his hold on the country through Palma Carlos, to limit the growing support of the political parties and isolate the communists.'[4] With all of the powers at his disposal, one may well ask why Spínola did not succeed at least in the first task?

The absence of the young officers from the government which they had helped to create was largely self-imposed. 'My experience taught me that I was right when I said that soldiers should not mortgage themselves to a government,' Vítor Alves told *Expresso* on 20 September 1975.

> Our original idea, written into the [MFA] programme, was that the government would be conducted essentially by civilians, with the eventual participation of one or more soldiers to guarantee the soldiers the development of the process. . .I and several others thought that soldiers should not enter the government. . .The presence of the MFA in executive positions would certainly have a corrosive effect, gradually sap our credibility. We live in a country which does not have a tradition of military rulers or, for that matter, soldiers in government [sic]. When it was insisted that soldiers run things, the sooner the country wanted to get rid of them.

This view was superseded in July when soldiers flocked into the second

Spínola's Summer

95

provisional government: 'It was decided that. . .it would be impossible for the civilian parties, all badly organized with the exception of the communist party, to lead the process [of revolution] effectively.'

Despite their small number and low government profile, the men of the Coordinating Committee remained the power brokers of the revolution: the MFA stamp of approval was required on nominations for high civil and all military posts. The committee sat as the supreme court of the revolution, slapping down policies and policy-makers judged incompatible with its advanced interpretation of the MFA programme. The junta ruled with a 'mandate' from the MFA and was charged with 'carrying out the MFA programme and the constitutional laws'. The Council of State, law 3-74 said, 'exercises its constituent powers in line with the Armed Forces Movement' and its seven military members were appointed by the president 'in agreement with the MFA'. Even cabinet ministers were charged with the 'excecution of the MFA programme'.[5] The leaders of the MFA then had a strong consultative role, and used it from the first. Initial differences between Spínola and the MFA leadership seemed minor, but were significant tests of strength which the young officers almost always won. This was apparent in the early hours when Spínola, in accordance with the agreed programme, wanted only political prisoners released from Caxias prison. The MFA, however, opened the doors to all detainees, even common criminals, with the exception of a Cuban officer taken prisoner in Guinea. And after a month or so of campaigning, they even managed that.

The MFA soon began to hedge on its programme in other ways. The PIDE-DGS was to be abolished at home, but 'restructured and purged' overseas and 'organized as Military Intelligence Police, as long as military operations require'. 'I reported to the Defence Ministry and saw Spínola on the 27th', one of his staff officers noted.

He had just signed the decrees abolishing the National Assembly and the PIDE. But in the colonies, the PIDE was to be transferred to military intelligence as had been agreed. About half-an-hour after he had signed, the Coordinating Committee asked for an interview. This was the first time that I had seen them: Alves, Antunes, Vasco Gonçalves, Contreiras and Crespo from the navy and Costa Martins from the air force. One of them held up the decree and said they could not accept the continuance of the PIDE in the colonies. Spínola explained that it would be transferred to military intelligence, and that this had been cleared with Costa Gomes. But the committee was adamant. They told him: 'we have given our word'. Spínola

96 *Spínola's Summer*

asked to whom. Everyone looked down at the floor. There was no reply.[6]

Spínola's only real victory in the early weeks – that of sending Caetano and ex-President Tomás into exile without trial, thereby almost certainly cheating the hangman – in fact proved a defeat. The MFA leaders were enraged at being cut out of a show trial which would have placed the old régime in the dock and provided them with a forum for their views and blood to baptise the new republic of virtue. But Spínola was having none of it, and packed his two prisoners off to Brazil, hardening differences between himself and his underlings. The soaring national prestige of the young officers, newly discovered by a press keen to tell their story, should have tipped Spínola off that the opposition was fast moving up to the first division. Soares described a situation which existed some months later, but one which had its roots in the early days of the Second Republic, as the country was introduced to its saviours:

> The soldier, to whom people attributed one thousand healing virtues, became the miracle man *par excellence*. Education was not healthy, send a minister-major; television needed pumping up, loan them a colonel; the Ministry of Health was sick, send a brigadier to help it toward recovery. All we needed was a marshal to exchange his baton for a cross and sit on the throne of the Cardinal-Patriarch to re-establish peace and concórd between church and state.[7]

The armed forces had not been so conspicuous in a European government since Vichy France.

Spínola and the first provisional government discovered that the tap of revolution, once turned on, was difficult to shut off. The first threat to the government's hold on the country came in a wave of strikes touched off by the *coup*. Galloping inflation had made wage demands a burning issue under Caetano, but managers backed by firm government were usually able to face down strikers. In May, workers demanding a monthly minimum of 6,000 escudos (£100) struck two national newspapers, the Church-owned Rádio Renascença and the important Lisnave shipyards across the Tagus from Lisbon. As strikes spread, the government installed on 15 May turned to its two communist ministers, party leader Alvaro Cunhal who sat without portfolio and Labour Minister Avelino Gonçalves, leader of the Porto bank workers' union, to dampen unrest. Soares had convinced the sceptical Spínola to bring

Spinola's Summer 97

the communists into the government for just such an occasion, arguing that Cunhal would be less dangerous tied to a desk.[8] The clandestine communist Intersindical was brought up from underground to replace Salazar's FNAT and channel discontent toward constructive ends. However, whether through design or weakness, the communists limited their attempts at strike control to some ineffectual finger wagging. As workers in textiles, chemicals, electronics, banking and other industries walked out, it became clear that Cunhal had little intention of intervening forcefully against shopfloor dissidents. On 26 May, the government decreed a 3,300 escudo minimum wage and froze all salaries over 7,500 escudos a month. Family allowances went up and controls were slapped on rents and prices. Promises followed to legalize the right to strike, to reorganize the financial market and, as a modest sop to the revolutionary blood lust, about 1,000 company directors compromised with Caetano were sacked. In most cases, however, the workers were unbowed. When influenced at all, as at Lisnave, it was by officers of the MFA who on several occasions used their growing prestige to talk workers back to their machines.

The government's inability to deal with mounting problems can be attributed in great part to fifty years of Salazarist dictatorship. The country's few experienced leaders were swept away on 25 April, leaving no politicians or political parties in the wings to take their place. Political exiles like Soares and Cunhal returned from Paris and Prague to enthusiastic popular receptions but it soon became clear that these men offered Portugal only theories of government, not political experience. Soares' courageous defence of political prisoners had won him a prison term and exile to France, where he taught at the Vincennes campus of Paris University; communists had suffered torture and even martyrdom at the hands of Salazar, forcing men like Cunhal to spend the best part of their lives outside Portugal, plotting to fit their country's experience into a Leninist revolutionary framework. The Portuguese communists were well organized for conspiracy, proving particularly adept at infiltrating the state administration and trade unions, but were temperamentally unsuited for government. The socialists converted their Portuguese Socialist Action, founded in Geneva in 1964, into a *bona fide* political party only at an April 1973 conference in Bad Münstereiffel, West Germany, their few hundred militants bound more by faith than party apparatus. The Popular Democratic Party (PPD), later to come to prominence as a union of progressive technocrats, was little more than a glimmer in leader Sá Carneiro's eye.

98   *Spínola's Summer*

Like many soldiers, Spínola's attitude to political parties was at best ambiguous. During the First Republic, the egotism and conceit of the politicians had pushed Portugal toward ruin. Since then, few potential statesmen had emerged from the opposition scrum. Parties and opposition leaders seemed more intent on making courageous stands than producing convincing blueprints for reform. Portuguese political life broke down into a mosaic of groups loosely formed around prominent personalities whose power was rooted in influence rather than popular support. They shouted slogans, political catchwords and clenched fists paraded before the world's television newsmen, revolutionary golden oldies lifted straight from a Spanish Civil War documentary, barely covered the personality cult quality of the new anti-fascist alliance. Spínola might well fear that the Spanish Civil War analogy, at least on the republican side, might be pushed further into fratricidal quarrels and even bloodshed among left-wing groups eager to hijack the revolution to their camp. Perhaps better that Portugal continue a modified authoritarian government for the present under his guiding hand, leaving the rhetorical dust of the revolution to settle and the moderate leaders of the PPD and Centre Democrats (CDS) to group support.

Like most post-revolutionary governments, Portugal's was handicapped from birth by the need to demonstrate the new régime's broad support. Every political group and faction, even those about to be gobbled up by events, must be fed a piece of the action. Cabinets named in these conditions seldom have the cohesion to vault even modest political fences and the first provisional government proved no exception. Socialists were given the ministries of Foreign Affairs, taken by Soares, Justice, occupied by Dr Salgado Zenha, and Communications, filled by the editor of the daily *República,* Raúl Rego. The communists took Labour and Cunhal sat without portfolio. They were reinforced by Pereira de Moura and Mário Murteira, both members of the left-wing Portuguese Democratic Movement, the MDP/CDE, in the Ministry for Social Affairs. Only one soldier, Spínola's friend Lieutenant-Colonel Firmino Miguel, sat in the cabinet as Defence Minister. The young technocrats and lawyers of the PPD had the pick of the remaining posts. Spínola topped this heterogeneous combination with Palma Carlos – a politically inexperienced academic lawyer whose undisguised distaste for Salazar had denied him a chair at Lisbon University – through whom he hoped to rule. Fully thirteen of the new cabinet had studied under Palma Carlos at Lisbon. 'He was a typical freemason, anti-clerical, republican by tradition, liberal and anti-fascist', wrote Soares, one of

Spínola's Summer 99

his old students, also tutored by Cunhal.

> He called himself a democrat, but he was more or less reconciled
> with the régime. We were somewhat surprised, therefore, when the
> MFA offered him the job: he was outside the political game, he did
> not know the people, he understood nothing about the communists.
> But he began with a minimum of friction. He did not infringe on
> the responsibilities of his ministers, coordinating rather than
> governing.[9]

That the political lines between the old and the new régime were hazy
is not surprising. Spínola's first choice for prime minister had been
Veiga Simão, Caetano's Education Minister, but he backed down when
advisers suggested that that really would be going too far. Those who
denounced the distinctly establishment nature of Spínola's choices for
office missed a fundamental feature of Portuguese-government and
politics — its domination by a small élite. It did not need a social
untouchable to call for the system's overthrow; there were plenty of
respected lawyers and academics in comfortable Lisbon suburbs to do
that. Revolutionary leadership, after all, has often been a patrician
prerogative. Cunhal, who married into the family of one of Salazar's
interior ministers, was in a way following in the footsteps of Lenin,
who had aristocratic relatives weighing down branches in his family
tree. Soares was on excellent terms with Jorge de Melo, whose many
companies he aimed to nationalize. Political leadership was
overwhelmingly in the hands of university-trained professionals, and
the central committee of the left-wing MDP/CDE composed of 25 per
cent lawyers, 15 per cent university lecturers, 10 per cent economists,
7.5 per cent publicists, 7.5 per cent engineers, 5 per cent doctors and
5 per cent school teachers was not appreciably different from that of
other parties.[10]

But if political divisions in the ruling élite were not reflected in
different social origins, the MFA added an element of class conflict:
misunderstandings between soldiers and politicians were in part due to
the social distance between them. Here were men trained in the Military
Academy which the middle classes had largely abandoned for the law
and arts faculties of Lisbon, Porto and Coimbra. If they had been to
university, it was usually to do sums in an unfashionable technical
course directly related to their military career. They sometimes made
alliances with parties in power, but they were trespassers — like beggars
in a Buñuel film who celebrate in the big house until the master returns

100 *Spínola's Summer*

to throw them back into the street. At its worst, the friction was almost racial: the Portuguese middle classes would squirm uncomfortably when some local MFA chief with distinctly Moorish features would burst uninvited into the television studio to read the latest decision of his branch meeting. You could almost hear the sigh of relief in Lisbon suburbs after 25 November 1975, when the 'different sort of people' were sent packing and the familiar white faces reappeared. The signs of relief were no less audible at the top of the MFA. After all, they too were an élite, and one which equally resented poachers: Alves and Antunes were so comfortable in their new milieu, that they decided to become permanent political fixtures. Others, sniffing the wind, were to consolidate their positions at the top of the army. A few like Carvalho, who never really understood what was going on, were swamped by events and pensioned off.

Judging by its constitution, the Council of State was yet another body to which Spínola could have looked for support: seven of its 21 members were named by the MFA, and here two of the movement's young turks, Vítor Alves and Melo Antunes, made their names. However, they were more than counterbalanced by the members of the junta and seven others handpicked by the President, as usual from among Lisbon's legal and academic establishment, but which also included two of Spínola's closest military aides, Colonels Rafael Durão and Almeida Bruno. As in the cabinet, disputes and divisions soon surfaced within the junta and Council of State to block effective action. In the left-wing naval tradition, Admirals Coutinho and Azevedo turned their guns on the Commander-in-Chief, expressing views closer to those of the Coordinating Committee than to Spínola's. Costa Gomes too became difficult to pin down, sliding already toward the position of neutral indecision which he was to occupy for the next two years and which, although it guaranteed his short-term survival, won him little respect.

Splits in the executive bodies deprived Spínola of a solid support base he needed to oppose the MFA. The junta had been created only as a dressy window display to entice the conservative Portuguese to buy the revolutionary goods inside. 'The Junta of National Salvation, created by the MFA, never existed except as a symbol for external consumption', wrote air force General Galvão de Melo, who sat with the seven.

> Through its image, composed of the images of its members, [it was] to give to the Portuguese and to the world a certain feeling of confidence and tranquillity about the revolution. . .The experience

Spínola's Summer

and the prestige of some of its members was a guarantee that, very probably, the 'captains' would not take power. It was a short-lived guarantee, because although other forces did not obstruct, divert or nullify its actions, the group very soon was compromised by serious differences between its members. . .which impeded any sustained, positive action. . .[11]

The paralysis of both the junta and the Council of State, combined with a hamstrung cabinet to shorten the odds between the General and the MFA. Revolutionary officers virtually moved in a political void.

In general, the meetings [of the junta] were not regular. They never started on time. We wasted time in sentimental and inconsequential discussions or talking about problems which did not merit attention from so important a group. On the other hand, serious problems, very serious ones like decolonization and the nomination of people for high office went begging! How could one expect so many millions of Portuguese to listen to these men when they, for their part, were so oblivious to the peoples' needs?. . .As for the Council of State, I found that it had to analyze voluminous documents and an excessive number of them for the time available. . .Discussions were at times excessively animated, with things sometimes approved out of boredom, ignorance or pure lack of interest. And that is all. What more can one say?[12]

A government machine more form than substance suited Spínola's temperament. Unfettered by political etiquette, he became Portugal's governor-general, the *coup's* commander in the field, the Father of the New Republic who would guide his children through the pitfalls of political puberty. Unfortunately, his attitude was contagious and soon caught by the MFA, the communists and other parties of the left, who all hawked a magic formula, a political snake oil which would instantly cure the country's ills. Soares complained:

He had an authoritarian concept and use of power, always intervening in business, never hesitating to short circuit the action of his ministers. He made the mistake of believing that he could govern a country — especially a country in revolution — like he administered a colonial province. He was president of the Portuguese Republic, but he acted as if he was still governor-in-chief of Guinea.[13]

102 *Spinola's Summer*

Spínola's style made him enemies among the political parties who resented his arrogance and meddling. However, rather than put stuffing into the government as a counterweight to Spínola's authoritarian streak, they kicked in with the young MFA officers who opposed him. The communists especially, acutely aware of their limited electoral potential, were among the first to push the MFA into a clash with the President, hoping to pick up the pieces. 'From the beginning of the revolution, the communists clung to the coat-tails of the MFA, never letting go, always ready to render any little service and inclined, of course, to whisper an opportune word', Soares noted. '. . .They were counting on the soldiers to impose their [communist] "order", which they could not do themselves because the people were not behind them.'[14]

The socialists kept the soldiers at a polite arm's length. Their leader, Soares, had written in *Portugal's Struggle for Liberty* published in 1973: 'We know what army intervention in politics means, even when it acts with the best of intentions and how, consequently, problems build up and become very complex.' Privately, he confessed that his marked uneasiness with the men on horseback was more personal: 'I do not understand anything military. I am always a little ill-at-ease in front of an officer in uniform, because I can never tell his rank.'[15] This did not preclude many socialists, including Soares, from looking to the army for salvation in the dark days of dictatorship. Soares claimed that he was predicting a military rebellion when the rigidly orthodox Cunhal was still plotting his textbook 1917 peoples' revolution. 'I was convinced that the army would overthrow fascism', he said.

> The communists were hostile to this idea and accused us, we socialists and democrats, of being vulgar putschists. The only hypothesis which they were prepared to accept was a popular uprising. Of course the action of the masses is essential in an anti-fascist movement, but it cannot succeed by itself, without a military conspiracy. History proved us right. In several hours, on 25 April, 1974, the army brought down a régime a half-century old. And immediately the people filled the streets.[16]

But without elections, an astrologer, not a political scientist, was needed to predict socialist strength. The question of support hung over Soares like a guillotine, with the communists and their Coordinating Committee allies holding the rope which could bring the blade crashing down at the first sign of bourgeois backsliding. This

Spinola's Summer

103

proved difficult for the Socialist leader accustomed to the comforts of his class. Leftists, lucky with a free weekend in Havana, begrudged Soares his receptions in European capitals, the ease with which he melted into the diplomatic world, the endless number of influential foreign editors who popped up on his doorstep to be ostentatiously entertained in well-known Lisbon night spots. For them, there was something too French about Soares, a glossy *Nouvel Observateur* socialist who uttered statements of dogma over sumptuous five-course meals, a Proudhonian rather than a Marxist, a middle-class radical of 1848 who refused to be photographed in jungle fatigues clutching a G-3, the fashionable double exposure of Che and Allende. And, most damning, he was a social democrat, an advocate of pluralist democracy who preached evolutionary change. But, for the moment at least, he was also inexperienced and slightly naïve, backed only by an embryonic party organization and quite willing to side with those offering an alternative authoritarian counterpunch, undermining Spínola and helping the country toward chaos.

Twice, in July and September, Spínola attempted to tip the political balance of power back in his favour. The first attempt left him empty-handed and the second out of a job. To consolidate his position, Spínola pushed his prime minister to strengthen and streamline the government. 'I do not have sufficient authority to re-establish order', Palma Carlos told Soares in late June. 'I need broader powers. I am going to ask for them.'[17] On 5 July, the Council of State debated the Prime Minister's request for reinforcement of his office, simplification of government machinery, postponement of elections to the Constituent Assembly to a date not before November 1976, a quick referendum for a new provisional constitution and election of a president of the republic. The implications of the proposals were obvious: new decision-making structures and a revamped constitution virtually would put the MFA, whose influence derived from their blocking positions in the deliberately cumbersome government, out of business. Spínola would cash in on his growing popularity in the country to regularize his position and powers and assure himself a further few years in office.

The Council of State, the political parties and the MFA rejected Palma Carlos flat. Everyone saw the General's hand behind the manoeuvre. Most of Spínola's supporters in the Council of State had no wish to provoke a confrontation with the MFA, and so vetoed the request on 8 July. The political parties, eager for an elected assembly with real powers and opposed to any modifications which would strengthen

104 *Spínola's Summer*

Carlos' and subsequently Spínola's power over their ministers, concurred. MFA leaders, keen to keep the momentum of the revolution alive, rolled the proposal into its grave. Palma Carlos handed in his resignation and after a few brief days of speculation, on 13 July, Spínola announced that Colonel Vasco Gonçalves would head a new government.

The choice of Vasco Gonçalves, an engineering officer with pronounced leftist sympathies, was a hard pill for Spínola to swallow; it was no secret that the General favoured Lieutenant Colonel Firmino Miguel in the chair. Vítor Alves, however, claimed that Gonçalves took some convincing by Spínola before he said yes. Perhaps the provisional President believed that general pressure on his military subordinate would win through. But if Vasco Gonçalves had a superior, it was not Spínola but Alvaro Cunhal. With Gonçalves at the helm for the next year, the government moved steadily to the left until it broke up on the rocks of the very disorder it had created.

Spínola's monumental July miscalculation produced a massive victory for the young MFA officers. Soldiers who had occupied only the Defence Ministry in the first government now flocked to occupy eight ministries in the new coalition − almost half the government. The MFA not only supplied the prime minister, but now directly controlled the important Labour Ministry. In addition, Alves and Antunes were brought in from the cold without portfolio, and together with Gonçalves formed a ruling trinity which in effect steered the country until it began to split apart in November. The July crisis also gave the Coordinating Committee official status for the first time by bringing it into the Council of State, which now swelled from 21 to 28 members. With 14 members, plus allies Coutinho and Azevedo, the MFA now held a majority interest in the body which was in effect the revolution's transitional legislature. The move was crucial for the course of the revolution, for the Coordinating Committee now not only ran the MFA, but also exercised a strong direction over the political life of the country. Once legitimized, it could use its status after Spínola's September fall to reinforce its position, first in the Council of Thirteen, composed of five military ministers, seven members of the Council of State 'designated by the MFA' and the commander of the MFA's military arm, COPCON, and then in the Council of Twenty. This group, composed of the Council of Thirteen plus the seven members of the junta, formed the basis of the Revolutionary Council from which the MFA later was able to command the political field.

Well settled into the government, the MFA left turned its attention

Spínola's Summer

to the problem which was to plague it to the end of its days – the lack of military muscle. Left-wing officers had abandoned field commands after 25 April, preferring the political manoeuvres of committees and cabinets to the monotonous military equivalent. Their hegemony in the general staff's fifth division – in charge of psychological warfare in the colonies and now bombarding innocent Portuguese with revolutionary clichés in an attempt at least to stun the country's critical faculties – and in the endless MFA organizations and committees, left them long on words but short on punch. They ran a high risk of being made to look ridiculous if one of their disputes with Spínola ever came to a showdown.

The Operational Command for the Continent – COPCON – was created on 8 July under the command of freshly promoted Brigadier Otelo de Carvalho, ostensibly to control 'vandalism', demonstrations and to ferret out right-wing arms caches. The Coordinating Committee had argued since 25 April that a force was needed to supplement the police which, under a cloud of its close association with the Salazar-Caetano régime, was reluctant to give parking tickets and even less keen to keep political demonstrators within the bounds of legitimate expression. Units of the Republican National Guard (GNR) sent to control a 25 May protest over the continued detention of Cuban Captain Peralta, captured in Guinea at the side of the PAIGC, simply melted into the crowd after taunts of 'fascists' reminded them of their harsh handling of Delgado supporters in 1958. The crowd's revolutionary *élan* was dampened only by water cannon wielded by Jaime Neves' commandos. Soon after 25 April, the Coordinating Committee set up an Operational Command for Coordination and Control – CCCO – for just such emergencies: 'We were aware that the population began to depend on the armed forces. . .and the armed forces had to resolve many diverse problems outside their normal routine', Carvalho noted.[18] But the few officers who staffed CCCO remained powerless to shift units in an army under the iron thumb of army chief of staff Brigadier Jaime Silvério Marques.

Spínola successfully blocked the extension of CCCO's powers while at the same time attempting to extend his influence among combat units. The left in uniform squirmed uncomfortably throughout May and June as the General carried out this 'military offensive', systematically visiting units to explain that the armed forces must set an example of 'political and ideological neutrality' and that a soldier's place was in the barracks, not at Belém. The point of the offensive was lost, however, with Palma Carlos' resignation.

106 *Spinola's Summer*

In the barracks at Alto do Duque, COPCON grouped a number of officers who, Carvalho hoped, would eventually command all 'operational' units of the three services. Its advantage, it was argued, was its ability to bypass the cumbersome military hierarchy in each of Portugal's three services and four military regions to act quickly in the event of an emergency. COPCON officers were designated in each of the units assigned to the command and given special bonus pay when on COPCON duty. Neves' commandos were given the honour of heading the COPCON list, which was eventually stretched to include the military police, the Lisbon first light artillery regiment – RALIS, the red regiment of the Portuguese army – the first engineers, the military administration school (EPAM), and the mixed detachment at the Fort of Almada among others. Carvalho retained the right to attach any unit to his command at short notice.

Despite its purely military appearance, COPCON was a supremely political creation. Under the direct orders of Carvalho, who in turn was responsible only to Costa Gomes, COPCON bypassed the chain of command, in particular army chief Marques and the army regional commanders, transferring operational control of the forces from Spínola to the Coordinating Committee. Carvalho soon dispelled any illusions that COPCON would act as a disinterested force if rolled into action when the President of the Republic considered 'the internal situation threatens peace and public tranquillity'. COPCON would define its own powers, which included the arrest and detention under military law of 'reactionary elements' both inside and outside the army. 'We are living through an exceptional period, which permits many things', he told journalists, '. . .a state of para-democracy. We are living in a revolutionary state in which the law must be made for us in accordance with what we consider needs to be done.'[19] COPCON units called in to arbitrate work disputes, pronounce upon the many occupations of flats, houses and farms following the revolution, and to control political demonstrations were instructed by Carvalho to act on the principle that 'the workers are always right' and to intervene only in acts 'not in the interest of the revolution'. In this way, Carvalho claimed to be acting according to 'revolutionary legality', even against laws and regulations made after 25 April which he claimed had been 'superseded by the revolutionary process'. The result was that COPCON actions often countered the rule of law,[20] and in the long run COPCON became an 'anti-force' bound by the flamboyant personality of its commander and attaching for the most part Lisbon units afflicted by the revolutionary malaise. The Lisbon and suburban red-belt orientation

Spínola's Summer 107

of COPCON was further accentuated after 11 March 1975, when Carvalho was named chief of the Lisbon military region. To begin with, however, COPCON provided the revolution with its Samurai, strengthening MFA lines of communication so that the Coordinating Committee could bully the political parties and even the President into strict adherence to the MFA programme.[21] The formation of COPCON set the MFA up as a state within a state. Its autonomy was forcefully demonstrated on 28 September when Spínola attempted to place Carvalho under arrest to reassert his control over the armed forces. The refusal of COPCON subalterns to take orders from the President snapped the chain of command and tumbled Spínola's last power bastion − the army. In his 30 September resignation speech, he complained that no president could govern unless backed by his own armed forces.

COPCON formed only part of the MFA's takeover bid for the army. Carvalho's meteoric rise from major to brigadier announced that revolutionary officers had thrown away the promotion rulebook. A 1 July law abolished the old seniority system, whose retention ironically had been the MFA's original *raison d'être*, and placed promotion in the hands of committees in each arm and service. These committees would forward their promotion choices to a joint chief-of-staff council which retained veto power over certain nominations, but otherwise could simply nod their approval. Experience, it was argued, demonstrated that soldiers should be left alone to pick their own superiors. Salazar's influence on past promotions was exaggerated as an excuse to cut the army free from government interference. The key to the whole structure was the nomination of the promotion committees, and here the law was intentionally vague. As before, politics formed the main promotion criterion, and advancement often boiled down to jobs for the boys. 'It was not too bad in the artillery, but I believe that there were irregularities in the infantry', one colonel observed, speaking of the promotion committees. 'There were both older and younger officers. The older officers did not know which officers to promote, so they asked the younger officers whom they should elect. They, of course, suggested their cronies, so that a clique took control.'[22] This new promotion system did wonders for the MFA's popularity among rank and file officers, and the Movement acquired a large following almost overnight. When 28 September became the Portuguese high command's 'night of the long knives', the promotion committees acted quickly to pack top positions with officers whose loyalty to the left was unchallenged.

108 *Spínola's Summer*

To free the army from state control was, after all, what all the fuss had been about. One of the first laws passed after 25 April stated: 'The structure of the armed forces is totally independent from the structure of the provisional government.' The defence minister was only the 'liaison between the armed forces and the government',[23] and exercised no governmental authority over the army. The same law also gave the chief of the general staff equal rank with the prime minister. In a single law, the Portuguese army leapt from the Third Republic to the Second Reich. It proved a long-term miscalculation, however, for despite long years of dictatorship, the Portuguese memory and political sense were well enough developed to shiver with apprehension at the spectacle of an army which set itself above the nation and the law.

The MFA, until now a small élite, moved to put down roots in the army. The fifth division, created to convince the overseas populations to remain within the realm, was reorientated to preach the gospel of revolution to men in uniform. 'Draw up and send out directives, plans and orders relative to the realization of the MFA programme', read its instructions.

> Keep the commander-in-chief of the armed forces informed of the attitudes of military groups and civilian representatives toward the realization of the MFA programme. Utilize the mass media to stimulate the conscience-raising of the armed forces to achieve its complete integration into the spirit of the MFA programme. Consolidate the confidence and mutual identification created on 25 April between the people and the armed forces.[24]

Dominated by radical Captain Valera Gomes, promoted to colonel by the MFA, the fifth division played an important part convincing the country that the dead hand of Salazarist reaction was behind Spínola's call for a 'silent majority' demonstration. Valera Gomes' group spread their activities into the civilian sector, notably through the 'cultural dynamization' brigades which covered the country to sell the revolution.

Not all MFA old boys were happy with the growing power of the Coordinating Committee. In August, a number of officer founder members under Major Hugo dos Santos met to discuss the leftward shift of the MFA. Dedicated professionals, they had joined the 25 April movement as an antidote to a régime which was leading both the army and the country to ruin. While not particularly avid Spínola supporters, they were dismayed that a few officers had picked up their revolution

Spínola's Summer 109

and run off with it. The result was a document which criticized the
growing military power in Portuguese politics: if the revolution
continued on its present course, it would lead to 'internal convulsions
which would affect the peace, progress and well-being of the nation'.
The blame was laid squarely at the feet of the Coordinating Committee.
This MFA presidium, they argued, had not been elected and therefore
could not legitimately claim its leadership role. It was hardly a model
of 'open government', given as it was to clandestine meetings in which
policy was decided independent of any consultations with the rank and
file. It had fallen under the influence of political factions and was
disrupting the smooth functioning of the army by dragging it into
political squabbles. The hierarchy had been challenged increasingly by
'overtly political' meetings of officers and latterly even of sergeants and
soldiers, and by a blatant appeal to 'opportunism with the appearance
of officers without the slightest mandate in key positions in the Armed
Forces Movement'. Misunderstandings ensued which drove a wedge
between the Movement and the armed forces. Santos also blasted MFA
propaganda in favour of the African liberation movements in the middle
of delicate negotiations. He called for the abolition of the Coordinating
Committee, democratically elected military representatives in the
Council of State, a minimum of soldiers in non-military jobs,
reinforcement of the hierarchy, the opening of the MFA to all officers
and sergeants who agreed with its basic principles and, in a reference to
the MFA's increasing recourse to the Salazarist ploy of posting
troublesome officers overseas, 'regular' assignments to the colonies with
strictly limited and 'comprehensible' exceptions. Finally, he demanded
a 'rigorous respect of protocol' in promotions, plus steps to accelerate
the advancement of the 'most qualified'.[25]

This back-to-the-barracks manifesto was shown to Costa Gomes who
authorized its circulation in the regiments and its publication in the
Lisbon evening newspaper *Diário de Notícas.* Left-wing naval
Lieutenant Vitor Crespo complained bitterly that its circulation and
publication had been approved by the Chief of Staff without the
approval of the Coordinating Committee. With his increasingly
characteristic indecisiveness, Costa Gomes withdrew his backing while
Crespo intervened to prevent publication. The leading 'Huguistas' were
exiled to Africa, clearing the field for the Coordinating Committee.[26]

Decolonization provided the provisional government with its most
pressing problem and ultimately with the issue which sunk Spínola.
The colonial wars had stoked the underlying discontent which flared
up in the military *coup.* The new governors proclaimed that their

110 Spínola's Summer

solution was 'political and not military', but were divided as to just how political that solution should be. Spínola's stand on the colonial issue not only placed him on a collision course with the MFA and most of the political parties, but also undermined his popularity and even authority within the armed forces. The General's views had been spelled out clearly in *Portugal and the Future:* Portugal was too poor and too backward to compete effectively alone in the international market place. The most optimistic forecasts suggested that Portugal, even by tripling her economic growth, could not overtake the least developed Common Market country within thirty years.[27] To survive, Portugal must turn to its empire and eventually perhaps to Brazil 'to construct a vast Lusitanian community with progressive autonomy for each country'.[28] Independence for the colonies was not acceptable: not only would it mean abandoning 'those loyal to our flag', but for Portugal it could spell eventual economic domination which would limit her political freedom of action. 'We are among those who believe that the overseas territories are the indispensable condition of our survival as a free and independent nation', Spínola wrote. 'Without the African lands, our country will be reduced to an unimportant backwater in all-powerful Europe, and will be deprived of all of the supports it can call upon to make our voice heard in the world. She will end up with no more than a purely formal existence in a political structure, but deprived of real independence.'[29] Without the commercial traditions of the Swiss or the Dutch, or the natural resources of the Belgians or Luxemburgers, Portugal would either be absorbed into an Iberian union or become a 'Soviet dagger stuck in the back of the West'.

Spínola's fear of foreign domination was an ancient Portuguese theme, and one echoed both by Salazar and the young officers of the MFA. The General's solution hinged on transforming the empire from a repressive nineteenth-century régime to a liberal democracy which would boast a true multiracial society with equal job opportunities and full black participation in government: 'You cannot resolve the [racial] problem simply by admitting that blacks and whites can sit together in the same bus. . .'[30] With the help of the armed forces, Spínola proposed extending his Guinea experiments in participation to the entire empire until the prototype of a western democracy existed in Africa as well as in Portugal. He told the *Diário de Notícias* in May:

In the modern world, when real political independence exists it is the product of genuine self-determination, and there can be self-determination only in an atmosphere where democratic institutions

Spínola's Summer   111

are functioning perfectly. We must conclude that such institutions
do not exist in the overseas territories, and consequently that their
inhabitants do not possess effective forms of expression and
párticipation and that what immediate independence really means
today would be nothing other than a negation of universally
accepted ideas.[31]

Under Caetano, Spínola's plans for a multi-continental Portugal sold
books to a public hungry for almost any solution to the colonial
problem; after 25 April, they met with almost universal opposition. While
the Coordinating Committee might agree with the President that
Portugal's primitive economy bound her future with that of the Third
World, their sympathies were firmly with the liberation movements,
whom they intended to help to victory. For the confirmed Marxists
among them, Spínola's 'liberal democracy' would act as a front for
continued black repression and big business exploitation of Portugal
overseas. Disagreement over the future of the colonies had clouded
relations even before the *coup*. When Spínola declared that the MFA
programme aimed to 'guarantee the continuity of the sovereign nation
as a pluricontinental entity', he in effect announced that he had won
round one of the platform fight by striking down the Coordinating
Committee's pledge to pursue total colonial independence. However,
his points advantage soon slipped away, for his views were shared by
almost no one of influence.

Politicians saw Spínola's Lusitanian commonwealth as little more
than a pipe dream. Most believed that Portugal's future lay in Europe
rather than with a vaguely conceived African union whose members
had little in common but language, and sometimes not even that.
Foreign Minister Soares noted that the Portuguese army, 'defeated and
totally demoralized', could not be expected to hold the liberation
movements at bay while a liberal democracy was constructed brick by
brick.[32] The General's call for one man one vote 'was to ignore, to
despise, the African reality'.[33] The whites, especially in Mozambique,
would never stand for it. One party systems were the rule in Africa,
and imported pluralist democracy could never take root.[34] Negotiations
with the liberation movements were undertaken with the President in
fundamental disagreement with his foreign minister and the MFA
hierarchy. 'Spínola distinguished between autodetermination and
independence, believing that he could alter the course of history in
this way', Soares noted. 'Our view was that there was no choice but
independence, the victorious conclusion of the struggles of national

112 *Spínola's Summer*

liberation.'[35]

'Soares' possibilities of negotiation were not only limited by Spínola's ideas and by the Portuguese financial interests who had confidence in him', wrote the staunchly pro-MFA Márcio Alves, one of many who hinted darkly at extra-Portuguese pressures brought to bear on the negotiations. 'He was also bound by the interests of the United States, South Africa and Western Europe in Portugal's African possessions.'[36] But if big powers and high finance did appreciably influence the negotiations, Alves provides no evidence. Spínola, Soares and the MFA were all firmly bound to a policy of national independence which could not be altered by a few phone calls from the Algarve villa of expatriate American Admiral Anderson or 'a conversation over port in a London club'.[37] The General argued for maintaining the colonies as a counterweight to the foreign influence in Portuguese politics that his opponents accused him of courting. Those with interests in Portuguese Africa, both strategic and financial, no doubt followed events there closely. But there is no evidence that continued Portuguese presence in Southern Africa was considered imperative either for the Americans who financed in part both the FNLA and FRELIMO, for Portuguese business interests who were among the first to voice serious opposition to the war, or even for a South African government apparently prepared to write off Rhodesia. If it was their aim to keep Portugal in Africa, or simply to put moderate blacks in power, then they failed miserably. If external pressure was applied on the negotiations, then it would seem to have come from the East, not the West: the Soviet bloc armed the guerrilla movements, and had in Alvaro Cunhal, a committed Stalinist, an agent prepared to unleash both industrial and military indiscipline to 'destabilize' the Portuguese government and undermine firm action.

As it turned out, Cunhal did not need to — at least not yet, and not for the sake of Africa. When Soares flew to Dakar on 17 May to meet PAIGC representatives, neither he nor Jorge Capinos, his pro-liberation secretary of state who had fled into exile to avoid military service, had any illusions that their instructions reflected the views of the MFA, or that they were in any way realistic, as Márcio Alves claims.[38] In a 6 May statement published in the *Diário de Notícias,* the PAIGC underlined its readiness to negotiate only on the basis of 'the total liberation of the peoples of Guinea and Cape Verde, and the recognition of the right to autodetermination of the other African colonies. Occupation troops will be regrouped and all hostile acts against the peoples of Guinea will cease.' In Mozambique, the FRELIMO's demands

Spínola's Summer   113

for 'complete and total independence of the Mozambican people and the liquidation of Portuguese colonialism' were equally explicit. Soares' proposal for an immediate ceasefire followed by elections supervised by Portuguese troops was rejected outright: 'As the Caetano government demonstrated that liberal fascism does not exist', announced FRELIMO leader Samora Machel, 'so too it is necessary to make clear that there is no such thing as democratic colonialism'.[39] The liberation movements had no intention of disbanding their forces before total independence was as good as theirs.

Samora Machel's contention that votes cast by illiterate blacks uneducated to democracy would be less than meaningless masked the revolutionaries' obvious conclusion that Portugal had come unstuck in Africa. Despite Spínola's instructions, Portuguese negotiators appeared almost eager to sign away their colonial claims. Soares' exuberant greeting of the liberation leaders, many of whom he had known in exile, created an informal atmosphere which precluded any hard bargaining. When Soares told the Algerian Ambassador to London, who hosted the Portuguese-PAIGC talks, that the two sides 'embraced and sat around a table, like friends who have a few common problems', the Ambassador expressed astonishment. 'That is rather extraordinary. You know that at Evian, French and Algerians only shook hands after we had signed the accord' (ending the Algerian war). Similar scenes occurred in Lusaka where Soares travelled accompanied by Carvalho. Zambian President Kenneth Kaunda's carefully choreographed 'protocole à l'anglaise' collapsed when the Portuguese delegation rushed around the negotiating table to embrace their opposite numbers. Throughout the negotiations, Carvalho, naïvely sent by Spínola to act as a brake on the Foreign Minister's diplomatic generosity, pushed him to further concessions.[40] Unable to sign agreements without Presidential leave, Soares fumed at Spínola: 'His [Spínola's] intransigence and his refusal to evaluate the situation correctly kept us from signing an accord with the Guineans in London much more favourable than the one we were obliged to sign three months later in Algiers', he complained.[41]

The army in the field gave Spínola his second shock. Encouraged by the revolution to believe that peace and repatriation were at hand, orders to fight on until a ceasefire could be negotiated were repudiated by soldiers in the bush. 'A cessation of hostilities was not officially proclaimed', Soares noted, 'but the fights became sporadic, and then ceased.' In many places, 'almost spontaneous' fraternizations between soldiers and their guerrilla enemies took place. The talks organized between Portuguese soldiers and PAIGC leaders at Dakar 'often became

114 *Spínola's Summer*

a series of embraces, a true fraternization between soldiers and guerrillas, who invited each other to interminable banquets. They left their arms in the cloakroom and sat around the table – to dine.'[42]

Colonial governors with pro-MFA sympathies played a leading role in this collapse of military discipline. Major Carlos Fabião, who headed Spínola's civic action programme in Guinea, was promoted to general and sent to take charge in Bissau. A career officer with a solid record, Fabião seemed to undergo a sea change with the revolution. His break with his old commander-in-chief and apparently with all conventional notions of military discipline soon became apparent. Soares wrote:

> One day, he [Spínola] told me very seriously: 'I am going to do something in Guinea which will help you with your problems. I am going to send thousands of portraits of me as president.' He did it. But the portraits stayed in the crates: General Fabião, who was then governor, did not think it a good idea to distribute them![43]

Not content to block the President's colonial politics, Fabião moved to dictate new ones. On 1 July, he chaired a meeting of 1,000 soldiers of all ranks in Bissau which unanimously demanded that: 'Overcoming all obstacles placed in its path by reactionary and neo-colonial forces, the Portuguese government, in accord with pertinent United Nations resolutions, immediately recognize the Republic of Guinea and the right of the people of the Cape Verde Islands to autodetermination and independence, the only course which will lead to a true peace.' The meeting further resolved that the government should parley with the PAIGC, 'not to negotiate the right to independence but to arrange the handover of power'. Lastly, it demanded repatriation of Portuguese soldiers as soon as possible, and called on those who remained temporarily 'to collaborate with the people of Guinea, contributing in this way to the payment of the historic debt engendered by Portuguese colonialism'.[44] Fabião claimed that his initiative was forced 'by the systematic refusal of the Junta of National Salvation to admit the political realities in Guinea'.[45]

Fabião's actions boosted the left-wing momentum of the revolution. His ideas on 'revolutionary democracy' in the army were airlifted back to Portugal after Spínola's downfall, when military assemblies were introduced and regularized. His military dictate also helped Spínola from power. Like the French Fourth Republic, the new provisional government was too shaky to resist a *pronunciamento* from its colonial capitals. Spínola's July bid for extended powers and early

Spínola's Summer 115

presidential elections aimed to restore his authority in the colonial army as well as in the country. The fall of Palma Carlos imposed a rethinking of his colonial stance. On 27 July, Spínola went on television to concede total independence of the overseas territories.

With Spínola's powers slipping away, Fabião's Guinea precedent was taken up, albeit on a slightly less spectacular scale, in Mozambique. While the PAIGC opted to let its war die a natural death, Samora Machel launched an offensive on 8 May backed by 122mm cannon and ground-to-air missiles 'to hasten the overthrow of Portuguese colonialism in Africa'. By the end of July, Machel claimed that his attacks had made ground in the north and splintered the morale of white colonists and troops. Whites in war-torn provinces had put out local peace feelers while soldier assemblies in several units had pledged solidarity with FRELIMO goals. Portuguese soldiers had little stomach left for the fight, and in August when Soares arrived at Dar-es-Salaam with Melo Antunes in tandem, only the conditions of retreat remained to be negotiated. Any lingering doubts were removed with the 26 August signing of Guinean independence. On 9 September, the Lusaka Accord provided for a provisional government headed by MFA militant Vítor Crespo to clear the decks for independence by June 1975. Embittered whites rose in revolt, and after watching from the sidelines for several days, the army moved in to restore order. The fragile calm was soon broken as supporters of the new black government settled old scores with their former colonial overlords. Coloureds and other blacks too closely identified with the empire suffered imprisonment, torture and even death.

Angola proved an equally tragic but altogether bloodier affair. To the by now familiar ingredient of disjointed Portuguese action resulting from conflicting colonial policies in Lisbon were added white and coloured minorities substantially larger than those in Mozambique and a split tribal-based guerrilla movement. In the north, the FNLA kept the evangelical fervour of its largely Methodist-educated leadership, drawing support almost exclusively from the Bankongo and their kin in Zaire. The Marxist MPLA held sway among the largely detribalized shanty town populations of Luanda and other central cities and towns, while in the south, UNITA, a fuzzy offshoot of the MPLA under Swiss-educated Jonas Savimbi, carried on the war with a minimum of arms and success.

Forced to bite his tongue as Soares and the MFA hacked Guinea and Mozambique free from the empire, Spínola intended to oversee Angola's future personally. If Angola could not be saved for Portugal,

116 Spínola's Summer

at least he could see to it that a moderate government would take power to guarantee the rights of racial minorities. To succeed, he had to shut out the Lisbon left and isolate the Soviet — and MFA — backed MPLA. His strategy hinged on the successful mobilization of Angolan power groups, which he called the country's 'vital forces', and rupture of the uneasy alliance between the liberation movements. It was not such a bad plan and might have succeeded but for anarchy, military indiscipline and direct Cuban intervention. Spínola believed the Guinea strategy of government based on hierarchies of tribal and racial groups would avoid the racist pogroms which had marred Mozambique's independence and keep Angola safe for Portugal and democracy. General Silvino Marques, whose brother sat with the junta, was despatched to Luanda as governor general. There he made contact with influential whites and blacks which were pursued by Spínola in Lisbon with a view to resurrecting the 'People's Congresses' in Angola. At the same time he looked to fan the natural distrust between the liberation movements, sending their common anti-Portuguese front up in smoke. Not surprisingly, the pro-Western, Zaire-backed FNLA was his first target. Through the good offices of Zaire President Mobutu, Spínola arranged meetings between Portuguese officers and FNLA leader Holden Roberto in Kinshasa, but failed to shake his temporary truce with the MPLA.

Spínola's opening moves were checked by increasing Angolan anarchy. Troubles touched off when white vigilantes moved into black Luanda to avenge the 12 July murder of a white taxi driver soon escalated into a full-scale fight between FNLA and MPLA supporters, mixed with random pillage and murder which Portuguese troops battled for more than a month to bring under control. Seeing the writing on the wall, some whites and coloured Cape Verdeans, the much resented merchants of the shanty towns, began to make for the capital's various embarkation points. MFA officers seized upon the disorder and Spínola's weakened position after Palma Carlos' dismissal to demand Marques' recall and replacement by Rosa Coutinho on 25 July. 'We made mistakes, that is certain', Soares confessed. 'Admiral Rosa Coutinho favoured the MPLA and restored its lost military force. His successor wanted to impose a more neutral attitude. The oscillations which resulted from Portugal's internal crises made our arbitration more difficult, less credible.'[46]

Saddled with an openly pro-MPLA foreign minister and colonial governor, Spínola appealed directly to liberation leaders. On 14 September, he convened a secret meeting of the three groups in the

Spínola's Summer   117

Cape Verde Islands to work out the shape of a future Angolan government. His proposal for a twelve-man provisional government composed of two representatives of each liberation movement and six from the various tribal groups and the white and coloured minorities was acceptable to Mobutu, Roberto and Savimbi. To circumvent MPLA warlord Neto, who had rebuffed all appeals to talk since May, Spínola produced two MPLA dissidents, Daniel Chipenda, an ex-Benfica footballer turned guerrilla, and Pinto de Andrade, to sign for that organization. On the face of it, Spínola had produced a diplomatic masterstroke: against the odds, he had succeeded in bringing both peace and a provisional government in which almost all political and racial interests would be represented. Neto and the radical wing of the MPLA were left out in the cold. But Spínola's victory led directly to his resignation, even as President Mobutu flew off to explain the deal in interested African capitals: Soares and Coutinho first read of the agreement in the Sunday papers, and were enraged. But Spínola stuck to his guns and the Coordinating Committee began to look for an excuse to dump him, which was not long in coming.

The Cape Verde agreement collapsed with Spínola's 30 September resignation. Garrison commanders in Angola were left to negotiate their own local truces, and on 15 January 1975, after five days of bargaining at Alvor in the Algarve, Portugal signed over the future of the country to the three liberation movements. Independence was set for 11 November 1975, until which time each party was to remain in position. The agreement lasted barely two months. Fighting soon erupted among the victors, with the Portuguese army unwilling to intervene. By the summer of 1975, an estimated 20,000 people caught between the warring factions had died and the civil war, complicated by Cuban intervention, had several bloody months yet to run.

Left-wing leaders defended their handling of decolonization: 'You cannot forget that decolonization began in the worst possible conditions', Soares wrote, 'after 14 years of war which was lost because our troops refused to fight any longer. This reduced our margins of manoeuvre in negotiations. . .In spite of everything, decolonization in its general lines was an incontestible success.'[47] Melo Antunes, who collaborated closely with Soares, expressed the same view in his own characteristically convoluted language:

[Decolonization] was conceived in accord with the grand principles imposed for the universal progressive conscience by history, by civilization and by modern culture, so the revolutionary plan was

118   *Spínola's Summer*

profoundly humanistic and expressed among other things the MFA's deep desire to let the new countries begin life with a clean slate without leaving neo-colonialist subjects or in any other way preventing their development.[48]

However, critics stuck left-wing officers and politicians with a substantial share of the blame for the Angolan civil war. 'The Junta of National Salvation sent destructive agents to Angola. . .among which come to mind Admiral Rosa Coutinho, Major Pezarat Correia, Major Emílio da Silva and Commander Correia Jesuino', wrote Cardoso da Silva, an artillery officer who served as personal secretary to Angolan Governor General Silvino Marques.[49] 'I must admit that all of this [decolonization] process ended by greatly benefiting the Soviet strategy and the Portuguese political factions tied to the Kremlin. This is true', said Captain Sousa e Castro. 'Many people say that decolonization could have been carried out differently. To all of these I ask: what would have it been possible to do? It is easy to say that it was a disaster.'[50]

But another outcome might have been possible had Soares not thrown in his lot with Cunhal and the Coordinating Committee to help his MPLA 'friends', rather than use his good offices to effect agreement behind the Spinola accord.[51] Neto held aloof from reconciliation, backed by the Soviet Union, Cuba and by demands of the domestic left for 'unilateral recognition' by Portugal of the MPLA.

The left's decolonization manoeuvres seriously discredited its leadership both with the army and in the country. Even for those who understood little or nothing about the policies which had bequeathed civil war, it was apparent that nothing had been done to protect Portuguese lives and property, not to mention those of black Africans. 'The whites in Angola were promised protection by the government', one officer said. 'They did not get it. Had I known that the colonies would be abandoned like that, I would have said no to the revolution.'[52] The failure even to attempt to organize and protect the orderly withdrawal of Portuguese civilians, using soldiers on the spot, remained one of the most serious charges levelled at the left-dominated provisional governments.

In his own defence, Soares argued that military indiscipline made such a course of action impossible. Certainly any continuation of the war was unthinkable after 25 April, and indiscipline was a predictable spin-off of the revolution. But the left must take the blame for the scope of this indiscipline: neither Lisbon nor Luanda was prepared to

Spinola's Summer

act with a firm hand. Coutinho's open encouragement of revolution seriously undermined the ability of officers to control their troops. Although politically more moderate, General Silva Cardoso, Coutlinho's successor on 28 January 1975, bent over backwards to demonstrate political neutrality, limiting military action to the defence of the governor general's palace and the airport. Political agitators active in barracks were not rounded up, military indiscipline went unpunished and officers received no orders. One naval lieutenant noted:

> One of our problems [in Angola] was the political turmoil in Lisbon. No one sent any orders. I evacuated all of the whites from a coastal town in the South after fighting broke out in the town between the MPLA and the FNLA with the Portuguese [civilians] caught in the middle. I had no orders; I just did it. We asked for extra ships to be sent from Lisbon to help with evacuation — this was in July (1975) — but they just said that everyone was on holiday. It took me three days to get several thousand people to Luanda.[53]

Evidence suggests that the army could have been organized to rescue its fellow countrymen. The increasing forced exile to Angola of 'professionals', officers who objected to the increasing disorder following the entry of politics into the barracks, provided an excellent framework for the restoration of discipline. The same naval lieutenant noted that the spectacle of human suffering did wonders for discipline on his troubled ship: 'These evacuations had a good effect on discipline. The men saw how distressed these people were, and they were just marvellous, giving up their beds and sharing their food.'

Had ministers and generals acted firmly to restore discipline and organize evacuation, much suffering and subsequent bitterness could have been avoided. That they did not is due in part to the confusion and lack of coordination brought about by the revolution. But the roots of inaction run deeper: the left feared that a disciplined army might intervene to halt the leftward course of the revolution; Angola could provide the base for a Franco-style invasion of Portugal. An indisciplined force therefore suited their political aims. To this was added the violent ideological distaste of many on the left for white Angolans, whom they regarded as oppressive colonialists and racists, receiving in their plight a sort of justice. Falling over themselves to ensure MPLA hegemony, the officers were quite willing to forego humanity. Many added a personal dislike of the colonial whites to their ideological objections. To a certain extent, the army's desertion of the

120 *Spínola's Summer*

white populations of Angola and Mozambique was the fruit of fourteen years of worsening relations which culminated in the January 1973 accusations of cowardice hurled at the army in Beira. 'I cannot forget that in general, the overseas white populations were hostile to the Portuguese forces', Captain Sousa e Castro, a member of the Revolutionary Council, told *Capital* on 2 January 1976. 'This is something people forget very quickly.' But it was not just whites who suffered. Coloureds, because of their superior economic and social status, and blacks who backed the wrong side, belonged to the wrong tribe or who were simply caught up in the general violence died in far greater numbers.

In this respect, the Portuguese experience differs markedly from that of the French. Most French officers who rebelled against the withdrawal from Algeria claimed above all to feel shame at abandoning those loyal to France who bore the brunt of guerrilla reprisals. They felt that the government had enticed them to give their word, to pledge that France would remain, and then forced them to betray it. No such sentiment seems to have affected Portuguese officers: 'There seems to be no feeling among any officers that they have abandoned people who were fighting for us, who were loyal to the Portuguese', one major observed. 'I think that this will come in time.'[54] Most officers were much too concerned with the future of their own country to worry overmuch about loyal blacks.

Rapid decolonization benefited neither Portugal nor her former wards. In the rush to divest Angola and Mozambique of their 'neo-colonial subjects' to allow the new governments to 'begin with a clean slate', Antunes and others overlooked the disastrous economic consequences of a quick Portuguese withdrawal. Industry in the former colonies was deprived of vital technicians, protected markets and the best part of their distribution system at a stroke. With the Portuguese went the skills and equipment necessary to keep factories and plantations ticking over. Industrial and agricultural productivity slumped 50 per cent in the two colonies, due largely, although not exclusively, to the lack of skilled management, and pushing the budgets of the new nations deeply into the red.[55] 'We have managed to avoid the worst', a FRELIMO leader admitted, 'but we do not have the experience to manage Mozambique's capitalist system.' Economists estimate that it will take at least five years for Angola and Mozambique to restore their industry to pre-liberation production levels.

The economic and political consequences of decolonization were hardly less disruptive for Portugal. The left appeared oblivious to the

Spínola's Summer

impact the arrival of almost one million refugees would have on Portugal. France was able to set up almost the same number of Algerian colonists in a new livelihood, but bitterness and dissension linger there even today. A country of barely eight million people with its economy in ruins, Portugal simply could not cope with the planeloads of colonists who were trucked to temporary accommodation in hotels, barracks, schools, prisons and even beaches. Their rush for jobs in an already underemployed population created explosive social tensions. 'The officers sold us out', said one *retornado*, in a café crowded with ex-Mozambicans. 'They did not think of the problems. There are 450,000 *retornados* in Portugal, without money or jobs. It was Rosa Coutinho who really sold us to the blacks. If he walked in here, anyone would be happy to put a bullet in his head.'[56] Soares too began to have second thoughts when he contemplated not only the mammoth social problems created by the newly impoverished arrivals, but also the potential electoral bloc for conservative political parties: 'Those repatriated from Angola', he admitted, 'weigh heavily on Portuguese political life.'[57]

While it was universally acknowledged that a solution to the colonial problem was urgent, a plan which dropped thousands of refugees into Portugal and gave the colonies over to régimes hostile to their ex-master added to the country's distrust of its new government. The officers were blamed for the friction and ill-feeling which inevitably grew up between *retornados* and natives jealously protecting their livelihoods. Attempts in 1975 to set up some *retornados* as cab drivers provoked vigorous protests from Lisbon taxi owners so that the former colonists were confined to Lisbon suburbs, forbidden to take fares to the centre. They, in turn, beseiged the National Assembly until run off by riot police.

The ignominious loss of the colonies without even the face saving creation of a paper commonwealth wounded the national pride of many Portuguese, who felt that Portugal would now sink into obscurity. Amália Rodrigues, Portugal's most celebrated *fado* singer, probably spoke for many of her countrymen: 'I am like a child perhaps, but I felt so proud of Portugal when she had all those colonies.'[58]

Notes

1. *Revue de Politique Etrangère,* June 1975, p.671. See also Alves, *Les Soldats socialistes du Portugal* and Insight, *The Year of the Captains.*
2. Insight, op.cit., p.90.
3. *Le Monde,* 4 February 1975.

122 Spínola's Summer

4. Soares, *Portugal, Quelle Revolution?*, Paris 1976, p.53.
5. Joxe, 'Le Movement des Forces Armées Portugaises', *Revue de Politique Etrangère*, Paris, June 1975, p.637.
6. Interview.
7. Soares, op.cit., pp.123-4.
8. Ibid., p.27.
9. Ibid., pp.51-2.
10. Maxwell, 'The Hidden Revolution in Portugal', *New York Review of Books*, 17 April 1975, p.32.
11. Galvão de Melo, *MFA, Movimento Revolucionário*, Lisbon, 1975, pp.13-14.
12. Ibid., p.14.
13. Soares, op.cit., pp.35-6.
14. Ibid., p.123.
15. Ibid., p.14.
16. Ibid., p.23.
17. Ibid., p.52.
18. Carvalho, *Cinco Meses Mudaram Portugal*, Lisbon, 1974, p.7.
19. Ibid., pp.43-4.
20. F.R. Allemann, 'Withered Carnations', *Encounter*, December 1975, pp.85-6.
21. Joxe, op.cit., pp.75-6.
22. Interview.
23. Law no.3-74, articles 19, 20.
24. Quoted in Joxe, op.cit.
25. Gomes Mota, *A Resistência*, Lisbon, 1976, pp.27-30.
26. Ibid., p.31.
27. Spínola, *Portugal et son Avenir*, Paris, 1974, p.29.
28. Ibid., p.50.
29. Ibid., pp.223-4.
30. Ibid., p.50.
31. Quoted in Insight, op.cit., pp.126-7.
32. Soares, op.cit., p.42.
33. Ibid.
34. Ibid., p.43.
35. Ibid., p.27.
36. Alves, op.cit., p.55.
37. Maxwell, 'Portugal Under Pressure', op.cit., p.26.
38. Alves, op.cit., p.54, and Soares, op.cit., p.38.
39. Quoted in Alves, ibid., p.55 from *Diário de Notícias* and *Diário Popular*, 13 May 1974.
40. Soares, op.cit., pp.40-1.
41. Ibid., p.36.
42. Ibid., pp.38-9.
43. Ibid., p.36.
44. Quoted in Alves, op.cit., pp.58-9 from *Boletim*, No.10, 11, February 1975.
45. Ibid.
46. Soares, op.cit., p.14.
47. Ibid., pp.43-4.
48. *O Jornal*, 2-8 April 1976.
49. *O País*, 23 April 1976.
50. *O Tempo*, 22 April 1976.
51. Soares, op.cit., p.45.
52. Interview.
53. Interview.
54. Interview.

Spinola's Summer

55. See *Le Monde*, 12 August and 3 September 1976.
56. Interview.
57. Soares, op.cit., p.45.
58. *The Times*, 5 August 1976.

5 THE STRUGGLE FOR POWER

During his five months as President of the Portuguese Republic, Spínola was often compared to de Gaulle, a comparison which he encouraged: a soldier turned politician, pulled from obscurity by military defeat, shunned for his clairvoyance by a government whose imagination had calcified in the depression and who emerged from the dust of a liberating army to transform the presidency from a comfortable sinecure into a power-house of government. Deprived of the right-wing supporters of a fallen régime and faced with a battery of Marxist parties and factions, as was de Gaulle to a slightly less traumatic extent after the decapitation of Vichy, he aimed his appeal to the nation — claiming to represent all Portuguese, not just those who paid party dues. People rallied to Spínola out of personal loyalty, out of respect for his honesty and confidence in his leadership, independent of, indeed often in opposition to, party loyalties. Even his 30 October resignation smacked of the French general. His speech, warning that 'crisis and chaos' were inevitable because 'the climate of anarchy in which everyone writes his own laws is increasing' appeared unduly alarmist, words spoken in a fit of pique by a man of immense pride who had been outflanked in a political skirmish which even the best-informed only half understood. The implication was that the resignation was only temporary. The General would retire quietly to some Portuguese Colombey-les-Deux-Eglises, where he would write and think and await his country's second call.

But the similarities were only monocle-deep. De Gaulle was a man of vision, a class politician able to outride party squabbles and political disputes to realize often revolutionary goals, yet whose sense of reality and limits avoided the disasters which could so easily have dogged his policies. Spínola was only a pale reflection of his French master. His plans for a pluricontinental Portugal, if inspired by humanity and patriotism, would have taken a piece of political alchemy to realize. Political commentators have criticized Spínola's 'bureaucratic' concept of political power.[1] But he was the opposite of an institutional politician, whose power was based on coalition and compromise. He saw himself as an Iberian Joan of Arc, a Portuguese El Cid who would turn the communists and leftists out of the country, or at least chase them back to the Alentejo. He met the opposition head on, forcing

124

The Struggle for Power 125

confrontations, rushing positions like a 1914 French commander – and with equally disastrous results. His offensives were no more than diversions which daily sapped his strength, for he had no organization, no heavy artillery, no reserves upon which an 'institutional' politician could call. Spínola hardened the MFA, allowed it to be transformed into a solid political force aided by the parties of the left, in particular the communists, and by bluff and blunder almost silenced the voices of moderation in the armed forces.

Spínola's last clash with the military left was destined to strip him of all power. The growing force of the MFA left wing backed by its political allies and the government's increasing inability to control strikes and growing disorder undermining the Portuguese economy, pushed Spínola to appeal to the nation's 'silent majority' for support in a massive rally set for 28 September. The political parties and the Coordinating Committee saw this as a hammer blow against their so far successful campaign for a socialist Portugal, an attempt by Spínola, denied elections, to legitimize and reinforce his office. 'We saw in this speech [on 10 September] that he [Spínola] was more determined than ever to provoke this swing [to the right], using the weight of the population which saw in him the symbol of possible liberalism', Carvalho noted.[2]

The Coordinating Committee and most members of the second provisional government thought the rally a bad idea. They claimed that it was simply a cover for a fascist takeover which would turn the clock back to Caetano, or beyond. Carvalho hinted darkly at a planned armed uprising, claiming that 40,000 arms, mostly from Spain, had already flowed into the hands of reactionary elements.[3] The COPCON staff drew up 'Operation Stop', a plan which would separate Spínola supporters from counter-demonstrators while detaining more than 100 officers and businessmen labelled as Caetano enthusiasts who might lend Spínola a hand. On 24 September, however, Costa Gomes scotched the scheme, reasoning that 'Operation Stop' would give the impression that COPCON was trying to prevent the demonstration.[4] The arrests, the first of many random detentions which were to mark the next fourteen months, were to proceed as planned, with a list supplied by the government.

Government opposition to the demonstration was solid. On 26 September, Spínola and Vasco Gonçalves argued publicly about the rally's advisability at a liberal party warm-up in the Lisbon bull ring. As they left, still hot with disagreement, fist-happy leftists turned up and shouts and scuffles ensued with police not always successfully

126 *The Struggle for Power*

separating the factions. The Intersindical and the communist and socialist parties called for road blocks manned by party faithful to prevent Spínolist support reaching Lisbon. In an acrimonious cabinet meeting of 27 September, Spínola categorically refused to call off the demonstration. By that afternoon, left-wing barricades blocked the Tagus suspension bridge and all approach roads to Lisbon, and radio stations occupied by leftists were calling for volunteers to man them. COPCON troops fraternized with those on the barricades, spread through the city to pick up men listed for detention and stood guard over the occupied stations assuring the left interference-free broadcasts.

In a long night of negotiations at Belém Palace between Spínola, the junta and the cabinet, Vasco Gonçalves first ordered the barricades dismantled and then retracted when the communists demurred. At 02.00 on 28 September, Carvalho was summoned from COPCON headquarters where he had been supervising the arrests to be told by Spínola to replace COPCON troops guarding radio stations with Republican National Guards. All stations were to close down with the exception of one which would broadcast government orders for the barricades' removal. Carvalho was also informed that COPCON would henceforth take orders from Costa Gomes. In the presence of Spínola and the junta, Carvalho phoned these orders to the Alto do Duque. However, Spínola's authority stopped at the end of the line. Increasingly suspicious that Carvalho was being forcibly held at Bélem, COPCON officers hesitated, and when staff officers attempted to pass on Spínola's instructions, told them that COPCON followed only Carvalho's orders.

Spínola soon realized that he was cornered at Belém. COPCON officers were becoming increasingly mutinous, threatening to force Belém to free Carvalho. General Diego Neto tried to bring paratroops and Marques cavalry to protect the palace, but without success. Spínola toyed briefly with the idea of paying COPCON a personal visit, but dropped it when it was suggested that he might find his name added to the lengthening list of those already detained. Unable to control his troops, Spínola released Carvalho. On his return to headquarters, the Brigadier ordered Republican National Guards to replace COPCON troops guarding the radio stations and manning the barricades. But Spínola was forced to admit that the forces opposed to to his rally were simply too strong, and at midday on 28 September he called it off. Troops and left-wing militants on the barricades turned back cars and buses headed for the demonstration.

The left moved quickly to clean out pockets of Spínolist resistance.

The Struggle for Power 127

On 29 September, Spínola rather optimistically proposed the dissolution of the Coordinating Committee. Full of its victory, the committee predictably countered with demands of its own which Spínola was forced to accept: the resignation of Generals Galvão de Melo, Diego Neto and Silvério Marques from the junta. His power emasculated, Spínola had no intention of presiding quietly over the socialization of Portugal. On 30 September, in dress uniform, he read his resignation speech before television cameras. His decision to step down, he noted, was motivated by the left's abuses of 'democracy and freedom'. He protested the 'anti-democratic' means by which decolonization had been rammed through 'against the interests of the African populations'. He criticized the 'internal convulsions' provoked by groups bent on sabotaging the Portuguese economic and political systems, citing specifically the occupation of radio and television stations as typical of the growing climate of anarchy.[5] Before the television sets had time to cool off, the junta elected General Costa Gomes to fill the new vacancy.

Spínola had disastrously misjudged his stroke. The left, its control of Lisbon radio and television stations complete and its grip tightening daily on many newspapers, claimed that the 'silent majority' rally was a rerun of Mussolini's 1923 march on Rome which announced the return of fascism. The fifth division's propaganda section hailed the break-up of a 'conspiracy under the cover of a demonstration. . .a counter-revolutionary plot'.[6] Carvalho was disappointed not to turn up any of the 40,000 arms which allegedly had entered the country, but noted that the 636 shotguns, 88 pistols, 240 clubs and 8,400 bullets confiscated by COPCON on the barricades, while minor arms, were held by people determined to provoke a confrontation which would give Spínola an excuse to intervene: 'They did not come to Lisbon to hunt partridges', he contended.[7]

The speed with which the left moved into positions of power led many to believe that the *coup* was little more than a phantom danger. '28 September was a conservative demonstration without any danger', a Portuguese journalist close to the socialist party claimed.

The communist party tried to convince everyone that it was a fascist *coup*. They placed popular barricades around the town. They collected many knives from people who arrived and said: 'Look, these people are armed. They came to pull off a *coup*.' But they were only penknives, the sort everyone carries to cut paper or bread. It was just a convenient way to get rid of Spínola.[8]

128　*The Struggle for Power*

Galvão de Melo, whom many cited as one of the kingpins of Spínola's *coup*,[9] denied that 28 September was anything more than a legal demonstration to which 'the political parties gave the most fantastic interpretations'.[10]

'The socialist party did not immediately appreciate the situation and even contributed to increasing the danger', Mário Soares confessed.

> The 'silent majority' demonstration was inopportune pressure. . .As for a reactionary plot, permit me to doubt it. One must realize that the huge mobilization effected that day led to a sudden acceleration of the process which the communist party and their allies knew how to take advantage of. . .We participated in the movement [28 September] in all good faith. But when we saw that the danger did not exist, or that it was not perceptible, we went home to take our normal lives up again. The others pushed their advantage to occupy the terrain. The manipulation of the press dates from this period. One started to see and pick out the reactionary monster at work everywhere. In this way, they hoped to snuff out all criticism, all honest criticism. They labelled as reaction everything which became a stumbling block to them, however insignificant.[11]

Spinola's rally had been no more than a tactical blunder, 'badly prepared and badly followed. If Spínola wanted a massive demonstration of support, he could have gone about it another way: make his speech at the United Nations, where I had prepared the way, and afterwards receive the nation's tribute.'[12]

Until this time, the MFA divided roughly into two groups: those represented by Spínola who believed that the armed forces should create the conditions for the free exercise of democracy and then return to the barracks, and the Coordinating Committee and their allies who were working hard to impose a socialist government at the point of a bayonet. More subtle nuances would later emerge, and indeed were already apparent, but for the moment the MFA forked into these so-called 'professional' and 'political' camps. In numerical terms, those favouring a return to the barracks outnumbered the opposition twenty to one, but they were utterly at sea in the political world they had helped to create. Most confined their political activity to the quiet hope that the whole political mess would simply disappear. Those few moderate officers who fully understood the danger stood up to be counted, but without real support were fed piecemeal to the Coordinating Committee.

The Struggle for Power 129

On 7 June at a meeting at Afeita across the Tagus from Lisbon, cavalry and air force officers proposed that the MFA disband and leave the running of the country to the junta and the provisional government. This demand was reiterated at a larger Lisbon meeting on 13 June and later in the petition circulated by Major Hugo dos Santos. That they did not succeed in imposing their point of view was due to their lack of a programme, organization and experience in dealing with a well-entrenched minority with professional political advisers, definite goals and support to achieve them. Moderate officers also suffered from the gnawing fear that the General's democratic tendencies were perhaps not well enough defined to prevent a lapse into a more autocratic political style.

28 September sealed the victory of the second 'activist' group, a victory which Spínola acknowledged. 'What became apparent to me was a new current of interpretation of the principles inspiring the MFA', Spínola told the *Expresso* on 4 January 1975.

A current which certainly was apparent in the preparatory phase of the movement, but whose exponents had adhered to the general consensus. . .After the revolution, differences on how to proceed toward the construction of a new Portuguese society again reared their head. These divergencies came from our diverse decision-making centres and aggravated a clear tendency toward radicalization. . .Its [the armed forces'] duty is to create the conditions for a free country. To take political power and surrender it to some force not elected by direct universal suffrage is incontestably treasonable.

'The tone was alarmist but the analysis was right in more than one case', Soares said of Spínola's speech. 'He did not describe the real situation of 30 September, but rather the one which we came to know several months later.'[13]

Professionals also faced a second handicap: as soldiers, they were expected to risk their lives for their country, but never their careers. The officer's notorious unwillingness to transfer battlefield courage to the civil sphere, to die for his flag but not his government, to indulge in cautious political fence-sitting in the midst of armed rebellion has not infrequently had governments tearing their hair. Portugal proved no exception. 'The vast majority [of officers] probably waited on the sideline to see which way the wind was blowing', Soares wrote. 'The MFA, covered with glory, contained only a few hundred

130   *The Struggle for Power*

victorious rebels.'[14]

In the first weeks of summer, congratulations were rolling in from all quarters; almost no blood had been spilled, discipline was holding up and the whole affair seemed quite jolly. All Portugal was debating the political options passionately but good-naturedly and many officers kicked in with their opinions. After 28 September, however, the political atmosphere turned decidedly sinister. Opportunistic officers seized on politics as a quick road to stardom, making speeches, stirring up indiscipline and issuing implicit threats against 'fascist' colleagues. 'Saneamento' was the order of the day, and many officers reckoned that if they were to stay on the payroll and out of jail, political discussions had best be held in private between consenting adults. Only the most courageous stood up to be counted, and they were soon alone and in Angola. 'After 25 April, you could go into the officers' mess and hear lively political discussions', a Military Academy instructor noted. 'It was really quite interesting. But after 28 September, not a word. You could not trust anyone. No one dared stand up to indiscipline because there was a real fear of being called right-wing.'[15] Desperate to dodge political torpedoes which could send their paycheck to the bottom, many officers resigned regiments to opportunism and indiscipline. 'Under the circumstances, it is only normal that officers were afraid to speak their minds', an army captain said.[16]

The officers who walked into the government were inevitably tailed by political camp followers bent on sifting for trinkets of influence and ultimately picking the pockets of the very men they followed. However, for the duration of the campaign, the advantages for both officers and the left were obvious: the left provided advice, support and companionship for officers dangerously short of all three. For leftists whose chances for immediate power through the polls were nil, the road to the top could be opened only by a tactical alliance with MFA activists.

The communists, by far the largest group to the left of the socialists, assiduously courted soldiers 'incapable of resisting the temptations of power'.[17] Early autumn opinion polls commissioned by several parties indicated that they would be the big losers in the promised national elections, gaining no more than 15 per cent of the vote. Cunhal's obvious task was to adapt party tactics to the exigencies of Western democracy like his French and Italian counterparts, setting his well-oiled party machine to the business of vote winning, gradually swelling his following until parliamentary influence or even power fell within his grasp. However, Cunhal was a man whose ideas were frozen

The Struggle for Power

131

in the past. His long, bitter struggles with Salazar had moulded him in the crude image of his persecutor. Like many politicians and soldiers, his knowledge of Portugal had grown rusty in exile. His long years in Prague had insulated him against the forces of change and left him untutored in the political conditions of the West. He was a Stalinist of the 1930s who dreamed of becoming the Lenin of his country, of creating a Saint Petersburg on the Tagus, a conspirator more at home in 1917 than 1974. 'Cunhal does not understand the Portuguese people', Soares complained. 'He wants to impose on them schemes that run against their psychology and their way of life. . .He is outmoded. Cunhal is Prague!'[18]

The communists aimed at an institutional takeover of Portugal. a bureaucratic hegemony through which they would gradually assume a stranglehold on the country. Every muscle·was strained toward seizing control of the press, trade unions, municipal councils, government administrations, even of the army itself. It was an attempt at a revolution on the cheap without the trouble of organizing a mass movement. 'The communist party methodically advanced its pawns one by one until the evening of the final assault', Soares claimed. 'It could have been a mass party, but in the end it was no more than a closed conspiratorial clan.'[19]

The tactical advantages gained in committees and assemblies, the great victories of 28 September and 11 March which seemed to clear the field of opposition gave the impression of an inexorable leftward march in the revolution. However, this was an illusion fed by a slanted, superficial press. It was not a war of great propaganda sweeps and political pincer movements, but rather more an ideological Passchendaele, a battle of attrition with each side locked into the business of trench-taking. Tactics and training threw the initial advantages to the Coordinating Committee, the communists and their fringe allies. But these evaporated as the country became increasingly disturbed by revolutionary excesses and as the moderate opposition mastered the minor tactics of political skirmishing. Each institutional conquest, each revolutionary gain evaporated in increasing desertion and disorder, forcing the left into new campaigns and alliances and building up a revolutionary momentum which ran away with itself. The great left-wing offensive of the summer and autumn of 1975 which had Western governments biting their nails was in fact a desperation move, a last-ditch bid for an elusive political victory which appeared ready to fall to the camp of moderation.

Communist strategy called for uncritical support of the MFA left

132 *The Struggle for Power*

while working into influential positions from which the party one day could spring to power. This demanded a series of tactical alliances, first with Spínola and then with Soares, to be scrapped when Cunhal felt strong enough to drop his temporary allies. Socialist support had been vital in preventing the silent majority' rally, but the rapid growth of that party posed the major political stumbling block for the PCP. Cunhal now turned his attention to eliminating his socialist rival.

The discredit and disorganization of political groups to the right of the socialists swelled Soares' ranks with a heterogeneous collection of social democrats, left-wing catholics, freemasons, Marxists and people who simply signed on to counterbalance communist influence in the government. Busy with his foreign ministry, Soares had left the party headquarters in the Bairro Alto in the hands of Tito de Morais an established opposition figure under Salazar. By the autumn of 1974, however, Soares recognized that the avalanche of support demanded a more effective party organization; Cunhal rightly judged the socialists' lack of organization and ignorance of their own strength to be Soares' Achilles heel. The first step was to be a party congress called for December to define party doctrine.

Soares' first secretary at the foreign ministry, Vítor Cunha Rego, was assigned the task of organizing the congress. His initial contacts with provincial socialists revealed the difficulty of the task ahead. 'He drew my attention to the extreme diversity of our adherents', Soares noted. 'No one really knew the troops we had under our command. They were hybrid. We did not speak the same language in Faro and in Braga, the [political] education was only rudimentary and the party line was often ignored. . .My ambition was to reinforce and renew the staff of the organization and, to do this, to attract the leaders of the young militant generations.'[29]

Among the new militants who joined the socialists was Manuel Serra, who had served in the merchant marine and as leader of the Young Christian Workers had an impeccable resistance record. Under Salazar, Serra's involvement with General Delgado had earned him prison and exile in Paris, where he had frequent contact with Soares who knew him as hostile to the communists and naturally friendly to the socialists'.[21] After 25 April, he toyed briefly with the idea of forming his own party but was enticed into the socialist party by Soares who allowed him to organize the Popular Socialist Movement (MSP) within the party itself. Soares later said:

He was not an ideologue: his political education was rather mediocre

The Struggle for Power 133

and for this reason he could not hope to play a major role in a party not short of thinkers. . .But he was a man of action, courageous and full of initiative. . .Yet he was very discreet, even silent, in party meetings. He seemed to take no interest. The reasons for his attitude became obvious later: he wanted to expand his movement at the expense of the party.[22]

Soares ignored warnings that 'Serra is working against us' and entrusted him with the job of organizing the party's security, information and propaganda. 'From the first day of the congress, I felt that a nasty *coup* was being prepared: the militants in charge of security were hostile to me and the reactions of many in the hall were unfriendly.'[23] No one seriously contested the political orientation spelled out by Soares. But on the third day of the congress, the 'Serra clan' unexpectedly presented a list of delegates whom they proposed to elect to the party's 150-man national committee, cleverly retaining the names of Soares and a few of the socialist old guard. 'Half drunk, the provincial militants did not understand what the quarrel was all about', Soares complained, and succeeded in imposing his own list only after the vigorous intervention of recognized party stalwarts.

Serra's influence did not cease with the end of the congress. In the national committee's first meeting, Serra, backed by a few trade unionists and young socialist leaders, again presented a list of candidates for the national secretariat and 40-member central committee. Soares again barely managed to discard the list in favour of his own choices, which included Serra and four or five MSP militants. However, before the new secretariat could hold its first meeting, Serra resigned. The reasons for his departure became clear with the January debate over trade union organization which for the first time found the socialists and communists in open opposition: a carefully orchestrated press campaign called on the government to dump the 'false socialists' and replace them with Serra's 'authentic revolutionaries'.[24]

'I have since become convinced that this affair was directed by the agents of the communist party', Soares said, claiming as his source of information officers who had played a part in the plan and defected to the moderates. 'Serra was probably not an agent but he worked in liaison with the men of the 5th division who were keen to "finish with the lawyers of the PS".'[25]

The PS-PC façade of revolutionary unity began to crack in the late autumn. The opening dispute appeared minor but announced political

134 *The Struggle for Power*

differences which would later bring the two parties close to blows. The Portuguese Democratic Movement-Democratic Electoral Committee (MDP/CDE) had grouped opponents to Salazar in a general anti-fascist alliance. The MDP/CDE had been given two seats in the first provisional government after 25 April, but the socialists claimed that the open party organization of the new republic made the MDP/CDE superfluous and pulled out, leaving it under communist control. Soares claimed that it was simply a PCP 'subsidiary', a 'PC bis' through which Cunhal hoped to pull votes and support away from the socialists. 'The affair attracted little attention abroad, but it announced PC duplicity and the hypocrisy of its unity speeches', Soares noted. 'The true battle began several weeks later, when Cunhal and his friends attempted to impose their ideas on trade union organization.'[26]

The debate over trade union control pitted communists against socialists in a struggle for the working-class movement, with the MFA acting as referee. It was crucial, for it marked the high point of communist influence in the MFA and indicated to keen observers the shaky support Cunhal enjoyed at the top. On 14 January, the communist-run Intersindical mounted a massive demonstration in Lisbon in favour of 'unicidade', or a single trade union. Cunhal argued that more than one trade union would split the working class, making the defence of their rights more difficult. This argument carried the day in the MFA Council of twenty by two votes, binding military ministers to the principle of 'unicidade'. 'It was a question of convincing the officers, slightly inexperienced in this sort of debate, that the working class and the PC were but one, that the workers recognized but one *avant garde,* the PC and none other', Soares said.[27]

'Unicidade' was opposed by parties over the entire political spectrum, from the PPD to the Maoist MRPP. The socialists especially denounced the communists for 'sabotaging democracy', interpreting 'unicidade' as another step toward a one-party state. Socialist justice minister, Dr Salgado Zenha, launched a stinging attack on Cunhal in the *Diário de Notícias.* This in turn ignited an immediate counter-campaign in support of Labour Minister Captain Costa Martins which labelled Zenha a 'heretic'. Lisbon socialists staged a massive rally against 'unicidade', while in Porto, bank workers voted out theor communist union chief, Avelino Gonçalves, labour minister in the first provisional government, in favour of the MRPP candidate.

The scope of the reaction obviously affected military ministers. In the 19 January cabinet meeting they voted the principle of a single trade union but meeting on the following day proved less willing to

The Struggle for Power

135

cede completely to the communist plan: Cunhal, Prime Minister Vasco Gonçalves and Costa Martins found themselves outvoted on provisions which seriously affected communist ability to transform Intersindical into a docile party tool. An additional five clauses stipulated that the law would be reviewed after a year, instituted a secret ballot in union elections to make manipulation more difficult, prohibited closed shops, granted individual unions the right to refuse Intersindical affiliation and ruled that this decision would be taken by all members, not just union leaders.

'Unicidade' registered the communists' highwater mark; its failure frustrated their hopes of gaining control of the trade union movement. Far from dazzling his socialist opponents with a display of force, Cunhal had revealed to Soares that his support stretched to the horizon. 'We had about 200 members at the time of the *coup,* and they gave us five to seven cabinet members', a socialist party official said. 'We did not realize how strong we were until January 1975, during the debate over the trade union law. We organized a rally in Lisbon, and the hall was packed. For the first time, we realized just how large our support actually was.'[28] The trade union debate put confidence into the socialists, who realized belatedly the extent of communist ambition. By standing up to Cunhal, Soares swelled his party's popularity with the vast majority of Portuguese worried by revolutionary excesses.

The breadth of opposition to 'unicidade', an encouragement to many officers to think again, was the beginning of the disagreements between communists and soldiers which finally ruptured the MFA in August 1975. 'This massive opposition [to 'unicidade'] caused a certain retreat within the MFA', Soares noted. 'Military leaders who understood that they had been manipulated but probably feared losing face did not totally withdraw their support for the PC position. The principle of one union was voted, surrounded by guarantees for internal democracy which were respected only at the price of hard battles.'[29]

The decline of communist influence among soldiers was forcefully underlined on 20 February with the unveiling of Antunes' 'Economic and Social Programme'. Nationalization was limited to a 51 per cent state ownership in all mines, oil and gas wells, to the great displeasure of Intersindical and the communist party which called for a takeover of the banks and insurance companies controlled by the large, family-owned conglomerates. Measures calling for fairer taxation, unemployment benefits, low-cost housing, health insurance and agricultural reform abolishing the share-cropping system widespread in the Alentejo simply moved Portugal into the post-war world. Despite

136   *The Struggle for Power*

Antunes' claim that his programme was 'revolutionary' and that anything more radical would destroy Portugal's already shaky economy, the parties to the left of the socialists were bound to denounce any plan which left the large companies intact.

After 11 March, they took their revenge in a series of wildcat occupations of farms in the Alentejo and of the banks, forcing the government to nationalize them. This hasty action worsened the already bad economic situation. Pushed by communists backed often by foreign militants, farm workers seized sizeable spreads in the south and attempted to run them as agricultural cooperatives. Although the acreage of land under cultivation increased, farm production slumped drastically. Farms which profitably employed 50 workers in the past now supported up to 350. Without the expertise to manage the new estates, farm workers slaughtered cattle and sold farm machinery to pay bills and salaries.[30] Efficiency was further undermined by political factions which disputed leadership of the new cooperatives. 'The Alentejo is headed for bankruptcy', Soares told the Portuguese on 9 September 1976 soon after his election as Prime Minister. His new government handed back over 100 farms 'illegally' occupied to their rightful owners and promised legislation to 'democratize' the running of the remaining agricultural cooperatives.

The banks too were hard hit by forced nationalization. 'We went too quickly and we must pay for our imprudence', Soares claimed. 'Banks which made enormous profits in 1974 are now, after nationalization, in the red', largely because the workers lacked the skills to run them.[31] In other industries too, management often walked out in exasperation after wildcat strikes and lengthy union meetings during working hours had pushed wages up by at least 80 per cent and brought production crashing down. Salazar's precious reserves, painstakingly built up over the years, were frittered away in a matter of months. 'Unfortunately, the banks were not the exception', Soares said. 'It was all of our production which in the space of a few months was gravely disrupted. On the brink of chaos, we wasted our last reserves'.[32] Agricultural and industrial disruption also encouraged the emigration of many of Portugal's skilled managers and technicians:

> Their spirit of initiative would certainly be useful in getting the Portuguese economy back on its feet. The worse thing is that they [the managers] took with them thousands of technicians whom we cannot replace quickly: only stability would encourage them to return. We must also regain the confidence of the small and medium

The Struggle for Power

industrialists who lived for two years in a state of disquiet and many of whom finally gave up. . .Who profited from this situation? The workers?[33]

Communist failure to dominate Portugal's political life was matched by the party's inability to bring the MFA into its camp. While it would be incorrect to say that a majority of top MFA men were communists – although communists or communist sympathizers were certainly strong among them, for the moment at least – they shared the fear that a free vote would expose the weakness of left-wing support and postpone perhaps indefinitely their plans for a socialist Portugal. PCP-MFA collaboration naturally opened the MFA to accusations of communist bias, which Carvalho denied: 'The communist party does not collaborate with the armed forces or vice-versa. The armed forces take their own decisions in total freedom. . .What does seem to me to exist is a certain alliance between the left-wing parties and the MFA.'[34] However, Soares believed that the communists and their military allies shared a common goal: 'The ideological dressing varied, but the intention remained the same: to impose, by dictatorship if necessary, a "revolution" which the people did not want.'[35]

The left in power argued that Portugal was not yet ready for democracy. Left alone, the people would be manipulated by clever politicians and tricked by capitalists back into economic servitude: 'I have always viewed political party debates with profound apprehension', Carvalho told *Expresso*. 'They provoke divisions in the mass of workers.'[36] The solution proposed was a period of political tutelage under the MFA, which would prevent press and party excesses while guaranteeing the 'socialist tendency' of the revolution. The MFA would become 'the sentinel of the people', assuring a 'Povo-MFA' alliance which would 'marginalize' the parties to prevent abuses of the nation's naïvety. 'The MFA understood from the very first that if the people were prepared for a revolution, they would have done it themselves', General Fabião stated. 'The "Povo-MFA" alliance was an attempt to stamp a dynamic on the revolution. The MFA wants to have on its side the sum of the progressive forces. . .By adhering to the "Povo-MFA" alliance, the left-wing parties risk marginalization.'[37]

Officers who vowed to make the MFA the 'vanguard' of the socialist revolution, the 'motor' of the ideological conversion of the nation, agreed that soldiers must take a hand in every aspect of the nation's economic, social and political life. To do this, the MFA had to be given legal status in the decision-making machinery, and the 'institutionalization'

138   *The Struggle for Power*

debate began which is raging to this day. An October 1974 communiqué from the Coordinating Committee suggested that the MFA and political parties should share the government, with the soldiers setting the political tone: 'Povo-MFA unity is essentially the triumph of democracy in the service of the people', it read:

> This unity must be cemented through the intermediary of the MFA through its contacts with popular organizations. . .always encouraging the political parties to seek unity with the MFA and with the people, rather than this or that interest group; always assuring, however, that this unity is above party quarrels. . .The formation of a front of progressive, democratic forces is very important, for in this way we will have a constitution truly of the Portuguese people and our young democracy will not waste its energies in debates, disputes and party struggles. . .Join the political parties in a progressive democratic front leading to an assembly. . . guaranteeing the restoration and consolidation of an economic and political democracy in Portugal.[38]

Vítor Alves denied that institutionalization of the MFA would transform Portugal into an authoritarian state: 'What is good for Peru or Egypt is not necessarily good for us', he said. 'It is true that Western opinion seldom associates the words "democracy" and "soldier". We hope. . .to prove that this new initiative associating the army and the people is possible. Democratize and decolonize are the two basic principles of the MFA, and the two essential goals of the new Portugal.'[39]

The institutionalization debate which spilled much ink over the next year cannot be understood as a simple squabble over the extent of military participation in the new republican government. Rather it masked a bitter struggle for control of the country among political groups who realized that the armed forces held the key to power. The 28 September victory of those eager to recast the MFA in the role of a superpolitical force above party quarrels, simply brought about the very disunity they sought to avoid. If the exercise of power in itself had not been sufficient to shatter the officers into factions, the influence of political parties on the army combined with the tensions between 'professional' and 'political' officers created an explosive situation. United in opposition to Spínola and the colonial wars, officers split on just how 'institutional' the MFA should be.

In November, the Council of Twenty met to consider Captain Pinto

The Struggle for Power   139

Soares' proposal that the MFA should book at least twenty seats in the Constituent Assembly to be elected in the spring. In this way, the MFA could keep an eye on the 'continuity of the democratic process'. Hoping that an MFA delegation would increase the electoral force of the left, communists and MDP/CDE stood alone among the political parties in their enthusiastic support for the proposal. Left-wing navy officers and the fifth division led a chorus of military support which was far from unanimous. Air force MFA delegates were especially sceptical, claiming that 'the participation of the MFA in the Constituent Assembly is contrary to the MFA programme, contrary to the promises made to the people, to the MFA and to the armed forces themselves. . .If the Assembly is not democratically elected, we will have the beginnings of a corrupted democracy.'[40]

To overcome opposition and define the limits of institutionalization, the Coordinating Committee took the problem to the MFA Assembly, designed to provide a legislative link with its uniformed constituents and to broaden support in the forces. One hundred army officers and fifty each from the navy and air force were selected to act as MFA watchdogs on government policy. But despite its careful selection, this assembly frequently put a brake on activist plans. From their first meeting in late December, delegates made it plain that they were not the rubber stamp which many 'institutionalists' had hoped. Moderate officers remained strong in a membership named largely from MFA leaders and regional and unit commanders. Divisions in the MFA leadership increasingly apparent after January were reflected in the delegates' reluctance to veer too far to the left. Backed by the socialists and the PPD, assembly moderates assured that Antunes' economic blueprint, debated in December, guaranteed a viable private sector.[41] Despite a January motion passed by the Assembly calling for the MFA programme 'to be carried out in its most progressive spirit',[42] representatives from the pro-Spínolist cavalry school at Santarém moved to scotch any attempts to sabotage the planned elections, uniting 94 per cent of assembly delegates behind a motion which read: 'Confronted with doubts about the political evolution of the country. . .we underline the will of the armed forces to guarantee the present plans of free elections in April 1975.'[43]

The MFA extremists pushed for the government to be given over almost exclusively to MFA control. Already in October, General Fabião had declared that the 25 April programme 'is not a political programme. . .[but] a minimum platform for the construction of a constitutional democracy. . .Thus, the programme will have to be

140　*The Struggle for Power*

carried out to its last details.'[44] In January, the left began a verbal offensive which it hoped would carry the MFA into power. Against a background of increasing political violence including the well publicized January siege of CDS delegates and British Tory MPs in Porto, the *Boletim* proclaimed that the MFA must become 'the motor of the historic construction of the political and social life of our young democracy'. Carvalho complained that the political parties were not defending the interests of the people and that the 'institutionalization' of the MFA in government was an absolute necessity.[45]

The left's offensive climaxed in early February when delegates were presented with a fifth division plan which would have greatly reduced the civilian voice in government. Attached was a suggestion that the MFA programme be 'clarified. . .instituting a social and economic policy which is truly in the service of the Portuguese people. The object must be the defence of the interests of the working class and the cessation of existing exploitation characteristic of the capitalist system', the fifth division statement read.[46] Delegates turned it down, opting instead for a course of 'moderate intervention' which bound the council to follow Assembly decisions. Regular Assembly meetings were also called for, as well as a more democratic election procedure. The Assembly ended its 17 February meeting by commissioning the Coordinating Committee to begin discussions with the political parties on future military participation in government.

Following the 11 March *coup* attempt, left-wing officers demanded that the MFA Assembly postpone the planned national elections indefinitely. This the Assembly refused to do, but they did vote a motion giving the MFA power of veto over any new constitution and creating a new Revolutionary Council from the Council of Twenty. Representing the views of the MFA left, the Revolutionary Council denounced the MFA Assembly as too 'élitist' and ordered it restructured into a constituent of officers, sergeants and soldiers.

The MFA Assembly topped a legislative network which grew through the winter, and spread markedly after 11 March. The MFA left clearly hoped that the more 'democratic' representative structures which bypassed the conservative military hierarchy would generate the steam needed to force through institutionalization. Each of the three services created its own assembly composed of members of the MFA executive organs, regional and regimental commanders, and representatives of the schools, sergeants and soldiers. At the base, unit assemblies discussed issues pinpointed after 11 March by the dynamizing groups at the instructions of the fifth division. In addition,

The Struggle for Power

'committees of well-being', set up in the navy before 25 April to discuss day-to-day problems, were extended to all services and given the mission of 'enlightening all personnel and making them aware of the execution and realization of the MFA programme'. Assemblies in each military region discussed how best MFA policy could be applied in the forces.[47]

The fluid composition and irregular meetings of the newly created organs, the influence of local extremists, the lack of a clearly defined relationship with the hierarchy meant that the new MFA structures provided no springboard from which any faction could vault to power. Furthermore, the attempts by many uniformed politicians to seize command initiative from the military hierarchy led to conflicts which drained much MFA sympathy in the ranks of professional officers. The MFA created a Supreme Council composed of between 120 and 130 'history-making' delegates who had taken part in 25 April just to define these links and 'assure a greater integration of the hierarchy in the revolutionary process'.[48] The Council was not particularly successful: many professional officers condemned the assemblies for contributing to growing indiscipline in the forces. 'I told Antunes when they began to create these assemblies that you cannot govern by mob rule, that this example will soon be followed by sergeants and soldiers', one captain observed.[49] The undemocratic nomination of unit delegates also fed fears that the revolution was falling increasingly into the hands of well coordinated minorities. 'We were told that so-and-so was our delegate and so-and-so appeared with a communiqué', an officer noted.

> When I asked a soldier who had picked him, he told me that 'they' had picked him, whoever 'they' were. I remember one meeting when an MFA delegate arrived with a communiqué which he read to the unit assembly. After he read it, the commander, in the true spirit of 25 April, asked if there were any questions. The MFA delegate was livid. He had not come to answer questions.[50]

After 28 September, the Coordinating Committee moved to purge the officer corps of men short on enthusiasm for the 'revolutionary vanguard' in vogue. The first effects were felt in the government, where moderate Lieutenant Colonel Firmino Miguel lost his defence portfolio, which was taken over personally by Vasco Gonçalves. Spínolist Communication Minister Major Sanches Osório was replaced by navy Captain Jorge Jesuino, one of several pro-communist officers who had floated to the surface in that service. Radical air force pilot Costa

142   *The Struggle for Power*

Martins assured left-wing control of the important Labour Ministry. Carlos Fabião was named army chief in the place of Silvério Marques and given a seat on the ruling junta, along with Lieutenant Colonel Lopes Pires. General Jorge Miranda and Lieutenant Colonel Mendes Diás sat for the air force, while the navy continued to be represented by Admirals Rosa Coutinho and Pinheiro de Azevedo, hopeful of radicalizing that body.

The purge of top officers initiated after 25 April was stepped up and extended downwards. In what was virtually a clean sweep of the senior ranks, Caetano generals like Kaúlza de Arriaga and Luz Cunha who had been among the twenty-five officers already axed for their links with the old régime were now joined in retirement by others whose professional consciences might one day stand in the way of an MFA monopoly. These *saneamentos* were not confined to the top echelons: an estimated eighty colonels and lieutenant colonels whose loyalty the MFA doubted were also placed on the job market.[51] The movement then conveniently shifted Spínola with a November 1974 decree lowering the retirement age of senior officers.

On 7 September, the navy announced it was sending home 105 officers between the ranks of captain and sub-lieutenant — 10 per cent of serving professional officers — in the second of a two-part operation aimed not only at those 'directly compromised with the old régime politically', but also at 'corrupt and inefficient officers'.[52] 'Many of the cases cannot be understood as consequences of a certain political or ideological behaviour', General Fabião claimed, 'but only as cases of ill-chosen careers. We have officers who would be excellent professors, doctors or engineers, but whose military qualities are absolutely nil.'[53] Nevertheless, to be a close relative of a high Caetano official was enough to put paid to the careers of many young officers.

Rather than solidify MFA support in the officer corps by eliminating men unsympathetic to the left, the purges had rather the opposite effect: the arbitrary manner in which they were carried out transgressed the almost sacred right to job security shared by soldiers and civil servants and was the first inkling many officers had that the revolution might not be in the best hands. 'The purges made us uncomfortable', one naval lieutenant noted. 'They were carried out by an elected commission. Some officers who were too closely connected with the old régime disappeared, as did some incompetent officers. What made us uncomfortable was the procedure. There was no way to appeal.'[54] Plans were announced for similar purges of the army and air force: 'of 4,000 officers, we will perhaps be left with 3,000, but

The Struggle for Power   143

cohesion will be reinforced', one MFA army officer promised.[55]

In fact, subsequent purges in the army and air force did not live up to left-wing promises, largely because professional solidarity often intervened to soften politics in those two services which, unliké the navy, were not dominated by a coterie of pro-communist officers. Professional solidarity weakened the MFA left, especially in the army and air force, by undermining its campaign to axe 'professionals' within its ranks. Many officers critical of the disorders provoked by 'political' officers suffered no worse punishment than a trip to Angola.

As the political situation deteriorated in the summer of 1975, more and more officers were booted out of their regiments, or jailed for some alleged misdemeanor, by self-appointed political committees usually working in tandem with local political groups. But professional solidarity acted as a career safety net and condemned officers would usually re-emerge, perhaps in a new post, after the intervention of a senior officer moved to rescue a comrade for old times' sake despite political differences. Such was the case of commando Colonel Jaime Neves who, removed from his command after a 'democratic' decision of his troops, was reinstated after Carvalho's personal appeal to a battalion assembly. 'I was invited to a dinner in the commando battalion sometime after the trouble there when some soldiers had attempted to throw out the commander, Jaime Neves', an ex-miliciano said.

> I was astonished to see one of the captains who had been involved in the attempt to purge Neves. I told another officer that I found it incredible that this man was still in the battalion. The officer replied that despite their political differences, they were still friends. They had been in the same post during the war. [56]

The extent to which the MFA was able to win adherents in the different branches and services of the armed forces poses thorny questions concerning the political orientation of military groups. In his study of the American army, sociologist Morris Janowitz described a resistance to modernization or 'civilianization' especially common in the traditional combat branches which boasted a tough warrior image. These men could expect a serious loss of status in a modern force dependent on missiles and push-button technology, and so resisted 'transformation into a technician or a manager'.[57] 'The history of the modern military establishment can be described as a struggle between heroic leaders, who embody traditionalism and glory, and military

144   *The Struggle for Power*

"managers" who are concerned with the scientific and rational conduct of war', Janowitz wrote.[58] This theory in part explains the conservative orientation of most American and European armies, the attachment to traditional values which pushed Massu's paratroops into the forefront of the right-wing military revolt in Algeria. The more technical orientation of the world's air forces and navies make them more open to technological change and modernization, and so more susceptible to new currents of political and social thought.

I.R. Horowitz, in his study of Latin American military élites, takes a different opinion, claiming that on that continent, at least, armies are the repository of radical ideas:

> We know very little of rivalries between military factions or military services, at either the organizational or ideological level. We know, for example, that as a general rule the army will be more liberal in its position than either the air force or the navy; however, we do not really know why. It might well be that this liberal-conservative dichotomy has nothing to do with Latin American characteristics, but is simply the function of the landbased nature of both army and civil functions, giving to its policies a realism perhaps less present in other branches of the armed forces geared to operating in the 'unnatural' environments of air or sea.[59]

The whole question of political tendencies in armed forces is much too complex to be reduced to general formulae. Most nineteenth-century theorists attributed the generally liberal politics of European artillery and engineering officers to their technical orientation, education and low social status *vis-à-vis* the aristocratic cavalry and more socially acceptable infantry. However, at least in France, the artillery acquired new status with the Revolution and a number of men, including Bonaparte, rose to high government and army positions from its ranks. In the nineteenth-century French army, the artillery formed a social and educational élite, and the material conditions of service rather accounted for its radicalism.[60]

Navies have always demanded greater professional skill in their officers. While colonels and generals could be helped up the promotion ladder by money, family and connections – until undone by some untimely campaign, like Cardigan in the Crimea – naval captains and admirals had to prove capable at least of keeping their boats off the Tagus bar. But despite the technical mastery required of naval men, European naval officers usually distinguish themselves by their

The Struggle for Power

conservatism. Retired British naval officers in Bournemouth and Bath do not provide the pillars of the local Labour parties. In 1940, French admirals narrowly beat the nation's bishops in the race to Pétain's front door when the cry went out to 'rally round the Marshal' while conspicuous place occupied by the French navy in the Vichy government prompted the Bishop of Lille to wonder if he would be replaced by an admiral upon retirement. Tirpitz' deliberate attempt to create a liberal navy from the anti-Junker, anti-Prussian German middle classes collapsed when his new officers slavishly aped their more socially acceptable colleagues.[61]

Nor is the most modern and technical of services, the air force, a bastion of advanced ideas: Hitler always complained that the Luftwaffe was the only German service totally committed to national socialism, while American air force General Curtis Lemay's obsession with force won him the nickname 'Stone Age' and the vice-presidential position on George Wallace's 1968 presidential ticket.

The political orientation of Portugal's armed forces also defies theory and the experience of other national armies. Despite Bandeira's contention that 'there are no historical antecedents that evidence a liberal tradition in the officer corps of the Portuguese navy',[62] most political observers agreed that if the MFA were the vanguard of the revolution, the navy was the vanguard of the MFA. On 1 February 1975, *Expresso* estimated that Vasco Gonçalves found his strongest support in the navy, backed also by some officers in the army engineers and artillery, and a few in the infantry. Moderate and Spínolist officers dominated the air force, the cavalry, the infantry and commando and paratroop battalions. While strict service agreements limited navy positions in the MFA Assembly and Revolutionary Council, the navy dominated the radical fifth division and was responsible for proposing and largely for organizing cultural dynamization campaigns. Its officers were also in the forefront of the push for the institutionalization of the MFA. The reasons for the navy's extremism evaded both officers and journalists, who speculated that sailors read radical literature during long sea voyages — a pastime shared by few of their contemporaries in other European navies.[63]

The Portuguese navy's left-wing traditions stretched back to the last years of the monarchy, when naval officers were prominent in radical politics. Recruited largely among the sons of liberal middle classes from Lisbon, Setúbal and the Algarve, naval officers brought their traditional family politics with them into the service. Competition for places at the Naval Academy was keen, standards were high, at least higher than

146 *The Struggle for Power*

at the army's Escola do Exército, and those who held its diplomas constituted, in Caetano's opinion, an officer corps 'distinguished by its culture, assurance and discipline, where everyone knew each other'.[64] The naval officer corps formed an élite, which scorned the archaic social conventions represented by the monarchy and its aristocratic supporters, upon whom it heaped the blame for Portugal's lamentable economic and social backwardness. A 1910 naval rebellion led directly to the proclamation of the First Republic, and naval officers were prominent in liberal governments in the first years of the régime. In 1936, three Portuguese warships mutinied and attempted unsuccessfully to join Spanish Republican forces. Portuguese communist leader Manuel Guedes claimed then that his party counted 300 sailor members and over 700 subscribed to the PCP newspaper, fully 14 per cent of the navy. Propaganda distributed by the Revolutionary Organization of the Navy (ORA) spread easily among sailors who, unlike soldiers, were required to be literate.[65]

The navy's attachment to politics continued through the Salazar period. Liberal traditions were kept alive at the Naval Academy where 'the new officers received the influence of the older generation'[66] through instructors like Pinheiro de Azevedo, Prime Minister in the sixth provisional government. Caetano also claimed that an old boys' society in the Academy formed ostensibly to maintain contact among graduates was in fact a 'sort of masonic lodge' with strong political overtones perpetuating left-wing traditions. The navy was never very far from politics: attached to the colonial ministry until 1911, naval officers provided the bulk of colonial governors and overseas administrators since 1736. Naval officers in the territories enjoyed a large degree of freedom and the Salazar government was never able to exercise the full weight of its authority over the miles of empty ocean. As the French government found with its colonial army, habits of independence built up over years, even centuries, proved difficult to curtail, and the Portuguese navy's fierce independence was often politically expressed.

When Portugal signed on with NATO in 1949 and reorientated her forces to the North Atlantic, new strains were placed on relations between Salazar and his navy. NATO money flowed in to raise the Portuguese armed forces up to Western standards while Portuguese military personnel flocked abroad to be trained in the latest tactics and techniques. Naval officers headed this exodus which in twenty years numbered around 3,000 men. Of 107 Portuguese officers trained in the United States in 1968, fully 95 were from the navy. In 1970, 26

The Struggle for Power 147

of 33 Portuguese officers sent to America came out of the navy.[67] Other naval officers were trained in Britain and West Germany. Naval officers abroad were acutely conscious of their lack of modern weapons and training and slightly humiliated by Portugal's dependence on her NATO allies for modern training and technology. Portugal's economic and social backwardness, her insignificance in the world balance of power, her antiquated régime and rotting empire in defence of which she was fighting an unfashionable war were all the more apparent to officers on the outside looking in. 'In frequent contact with foreigners, naval officers began to be sensitive to the argument which attacked Portugal because of its overseas war', Caetano complained. 'The books they read inclined them toward socialism.'[68] Even officers calling briefly in foreign ports felt that Portugal was NATO's poor relation. 'When we were abroad, we were embarrassed by the régime', a naval captain commented. 'We felt that people looked down on us, that we were a second-class country. I remember one trip to Canada: we were received by Canadian officers, but the reception was cool – correct but decidedly cool. It was the same everywhere we went.'[69] More than any other factor, this NATO mobility accounted for the growing separation between the armed forces and its Lisbon masters in the two decades preceding 25 April 1974. 'I have travelled in democratic countries throughout my career, on courses in Scotland, France and the US', an air force colonel said. 'I frequently bought books banned in Portugal, as did many of my colleagues, but we had no contact with the ideas of the guerrillas. We simply felt that things were not exactly as they should be in Portugal.'[70]

Naval officers got no career advantages from their élite recruitment, education and training. Low personnel turnover and small size gave the navy the lowest promotion rate in the armed forces. Only 3 per cent of naval deck officers – from whom all top officers were selected – could expect to become vice-admirals (admirals, like field marshals, are named only in exceptional wartime circumstances), rear-admirals or commodores. Even in the army, 4 per cent of combat officers could look forward to promotion to general or brigadier, while in the air force fully 8 per cent of pilot officers won promotion to the two top ranks.[71] Elite Naval Academy graduates vegetated in the lower ranks of the officer corps while contemporaries from the less select Military Academy who joined the air force shot up the career ladder. A Military Academy cadet who chose the air force could expect to reach the rank of major in seven years, while a classmate who entered the army looked forward to between an 11 and 13 year wait as a company grade officer.

148   *The Struggle for Power*

'A chap my age, 37, in the air force would already be a colonel', complained one naval officer who had topped his class at the Academy. 'And I have only recently been promoted to capitão-tenente, the equivalent of major.'[72]

The thirteen generals in the air force in 1973 averaged 56.6 years of age, its eight brigadiers named among the pilots 51 years and its twenty-three pilot colonels averaged 46.5 years. Brigadiers drawn from among the air force's engineering branches were also in their early fifties. Even though the army's 'rheumatic brigade' averaged 61.5 years in 1972, its brigadiers were still a relatively youthful 56.6 years old. Even after the massive purges of 25 April swept away all vice-admirals, rear-admirals and commodores, in the Portuguese navy, promoting a whole new leadership crop to the admiralty, the navy still lay behind the other services: in 1974, vice-admirals and rear-admirals were on average 57.5 years old. But if one eliminates the navy's two new vice-admirals, whose promotion was due exclusively to their political views, 57-year-old Pinheiro de Azevedo and Rosa Coutinho, who at 48 was promoted directly from capitão-de-fragata (lieutenant-colonel), the remaining rear-admirals averaged 59 years, still older than the army's average brigadier before 25 April.

The air force was Portugal's pampered service, and pilot officers had little reason to be discontent, unlike their colleagues in the army or navy. While muted opposition to the Salazar régime was widespread in the air force before 25 April, MFA delegates from that service were forthright in their opposition to the more extreme institutionalist demands of the left as the revolution progressed: A December memorandum from the air force council rejected MFA participation in a future national assembly as 'contrary to the MFA programme' and warned of the dangers of military dictatorship. It also cautioned that 'leftist tendencies' in the MFA could 'corrupt democracy' and endanger Portugal's geopolitical position'. The moderate politics of the air force made it difficult for the MFA left wing to find allies in that service. 'After 25 April, the MFA discovered that most revolutionaries in the air force came from the engineers, not the pilots', one officer noted. 'They had the devil of a time finding a pilot with left-wing views, and finally chose Costa Martins (for the Revolutionary Council) because he was the only leftist they could find. He is a courageous man, but not respected by the other officers. They simply had to use him because he was a pilot.'[73]

The career advantages which reinforced the air force's comparative contentment were bolstered by other material advantages. Air force

The Struggle for Power   149

officers in the colonies had been able to take their families with them to the relatively safe air bases, unlike army officers forced to live for months at a time alone in the bush, or naval officers plying back and forth between Lisbon and Luanda. Consequently, the air force suffered less than officers in other services from privation and war weariness.

Good career opportunities, material well-being, little war weariness and the absence of a left-wing tradition encouraged professional rather than political concerns in the air force while the navy simmered with resentment and discontent. When the *coup* carried off virtually the entire high command and when left-wing officers moved to capture the top after 28 September, few politically suitable pilots could be found. Consequently, the air force remained relatively free from institutional upheaval. In contrast, the navy contained any number of radical officers eager for power. The navy's liberal traditions assured, almost as a matter of pride, that men with advanced ideas would take over. Azevedo, promoted naval chief of staff, selected Captain Martins Guerreiro as his executive officer. Left alone in this key position, the pro-communist Guerreiro had a virtually free hand in the ministry, and was instrumental in organizing the extensive navy purges which surpassed those of the other services. Backed by a strong contingent of radical officers which included Rosa Coutinho, Ramiro Correia, Jorge Jesuino, Carlos Contreiras, Miguel Judas and Vítor Crespo, the left was better able to coordinate a successful strategy in this relatively small and centralized service. By the summer of 1975, however, the growing divorce between the radical vanguard and the mass of liberal officers led to a revolt in the Naval Assembly.[74]

Discipline is often mentioned as another factor determining a unit's political complexion. Well-disciplined paratroops and commandos held their heads above Portugal's growing tide of disorder, at least until their very discipline made them the special object of agitators' attention. A professional abhorrence of disorder, civil or military, would normally throw these men into the camp offering stability, while the tight grip kept by officers and NCOs on their men would nip any revolt in the bud. Yet, the air force, where discipline is usually regarded as slack, also remained relatively free from disorder. Air forces in general pride themselves on reducing the outward trappings of military life to a bare minimum, concerned only that everyone do his job. The Portuguese air force was no exception. 'Discipline in the air force was OK during the revolution', explained an air force sergeant. 'It always has been. It is hard to say why. The air force is very informal. If you were seated and an officer walked in, you just said: "How are you today, Lieutenant?" You only stood up for the commanding

150 *The Struggle for Power*

officer.'[75] Pilots bore the brunt of the fighting, and so gained the respect of their men. An air force colonel concurred:

> The air force has always been very democratic, even before 25 April. We treated soldiers as our fellows. People often said: 'Oh, you are not military men.' We forget about rank, we see the function. Each man has his job, and we must trust each other to make the plane work. The pilot must trust the flight mechanic to see that the engines run, and he must trust me to fly it. The atmosphere that reigns in the plane is transmitted to the base.[76]

Accessibility of officers, the *esprit de corps* built up through mutual contact between officers and men, and a common sense of mission appear more important than a strictly enforced military code as guarantees of discipline. 'The air force has a family life', a naval officer observed. 'There was not the division there was in the navy between younger and senior officers. There was more communication.'[77] 'If a man had problems and he saw the colonel passing, he stopped me and we talked about them', the air force colonel said. 'I was often invited to the NCO mess. We had a certain *esprit de corps* not present in the other services, a very informal atmosphere. Everyone simply did his job.'[78] Officers who made themselves available to their men escaped the worst ravages of indiscipline: 'I had few discipline problems because I had a reputation for being left-wing, a reputation which I let stand', a naval captain said. 'Each week I met with my men to discuss their problems. They were never political, just about food and drink which were difficult to come by in Angola.'[79] The same sort of 'family life' was evident in other more strictly disciplined units, like the paratroops, commandos and cavalry, where commanders were often more conscious of the needs and capabilities of their troops than in haphazardly disciplined line units where morale was savaged by a constant 'cost efficient' personnel turnover.

But while recruitment, education, career structure, the material conditions of service and war weariness may at a given time thrust one service or branch into rebel leadership, the political consequences of armed forces tribalism must not be exaggerated. There is no strict calculus which forces technical officers to the left and combat officers toward conservatism. Statements like: 'If you talk an engineering officer into a theoretical position, he will follow you like a dog', were frequently expressed to explain the left-wing views of Vasco Gonçalves, but most engineering officers were counted in the moderate military

The Struggle for Power

151

camp. Had politics split along branch lines, then the Portuguese armed forces, whose engineering, medical, administrative, support and general service (ex-NCO) officers found their career ceilings substantially lower than those of army combat officers, navy deck officers and air force pilots, would theoretically have been plunged into a heated military class war. But this armed forces petite bourgeoisie seems to have remained relatively inactive, preferring on the whole to leave revolution-making to their service aristocracy. This is not to say that rivalry and even jealousy did not exist in the services, as between deck and engineering officers in the navy, but it seldom degenerated into a bitterness which found political expression. Most support officers conceded to combat officers the right to higher rank. 'We told the engineering officers: "You think you are better than us"', a navy deck officer commented. 'But when they created the marines and they wanted fighters to lead them, they picked us, not you.'[80] Judas, a naval engineer, Correia, a doctor, and Costa Neves, an aeronautical engineer, sat with the Revolutionary Council, but, as noted before, their politicization seemed to owe little to their military education. Cadets or young officers with strong political views would sometimes convert small groups of friends, usually in the same service branch, to drag with them into power, but personal links seem more important than branch links in inclining officers toward revolt.

Notes

1. Joxe, 'Le Mouvement des Forces Armées Portugaises', *Revue de Politique Etrangère*, Paris, June 1975, p.676.
2. Carvalho, *Cinco Meses Mudaram Portugal*, Lisbon , 1975, p.18.
3. Ibid., p.14.
4. Ibid., p.22.
5. *República*, 30 September 1974.
6. *Boletim*, No.2, 3 August 1975.
7. Carvalho, op.cit., p.15.
8. Interview.
9. See Insight, *The Year of Captains*, London, 1975, p.171.
10. Galvão de Melo, *MFA Movimento Revolucionário*, Lisbon, 1975, p.45.
11. Soares, op.cit., *Portugal: Quelle Révolution?* Paris, 1976, pp.57-8.
12. Ibid., p.56.
13. Ibid., p.59.
14. Ibid., p.124.
15. Interview.
16. Interview.
17. Soares, op.cit., p.125.
18. Ibid., pp.31-2.
19. Ibid., p.120.

152 *The Struggle for Power*

20. Ibid., pp.79-80.
21. Ibid., p.81.
22. Ibid.
23. Ibid., p.82.
24. Ibid., pp.84-5.
25. Ibid., pp.85-6.
26. Ibid., p.102.
27. Ibid.
28. Interview.
29. Soares, op.cit., p.103.
30. Ibid., p.218.
31. Ibid., p.95.
32. Ibid., p.220.
33. Ibid., p.221.
34. *Le Monde*, 13 October 1974.
35. Soares, op.cit., p.125.
36. *Expresso*, 17 May 1975.
37. *O Século*, 13 May 1975.
38. *Expresso*, 22 February 1975.
39. *Le Monde*, 9 November 1974.
40. Insight, op.cit., p.199.
41. Joxe, op.cit., pp.683-4.
42. *Expresso*, 18 January 1975.
43. Ibid., 25 January 1975.
44. *República*, 30 October 1974.
45. *Expresso*, 1 February 1975.
46. Insight, op.cit., p.204.
47. Joxe, op.cit., pp.679-83; *Le Monde*, 27 August 1975.
48. Joxe, op.cit.
49. Interview.
50. Interview.
51. Figures furnished by the American Embassy, Lisbon.
52. *Expresso*, 7 September 1974.
53. Ibid., 16 November 1974.
54. Interview.
55. Niedergang, 'L'Armée portugaise ou la fascination du pouvoir', *Le Monde*, 6 February 1975.
56. Interview.
57. See Ambler, *The French Army in Politics*, Ohio State University, 1966, p.297.
58. Janowitz, op.cit., *The Professional Soldier*, Glencoe, Ill., USA, 1960, p.21.
59. I.R. Horowitz, 'The Military Elites', in S.M. Lipset and A. Solari, *Elites in Latin America*, New York, 1967, pp.169-70.
60. Porch, *Army and Revolution*, London, 1974, Chap.6.
61. H. Herwig, *The German Naval Officer Corps*, Oxford, 1973.
62. Bandeira, 'Military Intervention in Portuguese Politics', unpublished paper, York University, Toronto, August 1975, p.74.
63. See *Financial Times*, 11 March 1975.
64. Caetano, *O Depoimento*, Rio de Janeiro, 1974, p.178.
65. Bandeira, op.cit., p.76.
66. Caetano, op.cit.
67. Bandeira, op.cit., p.34.
68. Caetano, op.cit., p.178.
69. Interview.
70. Interview.

The Struggle for Power

71. Statistics based on figures taken from *Lista da Armada*, 1974; *Lista do Pessoal da Força Aérea, Vol. 1*, Quadro Permanente, 1973; *Lista Geral de Antiquidades dos Officiais do Exército*, Quadro Permanente, 1972.
72. Interview.
73. Interview.
74. *Expresso*, 20 September 1975.
75. Interview.
76. Interview.
77. Interview.
78. Interview.
79. Interview.
80. Interview.

6 11 MARCH

By the end of February, Spínola's resignation speech was beginning to appear less and less like the jeremiads of an embittered loser, and more like an accurate assessment of the revolutionary ambitions of the Portuguese left. Many Portuguese had adopted a cautious attitude to the revolution from the beginning, but in the euphoria following 25 April it was unfashionable, not to say dangerous, to say so. Now even Soares, the blinkers of revolutionary solidarity removed from his eyes by his clashes with Cunhal and by the real fear that the MFA was out to ditch the elections, began to manoeuvre towards something approaching Realpolitik.

The socialist leader's break with the communists was a crucial factor in re-establishing the political balance of power, perhaps even more important than the August revolt of the 'nine' officers against Gonçalvist domination of the MFA. For if the Antunes group was later successful in disorganizing Cunhal's general staff, it was only because they were backed by massive street support directed largely by the socialists. Soares provided moderation with an organized vanguard to lead the counterattack against totalitarian influence in the government and with slogans to break through the walls of rhetoric thrown up by the revolutionaries. Despite left-wing attempts to write him off as a false socialist, Soares provided a rallying point for those who thought things had gone too far — an overwhelming majority of the Portuguese people.

By the end of February, political good sense was slowly beginning to react to excesses of political behaviour, and moderation was clawing its way back into positions of influence. Moderate officers in the MFA Assembly who had staved off the more excessive demands put forward by the fifth division were disturbed by growing military indiscipline. Around Lisbon in particular, units seemed to have dropped all pretence to military efficiency and instead appeared bent on transforming the armed forces into a pale pink version of the Oxford Union. Time once spent in training and regimental duties was now consecrated to endless meetings and discussions which left officers short of authority. Consequently, most commanders were content, even keen, to get their soldiers out of the barracks, and handed out passes as liberally as if they were political tracts. And they might well

11 March   155

have been, for the effect was not dissimilar: soldiers gravitated towards
downtown Lisbon where, lounging on street corners and in cafés, they
fell easy prey to political agitators who no longer had to talk their way
past sentries at barracks gates.

Officers reading MFA communiqués or press statements concerning
discipline could only have concluded that common sense had deserted
many of their superiors, or that they had something more sinister in
mind. Since Spínola's departure, suggestions that traditional discipline
based on hierarchical authority was outmoded had been accepted as
official dogma. Army chief of staff General Fabião called for a new
'revolutionary discipline' which would reform traditional notions of
military hierarchy. He declared in October 1974:

> The old methods of the man who held all the power and could act
> as he pleased are finished. For the individual has been substituted
> for the group where the leader must impose himself not by the
> authority invested in him but through a lucid explanation which
> interprets and traces the line of conduct in the circumstances of the
> moment, in a way that it becomes clear to all his subordinates. The
> man alone, self-sufficient and omnipotent, will become a thing of
> the past, an extinct dinosaur. The Portuguese army must, like all
> other Portuguese institutions, be fundamentally democratized. This
> does not seem to me to run counter to the principles of order and
> discipline which must be at the base of every democracy. As to the
> form which this democratization of the army must take, I do not
> have well-defined ideas.[1]

A change of régime not infrequently causes progressive officers to
ruminate on the nature of military discipline. The French Revolution
pushed a small group of Prussian officers led by Stein, Scharnhorst and
Yorck to suggest that liberal use of the cat was perhaps not the way to
wring the best performance out of fighting men. The idea that soldiers
should be treated as human beings, as citizens with rights rather than
common criminals, which most of them were, slowly caught on in the
nineteenth century, putting men like Frederick the Great and Captain
Bligh out of vogue. Napoleon cultivated an image in line with the new
discipline: the emperor who rose through the ranks, 'le petit caporal'
who tweaked the ears of his troops and shared their potatoes, at a time
when the price of potatoes put them within the reach of the poorest
paid conscript. The French put their considerable battlefield success
down to a discipline based on patriotism and personal pride, on a freely

156 *11 March*

accepted authority, in stark contrast to the draconian discipline of their opponents. It was the military difference between the French and the British, between Napoleon, or rather his PR image, and Cardigan, the martinet of the Crimea, between Clark Gable and Charles Laughton.

Republican régimes especially have sought to introduce new disciplinary modes into their armies contending, quite rightly, that relations between officers and their men must be based on trust rather than force. The education and political conscience of republican soldiers, they argued, dispensed with the need for a tyrannical sergeant-major or boatswain to drive soldiers into attack or sailors up the yardarm. If orders were clearly explained and every man recognized the logic behind the command, then compulsion would recede into the past. Calls for disciplinary reform, however, are seldom motivated by an exclusive concern for military efficiency. Latin republican régimes especially, ever fearful of the reactionary potential of their generals, have often changed disciplinary regulations to keep the army off balance. French officers serving in the aftermath of the Dreyfus affair often discovered that radical republican attempts to restructure hierarchical relationships were in fact designed to lessen the authority of officers over their men in case anyone entertained ideas of marching on the Elysée. Military efficiency was the first victim of disciplinary reform. Calls for discipline based on mutual understanding were conditioned by electoral prudence and often boiled down to simple blackmail against officers, a means of obtaining leave for the mayor's son in the middle of autumn manoeuvres. At its worst, calls for a new discipline undermined the traditional authority of the hierarchy to the point where regiments lived in a permanent state of indiscipline verging on open mutiny.

Strict application of eighteenth-century discipline has never been a distinctive feature of the Portuguese army, even in the eighteenth century. Officers tended to suspect – rightly – that left-wing calls for a disciplinary facelift in the army were motivated more by fear of a right-wing *coup* than by sound theory. 'I am a soldier first and foremost', said air force Major Canto e Castro. 'I attended the Military Academy, I was in the African wars, I am a fighter pilot. I have only experienced a democratic discipline, never an iron discipline.'[2] Despite the good intentions of some, criticism of the authoritarian nature of military discipline was merely the latest card played in the left-wing bid to take over the country, a game in which control of the army was vital. Demands for a politically based discipline were aimed to ensure that soldiers would follow only those officers whose loyalty to the

11 March

revolution was beyond question. 'We must stress the grave risk run by all soldiers who believe revolutionary slogans such as "soldiers are apolitical"', the MFA *Boletim* announced. 'In this way they are trying to ignore the fact that the 25th of April was above all a political action, pretending to confuse politics with political parties. We must not forget that soldiers cannot be apolitical, because they have their programme, that of the MFA, whose defence makes all acts legitimate.'[3] Fabião's call for a new 'revolutionary discipline' was designed to guarantee that the Portuguese army could never again support reaction: 'Soldiers must take an interest in politics', he said. 'It is because they did not that we had fifty years of fascism.'[4]

Led by the fifth division, MFA leaders decreed that every Portuguese soldier be given a revolutionary vocation through programmes of 'internal dynamization' in every unit. The *Boletim* announced on 11 February 1975:

> The armed forces must depend upon their own resources; that is, introduce an internal dynamization whose primary purpose is political education in military units. This is crucial to unify the armed forces and make soldiers realize that they must aid the people at a more advanced level. The ideological and political line of the MFA, clearly laid out in its programme, must be explained to officers, sergeants and soldiers in the armed forces so as to give them a better idea of their mission. This will permit the mobilization of every man and will serve to avoid the divisions so desired and exploited by our enemies who try everything, through the influence of the political parties, to break MFA unity and its alliance with the people.

In February Fabião set out to apply these ideas in the army, creating 'internal information and public relations teams' in every unit in Portugal, Madeira and the Azores. To circumvent the conservative influence of professional officers, he decreed that sergeants and soldiers would sit on these dynamizing committees which he attached to the staff of each unit commander. Selected for their 'loyalty' to the MFA programme, which meant essentially the activist interpretation which the fifth division among others placed on it, the committees were to sit at least once a week to discuss political developments and decide the interpretation to be presented to the regiment. The committees formed the nucleus of the unit assemblies which were later made mandatory.

158   *11 March*

Internal dynamization was stepped up after 11 March. 'The internal dynamization of the units must be intensified', a COPCON order read, 'debating and analyzing the problems without restrictions, consolidating the cohesion [of units] to achieve a universally accepted discipline, the product of enlightenment, for only this will permit every soldier to carry out his patriotic mission of the determined defence of the interests of the Portuguese people.'[5]

The air force, accused of lacking enthusiasm in applying the new discipline, seized the initiative in creating a dynamization cabinet in the chief of staff's headquarters to coordinate the activities of unit committees. The idea was too good for Fabião to pass up, and he soon copied at army staff. The new Revolutionary Council lost little time in defining the principles which the cabinets were expected to hand down to their troops. Its instructions read:

Specify the socialist character of the Portuguese revolution. The Portuguese road to socialism implies a multiparty system which leads to socialism; a policy of national independence cooperating with all peoples of the world, especially with Portuguese speakers; the rejection of all dictatorship, especially of military dictatorship; the development of a cultural revolution as the base of a Povo-MFA alliance, an alliance free of all paternalism; the acceptance of the MFA as the motor of the revolutionary process until the day the process is irreversible.[6]

The decree creating the army dynamization cabinet underlined the importance of the politicization of the forces as a first step to achieve a socialist Portugal: 'Confronted with the socialist society we want to create, especially at this precise moment of the (revolutionary) process, reorganization of the army is clearly necessary,' the decree read.

This reorganization, beginning in its ideological base (political, judicial, cultural and moral) and extending to its infrastructures (organizations, institutions, etc.), must be the work of teams created for the job. . .The army dynamization cabinet (GDE) working at the army general staff, can draw together important elements to decide information and themes for unit debates. The suggestions will not be mandatory, but can serve as a means of testing reaction to reforms and subjects for studies which will be positively developed later. In this way, soldiers will not live in permanent expectation — they will know henceforth which line to follow — and baseless rumours will

11 March   159

consequently cease. Simultaneously, military units will adapt and orient themselves according to the agreed principles. The cadres will not feel marginalized, for their participation will be solicited as much as they like.

To politicize the armed forces without attaching them to a (political) party is a difficult task which must be undertaken. It is indispensable to give them a political education because of the role which is theirs.

Politicization and cultural education are intimately bound together.

The education must begin with the military schools, which must adapt themselves to the newly established models.

The team now created can dynamize these problems, but to do this it must be kept permanently informed of the development of the political process and must, liaising with the central dynamizàtion committee (CODICE, follow the evolution of Portuguese culture, which now has new creative horizons. Extensive contact with intellectual milieus will be a valuable source of information. The progressive political parties will also have an important role in this respect; they can and must help the armed forces to find the correct path. When the phase relating to elections is concluded, and if they do not engage in a syndicalist (or anarcho-syndicalist) struggle, it would be useful to hope for political stability (aided perhaps by the elimination of counter-revolutionary parties) which will permit a more creative, formative and educative ambiance.

The decree ended with a call for the army to extend its political dynamization to the entire country.[7]

Despite the vague and verbose idealism which characterized the decree, the creation of dynamization cabinets in the three services capped by a central dynamizing committee (CODICE) served as a brake on the fifth division's bid for ideological hegemony in the armed forces. The dynamization cabinets became the weapons with which the three service chiefs worked to undermine the influence of the communist-dominated fifth division, which until now had held a monopoly of information in the units. The cabinets split the political line handed down from the top; and if in the short run this contributed to the disorder fast gaining a grip in the forces, it at least prevented the fifth division dominating information and political directives. When the moderate counter-offensive began in late summer 1975, the dynamization cabinets became a source of criticism of unit

160   11 March

dynamization.

Not surprisingly, Lisbon and COPCON became the experimental laboratory for the new discipline and the first light artillery regiment, RALIS, its show window. Like many units permanently residing in the overheated political atmosphere of the capital, RALIS suffered from growing disorder after 28 September, so much so that its commander resigned in the early spring rather than bow to soldiers' demands for equal mess facilities with officers and a say in all command decisions. Carvalho promptly named Colonel Leal de Almeida to fill the post and radical Major Dinís de Almeida as the second-in-command. Active since the early days of the MFA, Dinís de Almeida stood to the left of virtually every politician and soldier in Portugal: the Marxist-Leninist UDP to which he and many of his soldiers belonged claimed as its slogan 'no one to our left'. His enthusiastic support of the new discipline and outspoken criticism of Portugal's continued presence in NATO made him the model of a 'political' soldier and an officer ideally suited to lead a unit in which eccentric political views were cultivated as a point of pride.

Under Almeida's influence, RALIS soldiers became the spearhead of the revolution, throwing themselves with enthusiasm into the battle against reactionaries, whom the UDP saw everywhere. Active in committees and in the forefront of demonstrations, they specialized in disrupting meetings of rival political groups, in particular of the Maoist MRPP.[8] RALIS became the focal point of the events of 11 March, and the bombing and strafing of its barracks along the highway to Lisbon airport seemed only to stoke its revolutionary enthusiasm. In the autumn of 1975, RALIS again succeeded in shocking even progressive officers when new recruits executed a carefully choreographed clenched-fist salute at the traditional swearing-in ceremony.

Left-wing claims that RALIS had solved the teething problems of political discipline and provided a model which should be imitated by all Portuguese regiments were frankly disbelieved by officers. 'People pointed to RALIS as a unit with revolutionary discipline and said that all units should become like that', one officer noted. 'They claimed that RALIS was disciplined, but they never let anyone look inside.'[9] Most pointed out the obvious danger of injecting politics into the life blood of a regiment: revolutionary discipline would work only if soldiers and the hierarchy were in perfect political agreement and this was extremely unlikely, given the unsettled state of Portuguese politics. An air force captain noted:

11 March

161

> If an officer expresses a political opinion inside his unit, he will command only those men who share his views. We have fourteen political parties in Portugal, so any stand in favour of one or another of them will assure him the obedience only of those who support that party. I told my soldiers: go to demonstrations, go to political meetings outside, read what newspapers you wish – but outside the base. This policy was not always successful, but I had no great problems.[10]

The drawbacks of revolutionary discipline were forcefully underlined when Major Tomé of the Lisbon military police supported the refusal of his men to embark for Angola to aid in the evacuation of refugees. 'Discipline will be re-established when the order of the hierarchy will place the soldiers on the side of the workers', he said. 'Indiscipline comes from the desire to assign soldiers a repressive role. Revolutionary discipline is established when soldiers are allied with the workers. Revolutionary officers are those who know how to bring about this alliance. The soldiers in my regiment were right when they refused to leave for Angola. That is not indiscipline, but a correct political response. . .and I am on their side.'[11]

For second-rate officers, calls for internal dynamization of units opened up a whole new career perspective. Men whose professional competence and capacity for hard work were suspect found a day spent organizing committees, exploiting regimental issues and denouncing 'fascist' colleagues infinitely preferable to the tedium of mastering the mechanics of their profession. Activists lived in hope of recognition in the new political imperium of the Portuguese army, a hope denied them in an army where promotion was based largely on seniority and professional competence.

All officers agreed that the most politicized officers after 25 April were usually among the worst in the armed forces. A colonel noted:

> Of one hundred officers in my command, about five wanted to organize meetings. These men were good for nothing. Before the *coup,* you would not have known that they were at all interested in politics. They simply wanted to take advantage of the situation to advance their careers. Discipline became less strict because the parties were disputing power. There was no legitimate government. The soldiers thought they were on holiday; they thought that they were there just to eat well – *finie la vie militaire!* The officers exploited this situation. They were very keen on marketing:

162 *11 March*

superficial politics, easy slogans, *la parole facile, la phrase clé.*[12]

A naval lieutenant concurred: 'Without a doubt, the most politicized were the worst ones. No one thought very highly of their professional competence.'[13] Rather than wed discipline to politics, the revolutionary discipline preached by these men simply dissolved many regiments into chaos. 'What is indiscipline?' an army major asked.'A few left-wing officers and sergeants led soldiers astray. I sometimes wonder if left-wing sergeants are not paid to disrupt the regiments.'[14]

Many political observers to the right of the communists believed that revolutionary discipline was an idea which could have been hatched only in the brain of a Stalinist: 'Revolutionary discipline was simply a communist party doctrine to disrupt the regiments', one socialist party official contended.

> Antunes, Alves, and Crespo went along with it because they believe that the MFA should assure a socialist régime, not a democratic one. Fabião is weak. He was a conservative officer close to Spínola. He simply got carried away. Carvalho is a romantic, naïve. Both he and Fabião were manipulated by the communists. If they had been successful, both officers would have been disposed of.[15]

Aware of Fabião's high professional reputation before 25 April, officers were equally puzzled by his apparent about-face. 'Fabião called me back from Mozambique to serve on his staff', a major who had served with him in Guinea remembered. 'In Guinea, he had been an excellent officer in every way. I was surprised at the change in his attitudes. I don't know why they changed. Perhaps it was simply the atmosphere at the time. After a month, it was apparent that we no longer saw eye to eye, so he invited me to go to Angola.'[16]

MFA leaders soon began to realize that politics, once introduced into the barracks, spread like the plague. This was especially true in Lisbon, where the Maoist Movement for the Reconstruction of the Party of the Proletariat (MRPP), made up primarily of university students, was busy telling every soldier in sight that the MFA was a 'bourgeois trick' and that COPCON was the 'new PIDE'. Growing indiscipline at first elicited only homilies from senior officers: 'We are in the process of transforming autocratic discipline into democratic discipline', President Costa Gomes murmured. 'This raises several problems in adapting all levels of the military hierarchy to the new command philosophy.'[17] Major Canto e Castro disagreed: 'People speak of revolutionary discipline', he said, 'I don't know what it is. If we were

11 March   163

a very rich country and could allow ourselves the luxury of a period of anarchy, I would say: This is a transitional phase of the revolution. But we are coming pretty close to chaos.'[18]

The spectacle of senior officers encouraging novel forms of discipline was like a cold shower to unit commanders who now realized that they could look to no one for help in keeping order among their troops. 'We knew that we would get little support from above', an army captain complained. 'Costa Gomes made things worse by his indecision. He said that he would punish the military police [after their refusal to leave for Angola], but he did nothing. I do not understand him.'[19]

Belatedly, left-wing officers began to realize that their appeals for political zeal had seriously undermined their operational potential by throwing open the doors to career opportunism and extremist groups. COPCON was hanging together by a thread and demands by soldiers for full participation in every command decision had made even simple orders difficult, if not impossible, to execute. Fabião woke briefly from his revolutionary somnambulance to tell soldiers that the new discipline 'cannot be equated with anarchy' and called on recruits to 'offer guarantees of a disciplined conscience and a spirit of abnegation'.[20] General Pires Veloso, a left-leaning officer later to lead the northern military region, also tried to define the limits of politics in the forces: 'We must give soldiers in training a truly progressive political education but not a political party education. Politics must not be permitted within the units. Army training must give soldiers this education to help them to rationalize consciously and know how to choose. But no one can practise his political choice within the barracks.'[21] The fifth division joined the chorus with a call for the soldiers to cease behaving like a mob, and even radicals like Carvalho and Dinís de Almeida reprimanded soldiers who equated the new discipline with the sound of breaking glass.[22]

By the end of February, the left looked to be losing its grip both in the country and in the army. The left-wing monopoly of great sections of the press and of the political slogans seemed to have paid few dividends. The political parties moved inexorably towards the 12 April election despite the best efforts of fringe groups to disrupt meetings of 'counter-revolutionary' parties such as the PPD and CDS. Political violence had become so commonplace that rallies often resembled a Celtic-Rangers football match, attended only by the courageous and the well-armed. Left-wing attempts to disrupt a PPD meeting in Setubal on 7 March had left two dead and seventeen wounded when police

164　*11 March*

opened fire on the agitators.

The PPD minister without portfolio, Magalhães Mota, seized the incident to launch a stinging attack on the MFA, which he blamed for permitting the new climate of violence. His attack found an echo in the army. In the first week of March, all career army and air force officers firmly rejected the MFA left in a vote for the army councils which sent delegates to the MFA Assembly. In the artillery, Carvalho, Antunes, Vasco Lourenço and Colonel Franco Charais lost their places to officers known for their close ties with General Spínola, among them Major Suárez Monje and brigadiers Orlando Costa, commander of the Coimbra military region, and Damião.Similar if less spectacular results were recorded in other arms. Rumours of *coups,* always rattling around Lisbon, seemed to take on a special significance as the feeling grew that the days of the communists and their MFA allies were numbered. It was whispered that General Spínola judged the atmosphere ripe for a comeback and the left needed a great stroke of luck to remain in power.

That luck came in the second week of March. The background to the events of 11 March may never be known; the version of the investigating committee, chaired by Rosa Coutinho, cannot be read as an objective account of events. In all probability officers close to Spínola had been plotting for some time and took their conspiracy off the back burner amid persistent rumours that the left-wing League of Revolutionary Union and Action (LUAR) planned an 'Easter massacre' of up to 500 officers and 1,000 civilians. Rumour had become the small change of Portuguese politics, but when this one hit the streets, a number of officers took the precaution of changing addresses or sleeping with a pistol under the pillow. Others probably decided to preempt the alleged communist Saint-Bartholomew with their own show.

Spínola later claimed from his Brazilian exile that he was only told of the *coup* after it had actually begun. The extreme amateurishness of the *coup* attempt lends credence to these claims, for the General's professional experience would almost certainly have caused him to shy away from such an ill-conceived venture. Under the command of businessman Miguel Champalimaud and Lieutenant Nuno Barbieri, the conspirators apparently felt that discontent over the political situation was so widespread in the armed forces that a simple gesture would provide the spark to ignite a spontaneous military revolt against the MFA. Air force Colonel Rafael Durão, Spínola's personal friend, offered his military base at Tancos across the Tagus from Lisbon as headquarters and his disciplined paratroops as muscle. Attempts to contact other

11 March   165

officers by telephone on the night of 10 March swung Major Monje and
General Damião behind the *coup* and no doubt tipped off Carvalho that
something subversive was in the air.

The *coup* organizers basically confined their action to a combined
ground-air attack on the RALIS barracks, from where the 'Easter
massacre' was expected to be launched. This was to be supported by
the seizure of several radio stations and an uprising at the Carmo
barracks of the Republican National Guard. Just before midday, RALIS
came under 'fire' from two antiquated Harvard T-6 trainers and three
helicopter gunships. One soldier died when what some claimed to be a
rocket and others a non-explosive training bomb pierced the roof of the
mess hall. Firepower was used sparingly, however: the 500 rounds and
99 anti-personnel rockets allegedly fired into the compound did damage
only measured in centimetres. 'With all the firepower available to them,
they could have flattened a unit if they had wanted to', an air force
captain claimed. 'The paratroops would only have needed to take the
wounded to the hospital.'[23]

Paratroops under the command of Captain Sebastião Martins then
surrounded RALIS, but by this time the aerial display had attracted a
large left-wing crowd and a few television newsmen. The Portuguese
proclivity to exchange words rather than shots again prevailed, and the
only violence was verbal. The attackers were finally dissuaded from
further symbolic action after Dinís de Almeida elbowed his way
through the crowd and in front of television cameras demanded an
explanation from Captain Martins, who could only stammer that he
was acting under orders. This explanation was obviously found wanting
by Almeida, who for several weeks had pioneered other disciplinary
ideas in his regiment. When Martins protested that 'there are important
individuals who are not satisfied with the way things are going', he was
told by the crowd: 'the people are not with you'. After declaring 'We
are not fascists. We were tricked. It is a scandal', Martins waited quietly
until the military police arrived to take him away; several of his men
threw down their arms and walked into the RALIS barracks to beg
forgiveness.

Elsewhere, the *coup* met with even less success. General Damião
secured the GNR revolt at Carmo, but appeared unsure of what to do
next. Alerted by general staff headquarters, COPCON forces
successfully kept rebels out of the radio stations and at 13.00 an army
broadcast called on all Portuguese to remain loyal to the MFA. At
Tancos, Spínola was putting through phone calls to a number of
commanders known to have doubts about the MFA leadership. But

166   *11 March*

Commando Major Costa Neves, Major Casanova Ferreira, head of the Lisbon riot police, and Captain Salgueiro Maia remained evasive. Although out of sympathy with the leftward tilt of the revolution, only a minority of officers were willing to risk failure and exile in an obviously ill-planned venture. Rebel officers had yet to learn the lesson of 25 April that meticulous planning was vital to the success of any military revolt.[24]

By three o'clock, Prime Minister Gonçalves announced that the plot was crushed. NCOs and soldiers at Tancos rose against the base command and Spínola, his wife and eighteen officers fled by helicopter to Spain and thence in Caetano's tracks to Brazil, probably eliciting at least a quiet laugh from the former prime minister.

March 11 ruined Spínola's already damaged reputation even among his most devoted admirers, who now relegated him from the de Gaulle to the Delgado league. The 11 March fiasco appeared a risible lunch-hour action: tank units were missing, too much was left to chance, and chance proved insufficient to overcome the natural reluctance of officers to fire on colleagues, even on those with whom one is barely on speaking terms. Many were obviously aware that civil war was a distinct possibility, and so were reluctant to fire the shot which might touch it off. The *coup* was so badly executed that many suggested that it could only have been a put-up job by the left, designed to consolidate their grip on the government. 'If it was a real *coup*, it was very naïve', an army colonel noted. 'There was absolutely no planning, no coordination. My corporals could have planned an operation better than that.'[25] Others found it very curious that Spínola had been let out of the bag at Tancos.[26]

The view that the 'Easter massacre' rumours had been deliberately planted to force the hand of officers unsympathetic to the left was further encouraged by the speed with which the MFA left, its influence on the decline only twenty-four hours earlier, moved to clean out the moderate opposition. 'The end of the story is clear', Mário Soares said. 'Like on 28 September, even more so, the "fascist menace" was exaggerated to throw out several troublesome opponents. Under the orders of the PCP, the fifth division mobilized its arsenal of conspirators and the pro-communist military faction installed itself solidly at the head of the MFA. . .'[27]

In an all-night emergency session of the MFA Assembly hurriedly called on 11 March, the left won back the ground lost in the previous weeks, and more. The recent elections to the arms councils favouring the moderates were made void. The Assembly cut the Gordian knot and

11 March   167

voted the immediate 'institutionalization' of the MFA. The Council of Twenty was replaced by a powerful Revolutionary Council, 'supreme organ of national sovereignty', responsible only to the MFA Assembly and made up of seven members of the junta, seven members of the Coordinating Committee, some of the military ministers and eight officers nominated by the MFA Assembly. Without even a cosmetic civilian presence, the Revolutionary Council stamped Portugal with an essentially military régime.

In a further — ultimately abortive — attempt to radicalize the leadership, the Council left in the cold Crespo, Antunes and Alves, once the *enfants terribles* of the MFA but lately suspected of a less than firm commitment to pluri-party democracy among many top MFA officers. Relations between Crespo and many of his navy colleagues in the fifth division had turned decidedly chilly, Antunes' provision for a capitalist sector in his economic plan had been denounced as a betrayal of the MFA's socialist principles, and Alves was accused of having 'grown apart' from the movement. Alves countered that the fault lay with the Prime Minister: 'After the victory of 28 September. . .General Vasco Gonçalves took a different attitude', he told *Expresso* on 20 September 1975. 'From November [1974], it became more pronounced.' When he returned from an autumn European tour and Antunes from Algeria, the pair found a 'barrier between us and Gonçalves, put up by his cabinet', Alves charged.

Crespo flew back from Mozambique where he was serving as high commissioner to confront Rosa Coutinho, who blandly told him that he would join the Council when he returned. Crespo insisted that as members of the Coordinating Committee, the three had a right to sit with the new Council. The left was forced to give in and on 27 March published a new list which included the three 'forgotten' members.[28]

Crespo's initiative was critical in preventing total domination of the MFA structures by 'Gonçalvist' officers. The Prime Minister obviously believed that his 11 March victory had so disorganized the opposition that he could cast adrift even progressive officers whose collaboration had become a hindrance. Crespo's decision to stand up to Gonçalves and Coutinho was the first setback to Gonçalves' plans to dominate the government and an important precedent for the group which revolted against the Prime Minister in August.[29]

The MFA left seized on the events of 11 March as a pretext to postpone the forthcoming elections indefinitely. Assembly delegates were told that the reactionary menace made it unwise to permit

168 *11 March*

elections until peasants and workers had recognized the advantages of socialism. To vote now would be to risk the revolutionary gains of the last months. Career officers refused to be persuaded, but the left retaliated by pushing through a motion opening the Assembly to milicianos, NCOs and soldiers in the hope of circumventing the conservative influence of the regular officer corps.

The reorganized 240 man Assembly was an attempt to turn the flank of the military hierarchy and stamp a revolutionary dynamic on the forces. Its 120 army delegates were drawn from the members of the Revolutionary Council, the four army regional commanders, MFA regimental and military schools delegates, members of the national committee of sergeants, and two officers, three sergeants and three soldiers elected in each of the military regions.[30] The navy and air forces were each allowed sixty delegates also elected and coopted in a similar fashion so as to guarantee a strong left-wing bias in the new Assembly.

The Assembly capped a legislative structure which reached down to the unit level and aimed to 'make every soldier an MFA militant'. An Army Assembly drawn from the army's 120 general assembly delegates, all generals and unit commanders, representatives of the Republican National Guard and the police and sixty soldiers elected from the units stood over affairs in that service. Assemblies were also created for each military region, and each unit was ordered to form a legislative branch in which the number of soldier representatives equalled the combined number of officers and sergeants. The dynamizing groups in the units set the tone of the political debate. A Naval Assembly grouped officer and petty officer representatives as well as sailors selected from dynamizing committees. The Air Force Assembly was chosen by the air force representatives on the Revolutionary Council from lists presented by airmen.[31]

From the beginning, the new structures drew heavy criticism from officers who claimed that the Assembly not only challenged the authority of the chain of command but also resembled no known form of democracy. Many delegates supposedly 'elected' were merely designated by the fifth division, largely from left-leaning units stationed in Lisbon or its surrounding red belt. More moderate regiments in the north and central region were under-represented. Army officers also thought it unfair that the more radical navy which made up one tenth of armed forces personnel should command one quarter of Assembly seats.[32] Discontent came to a head in late July when a large number of officers simply refused to recognize the

11 March   169

Assembly's validity.[33]

Many politicians shared the officers' lack of enthusiasm for MFA 'institutionalization'. Soares wrote:

> The institutionalization of the MFA after 11 March was an important step in this direction [eliminate the influence of political parties], at least, if one considered the way in which the 'theoreticians' of the fifth division intended using it. They managed to impose as a sovereign organ with exorbitant power, an assembly of 240 soldiers of all ranks of which no one knew the exact composition. No one had elected them: hurriedly designated by a handful of men carefully placed in key posts, they became overnight the immovable parliament of the MFA and later — why not? — of the entire country. . .It is this assembly, without representation, which simply decreed the first great wave of nationalizations and instituted the Revolutionary Council.[34]

The days following the abortive *coup* were marked by an increasing number of arrests and detentions of 'reactionaries' both in and out of uniform. COPCON troops spread over Lisbon to net suspected Spínolist officers and businessmen for questioning, often aided by keen vigilantes. In the first week, more than 100 people were dragged in, signalling the beginning of a wave of arrests which continued into the summer, filling Portuguese jails to capacity. Left wingers, ready in the old days to protest Salazar's detention of political prisoners at the drop of a hat, clearly were not opposed to political arrests in principle, shattering by a wide margin the records set by the Dictator. Carvalho claimed in a 27 April press conference that 1,331 political prisoners, mostly ex-PIDE agents, were held in Portuguese jails, but many journalists placed the number closer to 3,000.[35] The enthusiasm with which COPCON troops jailed suspected counter-revolutionaries earned their commander a court martial in the summer of 1976 for unjustified detention.

These numerous arbitrary arrests, designed to disarm and disorganize the moderate opposition, proved one of the left's greatest miscalculations. So long as detentions seemed to follow some logical pattern, so long as a case, however spurious, could be made against those detained, then many could hope that by remaining discreet they could avoid political retributions. However, once open season was declared on 'reactionaries' many officers began to realize that silence no longer guaranteed immunity from events in the capital. Self-

170 *11 March*

preservation, once the reward of those who kept quiet, now became the province of officers prepared to defend themselves.

Reaction in the country was similar. Many of the middle classes who had held aloof from the events of the past months were confronted with the bitter reality of the midnight knock at the door. Bands of COPCON troops led by officers whose new power had gone straight to their heads initiated many Lisbon families into the ways of authoritarian government. Raids on wrong addresses were not uncommon, and revolutionary soldiers often consoled themselves by cleaning out larders and bars, helping themselves to money and trinkets which caught their fancy. 'I saw officers who just loved to go to people's houses and arrest them', an army major commented. 'Young officers especially enjoyed it. They would be given an address and told: "this man was in the PIDE". Usually it was someone with no political interests at all. But it gave them a great sense of power. And I am not just talking of lower-class officers. Many were from good families.'[36]

'People simply disappeared', one Frenchman attached to the Portuguese forces said of this period.

> One day I met at a rugby match an officer whom I had not seen in some time. He had lost a foot in Mozambique stepping on a mine and had been given an administrative job. He told me that he had been in Caxias (the prison near Lisbon) for two months. They just came by his house one night and took him to prison. He asked for a lawyer, but they refused. He declined to answer any questions until told the charge against him. They told him nothing, kept him two months, and then released him. The tragedy is that when officers see people slapped into jail for no reason, it pushes them further to the right.[37]

Attempts to jail anyone who might aid the opposition were backed up by a drive to emasculate political parties. On 12 March, the Minister for Social Communication, navy Commander Jorge Jesuino, announced the banning of several extremist groups including the Maoist AOC (Worker-Peasant Alliance) and the MRPP. Both parties had proved a thorn in the side of the communists, who feared their growing influence in some trade unions and military units. 'The MRPP openly combats the MFA and has designated the "Social-fascist party" of Alvaro Cunhal as enemy number one', read an MFA report. 'It led a persistent campaign to denounce what it considered "The social-imperialist infiltration" of Portugal. Given its activity at the moment of the

11 March

elections the legalization of the MRPP was annulled.' The AOC had been recognized by the Chinese communists as the *bona fide* Maoists and their leaders invited to Peking.[38]

The parties allowed to remain in the campaign were presented with a 'pact' which they reluctantly signed for fear the MFA would tamper with the plans for Portugal's first free elections in fifty years. Reflecting Rosa Coutinho's guiding hand the 'pact' called for the 'parallel development of the Portuguese political parties and the MFA', but made plain that the MFA was to be the boss. The rules laid down for the next three years demanded a complete separation of civil and military powers; parliament would have no say whatever in military affairs; armed forces organization would be the exclusive province of the chiefs of staffs. The President would not be elected by universal suffrage, but chosen from among candidates vetted by the Revolutionary Council. Soldiers would also keep their hands on key defence and economic ministries, maintain the power of veto over much economic and social legislation and define the general lines of domestic and foreign policy through the Revolutionary Council. In what can be described only as a great leap backwards, the council of ministers was to be responsible to the President, not parliament, and if push came to shove, the President could dissolve any future civilian assembly.[39] 'We have a presidential military régime with political parties', *Expresso* declared on 12 April 1975.

The communists and MDP predictably signed the pact immediately; the socialists and PPD did so with great reluctance. 'We signed it because we understood that it was the condition *sine qua non* for the normal functioning of the elections', Soares maintained. 'Faced with growing economic upheaval, faced with the inevitable collapse of the state, we needed the elections above all, we needed to win. Realizing that politics is the art of the possible, we signed an accord with the MFA which allowed us to preserve the future. . .We did not want the Peruvian experience in Portugal.' He claimed that the 'suppleness' of socialist policy had allowed the political parties to avoid a potentially disastrous confrontation and gradually to negotiate a position of strength.[40]

The new cabinet also reflected the latest events. Named on 26 March, it placed leftists in commanding positions over the economy and the media, while opening the government to the MDP which the socialists, PPD and CDS had condemned as a PCP front organization. Left-wing soldiers under Prime Minister Vasco Gonçalves controlled the important ministries of labour (Costa Martins), education (José

172　*11 March*

da Silva), social communications (Jesuino), defence (Silvano Ribeiro), social infrastructure and environment (Augusto Fernandes) and the interior (António Metelo). The increasingly moderate Melo Antunes had foreign affairs. The MDP were given planning and economic coordination (Mário Murteira), finance (José Fragoso) and industry (João Cravinho), while Francisco Pereira de Moura sat without portfolio. Cunhal also served without portfolio, backed by Veiga de Oliveira with transport and communications. Soares sat without portfolio along with Francisco Zenha in the justice ministry. The PPD was given social affairs and Magalhães Mota sat without portfolio. Independents took agriculture, foreign trade and coordination between overseas territories in a cabinet which did not remotely reflect the election results one month later.

As election day approached, MFA leaders began to express doubts about the role of political parties in Portugal's future. Press conferences by Jesuino and Coutinho castigated the divisive influence of political party squabbles which, they claimed, had fragmented the nation. Jesuino stated categorically that the decision to permit political parties after 25 April 1974 had been a mistake, while Continho reaffirmed the MFA's determination to keep the revolution on its 'socialist course' even if this meant ignoring the election results. Carvalho added that the MFA might just stand on its own in the coming elections.[41]

If the MFA was to survive, its leaders decided that it must make its appeal over the heads of the political parties. Manoeuvres to ward off the coming elections had failed. The only way to squash the influence of the politicians and win over the many voters eyeing the political events in the capital with increasing scepticism was to beat the parties at the electoral game, to throw the power of the armed forces into a campaign to win the hearts and minds of the population, much as they had tried to do in Africa. The dynamization of the armed forces must be extended beyond the barrack walls to rope the nation into the revolutionary process.

'The participation of the army in national reconstruction is the army's most profitable and attractive goal in the next few years,' General Fabião's decree setting up an army dynamization council read.

To carry this out, we can apply the experience gained overseas, with the advantage of working in peacetime, with greater determination and with the cooperation of the people. The operation abolishing our country's oligarchic system is in the

11 March   173

hands of the armed forces, by virtue of its human and material
potential and its implantation in the country. The army engineers,
who already have a primary role in Portugal, must fully assume their
responsibilities by organizing themselves to assure scientifically the
army's contribution to national reconstruction. This represents a
professional opportunity which technicians have always desired.

It is not possible to mobilize the people for any purpose without
assuring them a minimum standard of living. The Povo-MFA
alliance will only be established after the entry of the armed forces
in the daily life of the people to achieve with their aid the concrete
tasks which correspond to their fundamental and immediate
aspirations. It is in this work, side by side, that true integration will
take place. Informal conversation will be the instrument of mutual
learning and of mutual cultural promotion. These lie at the base of
Portugal's cultural revolution.[42]

On the night of 11 March, the MFA Assembly voted to step up the
'cultural dynamization' programme begun some months earlier, and to
give it a definite political orientation. One of my intentions today is
to avoid confining our troops within the four barrack walls until
5 o'clock each afternoon', Carvalho proclaimed. 'On the contrary, I
would like to undertake a psycho-social action like we carried out in
Guinea.'[43]

Cultural dynamization was first suggested in a 17 November Naval
Assembly, when delegates called on the government to organize groups
of volunteers 'to realize an in-depth information campaign among the
least enlightened groups of the population, especially in rural areas'.[44]
The navy-dominated fifth division snapped up the idea and within a
week translated it into a plan for nationwide 'cultural dynamization'
which it sent to the general staff. The primary object of cultural
dynamization was to lift the country's standard of living through
public works projects. The idea of using soldiers in material
improvement schemes had been floated since the French Revolution,
and not infrequently applied with success. In underdeveloped countries
and frontier areas, the army often supplied the know-how and muscle
to build roads, bridges and railways; graduates of the Ecole
Polytechnique and West Point were instrumental in opening up French
Africa and the American West; many Latin American armies employ
their troops profitably in the business of nation building. Advocates
of army involvement in public works argued that society reaped benefits
while soldiers who would otherwise vegetate in unhealthy barracks or

174   11 March

bars were gainfully employed. In more developed countries, however, the idea often met opposition: critics complained that the army offered unfair competition for local contractors and labourers, while many officers objected that it distracted units from their primary role of war preparation.

In Portugal's case, it was undeniable that an intelligent use of the army in public works projects held many potential advantages, especially in rural areas where the benefits of Salazarist government had not stretched to roads, electricity, and water and sewage systems remained medieval. Properly organized and coordinated with the ministries, a system of public works projects would have pumped money into the countryside and brought the economic advantages of improved communication. Had the soldiers stuck to their original goal, the revolution might have produced some constructive results. However, it soon became clear that they expected something more from cultural dynamization.

The fifth division plan stated a second object for cultural dynamization, and this became paramount after 11 March. The MFA would set out 'to act politically by the presence of soldiers among the people, to explain the reasons behind the lamentable state in which the country found itself, to explain the MFA programme and discuss solutions, thereby creating the conditions for the general participation of the people in the national life'. Fabião, who under Spínola had directed the army's good works in Guinea, supported the plan with enthusiasm. He announced in November:

> We are going to rethink the army in terms of civic reconversion as is happening in Belgium. This will permit it to contribute to economic development and give social support to the populations. To a certain extent this will be a continuation of the programme already followed in our African territories, where soldiers built roads, constructed bridges and collaborated with civilians.[45]

Under the direction of MFA radical Ramiro Correia, the fifth division's 150 personnel were organized to lead the left-wing propaganda offensive in the country. A central 'dynamization committee' was set up in its Lisbon headquarters which sent orders to committees in each service, which in turn filtered them down to unit 'dynamization groups'. Regional and local committees in which some civilians were allowed to participate also spread. Political tourists and the curious could wander along to afternoon political discussions

11 March   175

directed by keen miliciano officers in the fifth division headquarters.
An Institute of Military Sociology was created from the old Institute
of Higher Military Studies to prepare volunteers to lead dynamization
teams into the country. A Centre for Enlightenment and Public
Information published the *Boletim* and handed out press communiqués.
Lastly, Correia directed a public relations service which dealt
specifically with social questions.[46]

In October, the central dynamization committee organized a dry
run for their rural invasion in Lisbon schools. Students aged between
ten and thirteen were treated to a curious revolutionary indoctrination,
beginning with a Wagner concert, Hitler's favourite and a composer
always claimed by the Nazis, followed by slides on Chile and a political
discussion between students and officers. The fifth division maintained
that these schoolroom chats prepared soldiers for their encounters with
backward peasants, 'to whom the political parties almost never speak in
a comprehensible language'. This academic exercise was carried out
before Lisbon television cameras which the dynamizers hoped would
demonstrate their good intentions to the world outside.

The age group at which this first dynamization experiment was
aimed set the general tone for the 2,000 dynamization meetings
organized between October 1974 and March 1975. Correia directed
his offensive especially at the staunchly Catholic north and centre
where the conservative PPD and CDS were strong among a population
of poor but proud and independent farmers whom he hoped to save
for socialism. Officers spread out through small northern villages
mouthing the basics of a political education. The *Boletim* declared:

> There are thousands, perhaps millions of Portuguese, the parents
> and grandparents of the two million emigrants who work in Europe
> and America, who cannot read and whose houses are mud walls
> penetrated by the wind, rain, sun and snow. There are men and
> women who often have no electricity, no fountains, no roads. They
> are old and poor but they vegetate without medical help, with no
> cultural reality but their own, sometimes without even a cemetery
> where they can rest after death. For these Portuguese, public
> liberties, the eradication of the PIDE, decolonisation, trade union
> freedom, the right to strike, free elections, the start of anti-
> monopolist measures, all of these are realities which have no part
> in their daily life.[47]

As might be guessed from the above text, the main priority of the

176 11 March

cultural dynamizers was not the improvement of living conditions, which were often appalling, or even a campaign against illiteracy, but rather a political education aimed at breaking down deep-rooted rural hierarchies ruled by the Church. Conscience-raising sessions were organized in villages where peasants were rounded up to be lectured on the meaning of imperialism, socialism and communism, to be explained the drift of Portuguese politics 'to unmask reaction, denounce fascism'. 'We can proclaim communism in villages where the communist party would be stoned', an MFA captain announced.[48] The *Boletim* published lengthy reports on the inadequacies of living conditions in many villages, claiming that reform was sabotaged by 'campaigns of counter-revolutionary propaganda and the ignorance of the populations'.[49] The immediate task was not to reform rural living conditions, but to exploit them to create dissatisfaction in the provinces, if possible to create a revolutionary situation which would catapult the MFA into power in the strongholds of reaction.

To realize this plan, the MFA left looked to discredit the political parties as the elections approached. The committee investigating the events of 11 March under the direction of Rosa Coutinho did its best to implicate the socialists, whom opinion polls tipped as the strongest party. *Avante,* the communist party weekly, printed a telegram from the Spanish secret police linking Soares and Spínola which Soares claimed was forged. The committee members put this to Soares citing as evidence an article in the French satirical weekly, *Canard enchaîné,* but backed down when the socialist leader noted that the same article accused Prime Minister Vasco Gonçalves of being a member of the communist party. Next the committee confronted him with the fact that on 11 March he had received a phone call from police Major Casanova Ferreira, whose rejection of Spínola's invitation to join the *coup* had not spared him a prison sentence. Soares pointed out calmly that it was still illegal in Portugal to tap telephones. Lastly, the committee lamely asked why he had on 11 March placed two guards on his door instead of one.[50] The failure of the investigation did not prevent the release on the eve of the elections of preliminary reports on the 'silent majority' rally on 28 September and the 11 March *coup* (both of which pointed accusing fingers at the socialists and PPD). An electoral law forbidding campaigning on the last 'day of reflection', stopped any rebuttal from the two parties.

As the elections approached, MFA leaders desperately searched for a way to sabotage the vote. Carvalho claimed that dynamization teams reported that the parties 'were not doing their job properly' in the

11 March 177

provinces, implying that they were depending on the ignorance and inertia of the populace to carry the day. To gain time, the elections were put off until 25 April for 'technical reasons', the Revolutionary Council citing the need for the many left-wing parties to find a more imaginative symbol than the hammer and sickle with which to confuse voters.

The MFA decided to play the African card to the hilt, extending the overseas parallel to torpedo the political process. Using the same argument that FRELIMO leader Samora Machel hurled at Spínola, they claimed that elections were meaningless in a population uneducated to vote for their own interests. Portugal stood very near the bottom of Europe's economic table, and judged by every indicator – national GNP, average annual wage, literacy rate, etc. – had much more in common with developing nations than with her wealthy neighbours to the north. The idea that Portugal had an extra-European orientation was not a new one, having already fuelled centuries of Portuguese expansion overseas. In periods of national isolation or decline, it usually enjoyed a revival, anti-Europeanism translating a refusal to recognize the realities of Portugal's international position and the reaffirmation of an inward-looking Lusitanian culture. The proposal that Portugal cast its lot with the Third World stood at the base of Spínola's *Portugal and the Future*, and ironically provided the link between Salazarist minister Franco Nogueira's 'African' conceptions of Portugal's world role which the Dictator successfully integrated into the ideology of the New State and her Third World vocation which the left took from storage after 11 March. 'How can you make these Portuguese participate in their own destiny, if they themselves shut out the political parties and sometimes stone them', the *Boletim* declared on 11 March. 'In Europe's 89,000 square kilometres there is underdevelopment, a piece of the Third World, the remains of feudalism.' That 'piece of the third world' was Portugal. Antunes, foreign minister in the fourth provisional government, also called for Portugal's 'opening to the countries of the Third World and those of Lusitanian orientation' as part of a policy of 'national independence'.[51]

The MFA decided to assume the only role it believed progressive political forces could play in an underdeveloped country – that of a national liberation movement which would unite all strains of progressive political opinions and so eliminate divisive party quarrels. Carvalho told the MFA Assembly on 19 May that only by becoming a Portuguese liberation movement in the FRELIMO model could the MFA see the Povo-MFA alliance through to a successful conclusion.

178   *11 March*

He said:

> It is evident that the Portuguese revolution has been jeopardized by
> divisions caused by the political parties. The only way to end their
> quarrels is for the MFA to assume the role of a supra-party political
> force, like a liberation movement, banishing the influence of the
> party leaders and taking away their support so that they adhere to a
> determined ideological line. If all the [support] bases are stolen
> from the political leaders and they adhere to the MFA as the nation's
> political force, so transforming the MFA into a liberation movement,
> I am convinced that the country will be given an enormous push
> forward on the revolutionary road to socialism.[52]

The absorption of the political parties into the new 'liberation
movement' posed the problem of what to do with all of those out-of-
work politicians. By the end of the summer, Carvalho would suggest,
some thought only half seriously, that they be executed, but for the
moment he sought a more diplomatic formula: 'If the MFA is really a
true liberation movement and we have a link between the people and
the MFA, the politicians can serve as political technicians in the conduct
conduct of the country's politics', he said. 'We can follow this path: the
MFA is a liberation movement, the political motor of the Portuguese
revolutionary process tightly bound to its support, to the masses, the
Portuguese people with whom they will drive the revolutionary
movement, containing as politically enlightened elements, political
technicians, the nation's great political leaders. We will then have
practically a quasi-dissolution of the political parties.'[53] Article 1 of the
'Povo-MFA' programme adopted by the Revolutionary Council on 21
June and approved by the MFA Assembly gave this idea official sanction:
'The MFA is the liberation movement of the Portuguese people.'[54]

Not surprisingly, the politicians frowned on a scheme designed to
put them out of business. Mário Soares gave MFA leaders full marks for
imagination, but thought less of the practicality of their politics. He
remembered:

> In June 1976, the MFA proclaimed itself a 'national liberation
> movement' of the Portuguese people. Psychoanalysis would probably
> be more useful than politics in explaining such a pretension:
> battered and bruised after 14 years of war, these soldiers could find
> nothing better to purify themselves and win through than to identify
> with their victors. A curious transference which raised more than one

11 March 179

smile among African nationalist leaders. . .But it well illustrated the desire, strong among the communists and their partisans in the forces, to marginalize the parties.[55]

Arguments that Portugal belonged to the Third World and was led by its own liberation movement combined a refusal to recognize the pressure of public opinion, especially after the electoral victory of the socialists and PPD resoundingly defeated the MFA 'vanguard of the revolution' thesis, with the left's desire to turn its back on the realities of power politics. By accelerating the revolutionary process, by attempting to drag Portugal kicking and screaming out of Western Europe, the left was inviting political reprisals. A despairing Kissinger seemed to have already written off Portugal, concluding that, like Cuba, it would inoculate Europe against communism.[56] Spain, however, could not be expected to stand quietly by while a left-wing régime put down roots next door. The range of options open to Madrid if Lisbon failed to put her house in order ran from economic arm-twisting through her control of much of Portugal's power and water supply, through serving as a friendly base for counter-revolutionary forces. Madeira and the Azores would almost certainly cut loose from the mainland if things went much further. Cunhal remained oblivious to these arguments, encouraged by Moscow, which calculated that a communist régime on the Tagus would be better than gold in the bank: either they would have a base on the Atlantic or provoke an American military reaction which would offset their propaganda débâcle in Prague. 'When the revolution is within your grasp, you don't let it escape for those sorts of considerations', Cunhal told Soares.[57]

As had happened so often in Portugal's past, the new African thesis was preached by political dropouts and boiled down to little more than a left-wing attempt to rationalize its weakness. Soares argued that it ignored both Portugal's economic ties with the West and some 800 years of history: 'Of course we lag behind Europe, but in her we find the essence of our identity', he said. 'A civilization, a culture, habits, aspirations, desires and even a common standard of living. Eighty per cent of our economy is bound to the West, and more than one million Portuguese sell their labour in France, Germany, Canada. . .Where is the Third World in all that? Reality is stronger than beautiful speeches about the merits of an opening to the Third World.' While Portugal should certainly not turn her back on Africa, he maintained her future lay with Europe.[58]

The elections proved that economic backwardness was a weak

180 *11 March*

criterion upon which to award a country the status of belonging to the Third World. 'We are neither the Cuba of 1959, with a one-crop economy, nor Algeria, which people so often claim, who does not have the technicians to realize her ambitions', wrote Portuguese intellectual Eduardo Lourenço, a critic of left-wing fears of fully integrating Portugal into Europe.[59]

The MFA's African experience led them into error by creating a distorted image of their own country. A few cursory visits home and the yearly drafts of peasant conscripts were the only keyhole through which many younger officers who spent most of their adult lives in Africa could view Portugal. 'What we saw was that Portugal was itself part of the Third World', one MFA officer noted. 'Lisbon and Porto were an illusion, the country within was underdeveloped, with an illiterate and exploited peasantry.'[60] But what they saw through these conscripts was not the mirror of Portuguese reality but rather a sociological peep show, what was left over after removing the more intelligent, educated, or simply lucky who joined the navy and air force, became milicianos, used influence to secure a comfortable rear job, wrangled a medical deferment or simply took to the hills. Certainly, marginal strata exist in certain areas of the country which are an affront to any concerned person. But Portugal was not the jungle, nor were the Portuguese Africans squatting in the bush.

The MFA seriously misjudged the people whom they pretended to govern. They earned much popular gratitude by toppling the Caetano régime; by attempting to take its place on the spurious grounds that the Portuguese were incapable of managing their own affairs, they gave a modernizing Western European country a Third World government. 'Experience with military governments suggests that rule by the armed forces can serve as a preparation for democracy and civilian rule, but only if the military régime has 1. comparative freedom from pressures to act "efficiently" in terms of quick economic or technical "progress" and 2. a clear commitment and knowledge of the means to civilianization or democratization as an eventual goal', wrote Wilson McWilliams. 'Neither is highly probable.' McWilliams continues that soldiers are unlikely to play a dominant or directive political role in countries where they lack the skills to direct a complex social and economic structure and where organized opinion supports an established political system and culture.[61]

If the political conscience of MFA officers developed in the African bush, as many have claimed, it seems never to have left it. These men seemed oblivious to the fact that a long, at times even glorious, history

11 March 181

had bequeathed the Portuguese a language, a developed sense of
cultural homogeneity and a national unity rare in countries split by
tribal, racial or linguistic divisions. Portugal has attempted most forms
of government from monarchy, through republic to right-wing
dictatorship, and come perilously close to a communist régime, leaving
a residue of institutions, habits, memories and traditions even if the
régimes were transitory. Few Portuguese, least of all the less privileged,
took kindly to officers, however well-intentioned, who unflatteringly
compared them to primitives. Voting levels, usually accepted as an
indication of the populace's integration into the national community,
demonstrated a staggering degree of political awareness, even in the
country's most remote corners. The 92 per cent voter turnout on 25
April 1975 must have come as a great disappointment to MFA officers
who looked for something more along the lines of Mexico's 48 per cent
or Brazil's 40 per cent. 'The people, by a vast majority, showed the
soldiers that they were ready for democracy and could pass up the
instruction', Soares said of the election results.[62] By this indicator,
Portugal had proved more Third Republic than Third World.

The election results were even more surprising given the MFA's
blatant attempts to make the political parties flop. Carrying out
Carvalho's threat, the Revolutionary Council devised a way for people
to vote MFA as a protest against the 'political party game'. Claiming
that the nation was 'badly informed' by the politicians, soldiers called
on voters to leave ballots blank as a sign of solidarity with the MFA:
the *Boletim* statements by MFA leaders in press and radio, and cultural
dynamizers in the field announced that 'a blank vote is an MFA vote'
in an appeal for popular endorsement of a military régime. MFA leaders
calculated that at most 80 per cent of the electorate would turn up at
the polls, and fully 40 per cent of these would cast blank ballots.[63] If
50 per cent of the electorate boycotted the elections or voted blank,
the MFA could claim that much of the electorate was 'undecided' and
denied the political parties the popular mandate they needed to govern.

The impression given of a triangular showdown between the MFA,
the communists and parties of the extreme left, and the moderates
grouped under the socialist, PPD and CDS banners, was somewhat
deceptive. The communists looked to corral the votes of the industrial
centres and the traditionally radical south. A large 'undecided' vote in
the north and centre, where they had few illusions about their strength,
would fit nicely into their plans for neutralizing the moderate opposition
opposition before taking on the soldiers for command of the country.

The moderates barely got a mention in the largely communist

182 *11 March*

dominated daily press and television. Statements by Soares and PPD leader Sá Carneiro were buried under an avalanche of reports of the latest communist political demonstration at Beja and the minutes of a party meeting in Setúbal. Their campaign appearances in Porto or Braga were preempted by a televised PCP rally from the Alentejo, where party militants rhythmically chanted 'PCP', 'Spain will overcome' and 'Soviet Union', all under the beatific gaze of 'Comrade Alvaro'. Balanced reporting was left almost exclusively to the *Expresso*, one of the few newspapers which had escaped the communist press net. And it had only narrowly avoided a takeover after communists denounced *Expresso* as a reactionary publication and claimed that its editor had been involved in Spínola's 11 March fiasco.[64]

The election results came as a shock to MFA leaders. The low-key campaigns run by the socialists and the PPD, avoiding confrontations which could have provoked violent reprisals and instead concentrating on the need for progressive reform, had paid off. The final poll put them well in the lead and in a position to oppose left-wing attempts to curtail their powers:

Table 1

	Votes	%	Seats
Socialist Party (PS)	2,145,392	37.87	116
Popular Democrats (PPD)	1,494,575	26.38	80
Communist Party (PCP)	709,639	12.53	30
Centre Democrats (CDS)	433,153	7.65	16
Portuguese Democratic Movement (MDP)	233,362	4.12	4
Popular Democratic Union (UDP) (Maoist)	44,542	0.79	1

The communists came off strongest in the Alentejo where a largely landless peasantry saw in Cunhal their best hope of keeping many of the large estates they had occupied. However, results in the Algarve to the south and in the Lisbon and Porto industrial belts where communists were firmly implanted in trade unions fell far short of expectations, oscillating between 65 and 17 per cent of the vote. Communists in the north had notched up a dismal 5 per cent. The PPD had shown its strength in the north while the socialists had done best overall, proving especially strong in the large cities. Only 7 per cent of

11 March

the votes were blank, a massive rebuff for the MFA and cultural dynamization.

Socialist reaction to the elections was predictably ecstatic: 'Portugal is now entering a new era', Soares announced. 'The other parties will have to realize that only the socialist party can legitimately claim to be the most representative of all the Portuguese parties. It means a new direction for socialism after a year dominated by the parties of the far left.' The PPD also interpreted the results as a rejection of any 'paternalistic solution'. Eager to keep his fragile coalition intact and avoid charges that the PS was reactionary, Soares pointed out that socialist and communist votes combined constituted a clear majority for the working classes. He was savaged both by the communists and the MFA. The communist-controlled press and radio claimed that the elections were 'unimportant' and did not 'reflect the profound feelings of the masses'. They explained that the high socialist poll was in fact a victory for cultural dynamization, which had managed to put the word 'socialism' into the everyday vocabulary of backward peasants: seeing the word on the ballot, they voted for it. The socialist vote could not be interpreted as a vote for the socialist party, but for the 'MFA's socialist option',[65] an argument whose force was somewhat diminished by the fact that at least four parties on the ballot had social or socialist in their name. Charges that voters in the north especially were intimidated by priests or vigilantes in the pay of landlords and capitalists into voting PPD or Centre Democratic were not without some foundation. Social pressures certainly existed in varying degrees in small towns where the secret ballot was secret in name only: the one communist voter in a village solidly behind the CDS or PPD cannot remain anonymous. But pressure worked both ways, and the votes gained in this way in the Trás-os-Montes were at least partially offset in the Alentejo.

In a sense, however, communist and MFA claims that the socialists should not crow too loudly were well founded, although for reasons they refused to recognize. The socialist victory was not simply a vote for socialism, but a vote against the PCP and MFA and for the man who appeared most likely to turn them back in their tracks. 25 April 1975, spelled a clear rejection of Cunhal and his 'putschist' politics. even among the trade unionists upon whom he had counted for support. 'In April 1974, I would have voted without hesitation for the communists as the most committed opponents of Salazarism', a Lisnav metal worker said. 'But I am a year older in April 1975. I have realized one thing: they don't care a fig for democracy.' 'I supported

184   *11 March*

the illegal PCP before the *coup d'état*', said a railway worker in Figueira da Foz. 'But we Portuguese cannot sleep with our fists clenched. . .This isn't East Germany.'[66] The socialist victory margin would have been impossible without support from large numbers of industrial workers in Setúbal, Lisbon, Porto, Beira and other cities, 'who would never have dreamed of voting socialist if the PCP had resembled the Italian communist party', noted an Italian journalist. Even socialist party militants admitted that Cunhal had been their best campaign worker: 'We cannot take all of the credit', a socialist lawyer in Setúbal admitted modestly.[67]

To underline their contempt for the election results, the communists and their MFA allies moved to hijack the 1 May celebration of Portugal's first free elections in fifty years. Filling the seats of the Lisbon bull ring with his supporters, Cunhal transformed the rally that government and party officials were to attend into a PCP demonstration. Arriving PPD delegates were jostled and turned away by communists waving flags and acclaiming their leader, who had taken the podium with Vasco Gonçalves. Soares found his way barred by an Intersindical official who refused to allow him on to the podium: trade unionists grouped to keep out his followers. Believing at first that there must be some mistake, he explained that he had an official invitation, but got no further. He then attempted to speak to his supporters outside, but was forced to abandon the attempt after whistles and shouts from communists made his voice inaudible. 'The objective was clear', Soares said of the '1 May scandal'. 'Show the soldiers and their political opponents, everyone, that the elections had changed nothing, that "their" revolution was continuing as before. A monumental error. The people do not like to be taken for asses and object when someone steals what they had paid for dearly.'[68] When the socialists protested officially, the communists attacked Soares for having disrupted the celebration. The socialists replied with a massive Lisbon demonstration on 2 May which called on the government 'to respect the popular will'.

The decision to press cultural dynamization taken by the MFA Assembly on 11 March was applied vigorously after the elections demonstrated, Jesuino claimed, that 'it takes more than one year for millions of citizens to acquire a political conscience'. Politicized COPCON contingents, fresh from indoctrination sessions at the fifth division's Institute of Military Sociology, joined volunteers working in the north to reverse the setback inflicted by the politicians. In May, the Revolutionary Council ordered units to take up residence in the areas they aimed to dynamize, hoping that reforms imposed on the

11 March

reluctant population would stick: previous 'civic promenades' had proved only that the influence of dynamization teams evaporated when the last lorry disappeared around the bend. Peasants then moved to throw out the municipal councils imposed by the visiting soldiers, to move families encouraged to occupy the vacant houses of 'absentee landlords', usually emigrants who had sent their savings home, and to forget their force-fed catechism. Technical cabinets to coordinate activities were set up in the army engineers and in the economy, agriculture, fishing and health ministries; Military Academy cadets were trucked north to help the peasants with their planting. 'Fundamentally, our actions will be a political action to create a more immediately social base for the revolution', fifth division chief Ramiro Correia said:

> The armed forces at this moment are completely different from what they were on 25 April or 28 September and this is the result of a dialectical process through contact with reality. Personally, I am conscious, for example, that when the population in its totality voted for socialism, it was due for the most part to the efficiency of our action in educating the country.[69]

Cultural dynamization efforts were particularly aimed at the town of Bragança and its surrounding countryside. In the 25 April elections, 43 per cent of the region had voted for the PPD, 25 per cent for the socialist, and 13.5 per cent for the CDS, while the communists and MDP finished last with 2.7 per cent and 3.6 per cent of the vote respectively. The communist-controlled press categorized its population as 'religiously reactionary', although in the 1958 presidential election the district had voted overwhelmingly for General Delgado, and COPCON sent a contingent of 38 soldiers from Lisbon to 'dynamize' the population. The soldiers immediately established close relations with local communists: 'The soldiers would spend their evenings at the PCP headquarters, and then would go to the people and present communism with arms in their hands', one resident said. They bolstered PCP domination of the municipal council, which had already come under fire for its blatant favouritism of party members: in one lottery organized by the council, the only MDP militants among 700 people entered won both draws. Finally, on 22 August, popular patience broke and the headquarters of both the PCP and MDP were sacked by angry townsfolk in what was described as Bragança's 'anti-cultural dynamization riots'.

Steps were soon taken to bring cultural dynamization which had con-

186 *11 March*

tributed to similar riots throughout northern and central Portugal in the late summer, to an end. In July Soares accused the fifth division of being nothing but a tool in the communist plan to take over the country. His demand found an echo in the infantry assemblies of 19 and 25 July, which voted for the fifth division's dissolution and the dismantling of cultural dynamization. Finally, on 27 August, the activities of the fifth division were suspended.

The left blamed the failure of cultural dynamization on the influence of reactionary priests, fear of wealthy capitalists and landowners upon whom many depended for jobs, sabotage by unfriendly Lisbon bureaucrats and the general mistrust and ignorance of a rural population. 'It's all right to take decisions here, but in a few days you will leave', one peasant reportedly told a soldier. 'The bosses, on the other hand, will stay and we will have no one to protect us. Who will give us work then?'[70]

The dynamizers, however, must shoulder the lion's share of the blame for their failure. 'The distrust and anguish of our people was not, as certain authors pretended, the fruits of a concerted Machiavellian manoeuvre, the concealed Portuguese reaction financed by international fascist finance', wrote Gomes Mota. 'But rather the result of diatribes, of the insubordination of many soldiers responsible for sectarianism and the violence of totalitarian forces.'[71]

Rather than concentrate on civic improvement or even social justice, dynamizers and their communist allies too often indulged in the crudest sort of anti-clericalism, geared not only to raise the hackles of the Church, which until the summer had remained relatively silent, but to shock the sensibilities of a deeply religious population. Catholics on the receiving end of the barrage of radio and press reports and soldiers' speeches denouncing the north as 'backward' and 'reactionary' naturally reacted unfavourably. 'Reactionary? Who is reactionary?' asked one villager in the north. 'Why do they always accuse people in the north of being reactionary? We do not follow Spínola or Cunhal. All we want is bread for our children and a doctor for our ills.'[72] A left-wing student reported that the tactless and often brutal behaviour of dynamizers, who sometimes went so far as to threaten their audiences with physical violence, had made people suspicious even of those working on literacy programmes: 'The people. . .did not like the way they were approached, to be told that they were savages and that they must be brought back to civilization', he said. 'It cannot be very pleasant to be invaded and be told nice things which class you among the "niggers" of Portugal.'[73] 'This word reactionary. . .was applied curiously to the people of the north', said air force Major Canto e

11 March   187

Castro, later one of the 'nine'. 'But the people of the north are not reactionaries. This revolution was made for the people, for the peasants who live as if in the middle ages. Through demagogy, we almost forgot about them.'[74] It is an enormous error to consider the people – in this case the *transmontano* people – as stupid and primitive', the *Expresso* wrote on 13 September 1975. 'One must not confuse. . .under-development with imbecility.'

Some of the more lucid officers who worked with the fifth division admitted that their miscalculations never allowed cultural dynamization to get off the ground. One said:

> When you want to carry out cultural dynamization you should study the local people. Private property is very important in the north. Everyone has a small piece of land or a cow. The soldiers should have kept the feelings of those people in mind, and especially respected their religious beliefs. They worked in the north like they worked in the south: in the south, the people have nothing and were more receptive. Often soldiers would tour the villages with troops of actors, including girls with short skirts. You simply cannot do that sort of thing in these small villages. They did not do much to improve the lot of these people, but they did talk a lot of politics.[75]

The uncompromising political character of cultural dynamization and its often abrasive application is explained in part by the fact that while inspired by the army's African experience, in particular that of Spínola's Guinea command, it was applied by men who more often than not had never set foot on the continent. Calls for cultural dynamization had come first from the Naval Assembly and were pushed through by a fifth division largely controlled by radical naval officers whose ideas had not hatched in the jungle. Although it is impossible to ascertain the origins and war experience of the 150 men who made up the fifth division, much less of the many soldiers sent to preach politics in the field, it seems unlikely that even a significant proportion had ever seen African service, much less engaged in the army's 'hearts and minds' campaigns in Guinea. Had this been the case, they might have had a more realistic view of the potential and limitations of cultural dynamization. 'Most of the people I met had never been in the colonies', said a captain who served several months in the fifth division. 'Most were young second lieutenants, milicianos. Most of the people whom the 5th division sent out were selected in the units for their political opinions. I think that this included many deserters – men who

188   *11 March*

had fled the country to avoid military service and then returned after 25 April to serve as milicianos. I cannot prove this, but we felt this to be the case.'[76]

Many foreign observers took too many MFA reforms at face value. Kenneth Maxwell observed:

> Much of what they [MFA] have done shows how serious and far reaching their intentions are. The 'cultural dynamization' teams which have spread throughout the country, and whose activity was critical in informing the people of their duty to vote and how to go about it; the central role the army had defined for itself in the social and economic reconstruction of Portugal; the myriad committees of soldiers, sergeants and commissioned officers, that are functioning in quasi-legislative bodies within the army.[77]

But cultural dynamization was little more than a medicine show, part of Portugal's 'Boys' Own' revolution carried out by keen scouts whose efforts seldom exceeded the level of enthusiastic amateurism. 'In August, about 100 cadets were sent up north', an officer in the Military Academy remembered. 'They worked in the field with the peasants who were used to working from dawn to dusk. After two or three hours they were exhausted. Anyone who knew them at all well would know that it was the peasants who should have come to dynamize the Academy, to teach the cadets how to work.'[78] Advice on the vote usually boiled down to an order to stuff the ballot box with blank papers as a sign of MFA sympathy. Most people who came into contact with cultural dynamization teams could hardly wait to vote PPD or CDS. Their social and economic contributions to Portugal's reconstruction appear to have been largely negative, while the soviets of soldiers, sergeants and officers simply proved the generally accepted tenet that armies function poorly without discipline and that governments usually function better if their soldiers sit in the barracks and not in the cabinet.

Of all the left-wing revolution programmes, cultural dynamization proved the most disastrous. Launched to win the population for the revolution, its effect was the exact opposite.The army dynamization cabinet (GDE) blamed the mishandled cultural dynamization campaign for the MFA's failure to win the confidence of the population. The GDE's November report read:

> Cultural dynamization was one of the great touchstones of the entire

11 March   189

process which began on 25 April...It served to prepare and organize by bringing the people into contact with the MFA and thereby with its own idea of the revolution. But although its intentions were good, it did not work out that way in practice. And this, it must be said, sometimes defrauded popular expectations and blackened the image of the revolution. We know that a revolution which serves as a transition from a capitalist state to a socialist one has to transform the socio-cultural reality which motivates it without tearing the social fabric upon which it acts. Thus, the revolution must respect the habits and socio-cultural values of the population. This did not happen in most cases and sometimes there were grave insults to the values — moral, traditional and cultural — of our people, which led naturally to the rejection of the men of the MFA.[79]

Notes

1. *República*, 10 October 1974.
2. Quoted in Fremontier, *Les Points sur les i*, Paris, 1976, p.58.
3. 1 September 1974.
4. *República*, 10 October 1974.
5. *Expresso*, 25 April 1975.
6. Alves, *Les Soldats socialistes du Portugal*, Paris, 1975, pp.116-7.
7. *Boletim*, No.21, 17 June 1975.
8. See *Expresso*, 31 May 1975.
9. Interview.
10. Interview.
11. Quoted in Fremontier, op.cit., p.58.
12. Interview.
13. Interview.
14. Interview.
15. Interview.
16. Interview.
17. *Le Monde*, 5 June 1975.
18. Fremontier, op.cit., p.58.
19. Interview.
20. *Expresso*, 18 October 1975.
21. *O Jornal*, 23 December 1975.
22. Insight, *The Year of the Captains*, London, 1975, p.196.
23. Interview.
24. For *coup* events of 11 March see *Boletim*, No.16, 23 April 1975, which contains preliminary report of Investigating Committee and Insight, ch.12.
25. Interview.
26. See Soares, *Portugal: Quelle Révolution?* Paris, 1976, pp.106-7.
27. Ibid., p.107.
28. Alves, op.cit., p.98.
29. Gomes Mota, *A Resistência*, Lisbon, 1976, p.62.
30. *Le Monde*, 27 August 1975.
31. Ibid.

190   *11 March*

32. Percentages based on figure in Maxwell, 'The Hidden Revolution in Portugal', *New York Review of Books*, 17 April 1975, p.30
33. *Le Monde*, 28 August 1975.
34. Soares, op.cit., p.126.
35. R.C. Fields, *The Portuguese Revolution and the Armed Forces Movement*, New York, 1975, p.176.
36. Interview.
37. Interview.
38. Alves, op.cit., p.165.
39. *Expresso*, 5 April 1975.
40. Soares, op.cit., pp.109-10.
41. Insight, op.cit., pp.237-8.
42. Quoted in Alves, op.cit., p.119.
43. *Revista do Povo*, 1 November 1974.
44. Alves, op.cit., p.106.
45. *Expresso*, 16 November, 1975, quoted by Alves, op.cit., p.111.
46. *Le Monde*, 15 August 1975.
47. Quoted in Alves, op.cit., p.108.
48. Niedergang, 'L'Armée Portuguaise ou la Fascination du Pouvoir', *Le Monde* 5 February, 1975.
49. See for instance the *Boletim* of 11 and 25 February 1975.
50. Soares, op.cit., pp.108-90.
51. *Expresso*, 22 February 1975.
52. *Expresso*, 24 May 1975.
53. Ibid., 17 May 1975.
54. Ibid., 21 June 1975.
55. Soares, op.cit., p.125.
56. Ibid., pp.66-7.
57. Ibid., p.63.
58. Ibid., p.65.
59. Harsgor, *Naissance d'un nouveau Portugal*, Paris, 1975, p.205.
60. Maxwell, 'The Hidden Revolt', op.cit., p.32.
61. McWilliams, *Garrisons and Governments*, San Francisco, 1967, p.28.
62. Soares, op.cit., p.114.
63. Insight, op.cit., p.242.
64. See Harsgor, op.cit., pp.184-5.
65. Soares, op.cit., p.116.
66. Harsgor, op.cit., pp.189-90.
67. Ibid., p.191.
68. Soares, op.cit., pp.119-20.
69. *Diário de Notícias*, 1 April 1975.
70. Alves, op.cit., p.110.
71. Mota, op.cit., p.13.
72. *Expresso*, 13 September 1975, report on Bragança riots.
73. Harsgor, op.cit., p.155.
74. Fremontier, op.cit., p.33.
75. Interview.
76. Interview.
77. Maxwell, 'Portugal under Pressure', op.cit., p.28.
78. Interview.
79. *Expresso*, 19 November 1975.

7 THE RESISTANCE

By the early summer of 1975, Portugal's prolonged political crisis was beginning to wear the patience even of her reputedly phlegmatic population. Decolonization, the growing economic crisis, cultural dynamization, a half-understood political debate raging in the capital, and a thousand irregularities in the running of the press, local governments and military units had aggravated the country's natural divisions. Portugal was increasingly split between socialists and communists, between north and south, between Lisbon and the rest.

These divisions were mirrored in the armed forces. To the extent that it is possible to subdivide the burble of ideologies and personalities which made up the MFA, by May one was able to detect three vaguely coherent groups. The first and the most successful to date was led by Prime Minister Vasco Gonçalves. Accused of pro-communist sympathies, 'Gonçalvist' officers were strong in the government and in the fifth division, lending credence to charges that Cunhal aimed to effect an institutional conquest of the country. 'He was not naïve', Soares said of Gonçalves. 'He consciously helped the communist attempt to install a popular democratic régime in Portugal. For him, this was a mission: to encourage PS and PC unity, then blend them into one party. A classic schema. . .I don't know if he paid [PC] dues, but he served the interests of the PC and he spoke their language. A conscious object of their manipulation, he stayed faithful to his assigned role to the end.'[1]

The fifth division was a Gonçalvist stronghold. Led by tested militant Valera Gomes, backed by Ramiro Correia, a navy doctor prompted to organize cultural dynamization, the fifth division worked to transform the army into the revolution's cutting edge. Vasco Gonçalves axed Defence Minister Firmino Miguel after 11 March, and personally took over the defence portfolio, naming radical officers to key positions in the ministry.[2] Naval captain Jorge Jesuino replaced army Major Sanches Osório, a close friend of Spínola, in the ministry of communications. Jesuino's grip on the media was tightened through the Serviço de Detecção e Coordenação das Informações, organized by Almada Contreiras, Pereira Pinto and army Captain Ferreira Macedo, who vetted the ideological content of radio and television programmes, while keeping a close watch on the national press. Radical air force pilot Costa Martins was handed the labour ministry and with it the

191

192 *The Resistance*

task of assuring left-wing domination of the economic life of the country. 'In the name of "economic sabotage", they decapitated administrations, changed managers, "purged" cadres, arrested citizens, exiled technocrats and infiltrated "committees", all under the direction of Rosa Coutinho, chief of support services of the Revolutionary Council, and the Machiavellian lieutenant of Rosário Dias, the economic adjutant of the Prime Minister', wrote ex-naval lieutenant turned journalist, Gomes Mota.[3]

Jacques Frémontier, correspondent of the French communist party newspaper *Humanité,* held that PCP designs on Portugal were exaggerated by hostile politicians and an unfriendly press. He argued that no links between communists and the fifth division existed, that claims made for the disproportionate influence of communists in local governments, especially in the north, were grossly exaggerated, and that while communist-backed unions were active in many strikes and press seizures, it was not always with the blessing of Cunhal but rather the result of agitation by groups on the extreme left.[4]

Frémontier's contention that Cunhal was not directly responsible for much of the disorder attributed to him cannot be disputed. Many politicians, journalists and the people in general laid the responsibility for upheaval in factories and barracks, illegal occupations of banks, farms and houses and growing violence squarely at the door of the PCP. Cunhal's reputation no doubt suffered from the initiatives of local communists and the excess revolutionary enthusiasm of the left in general, all in the name of communism.

However, while the PCP cannot be saddled with the responsibility for every strike, misdemeanour, or excess of behaviour which rapidly turned Portugal against the revolution after 11 March, the disorder fitted communist strategy nicely. Melo Antunes said in mid-November 1975:

We are convinced that there is a plan — a communist plan — inside the army to disorganize systematically the chain of command. At the same time, small groups install themselves in key posts and operational commands. It is the [extreme] left which agitates against the 'bourgeois' army and which forms the future action groups. But it is the PC which drew up the master plan and is most keen that it can reap the benefits. The same tactic has been followed in civilian society: for the moment, the communists do not want to overthrow this government in which they sit. . .Their best tactic for the present is to make propaganda and agitate. This government is useful as a

The Resistance

scapegoat. They can criticize it, paralyze it almost completely, prevent it from operating and then denounce its inefficiency. They can extend actions like those of these last weeks – the occupation of parliament, sequestrations and intimidation. All of this aims to create a climate of tension, to terrorize the country, to paralyze the state. One day, the country will be exhausted, totally disorganized, almost without resistance, undermined everywhere. Don't think that I am exaggerating; the process is well under way. Everyone will tell you that Portugal can become ungovernable any day now. . .And when it is no longer possible to govern the country at all, we will come to the second phase, that of the real conquest of power. And this will be carried out, initially, with the conquest of the army.[5]

The PCP encouraged the escalating climate of violence in the summer and autumn of 1975. Fremontier narrowly limits party influence to card-carrying members, treating the MDP and widespread 'independent' influence in local government as a separate category and refusing to acknowledge the strong PCP sympathies among 'Gonçalvist' officers in the government and fifth division. Even back in the Salazar days, Vasco Gonçalves and Vaera Gomes had enjoyed close links with the communists. Once in power, Gonçalves leaned heavily on the communists and MDP for political support. Jesuino, Contreiras and Macedo in the information ministry facilitated the takeover of many newspapers by 'workers committees', which, if not always instigated by the communists, usually left them generously compensated in positions from which they could direct news, all with a view to silencing their powerful socialist rivals. Jesuino named pro-communist or communist editors and deputy editors to the large Lisbon dailies *Diário de Notícias, Século* and *Diário de Lisboa* after workers threw out the moderate management.[6] In the labour ministry, Costa Martins leaned heavily on his under-secretary, MDP militant Carlos Carvalhas, and communists Eugénio Rosa and Barros de Moura, all of whom worked to extend Intersindical's control over the trade union movement.[7] While Gonçalvist officers may not have paid PCP dues, the similarities in political aims and ideology and the ease with which they worked together made differences between them academic.

The communist affinities of many fifth division officers were also clearly apparent. Ramiro Correia prided himself on his revolutionary ideology. He had edited a book of Portuguese revolutionary songs in Russian and sponsored a text on 'who are the people and who are not', reproduced from a PCP publication.[8] While some fifth division

194   *The Resistance*

officers denied having formal links with the communist party, they counted the PCP as a firm ally: 'I have never in my life spoken with a leader of a political party', fifth division spokesman air force Captain Paulino said. 'And they say that I am a communist! And as I am one of those responsible for the information section, they say that everyone is like me, that all my comrades are communists! What has happened is the class struggle. In the class struggle, the MFA is on the side of the movements which support the workers. And the communist party is on that side.'[9]

A second political cleavage within the MFA was represented by COPCON and its flamboyant commander, Otelo de Carvalho. Influenced by groups on the extreme left, Carvalho championed a concept of society based on 'popular power', with government entrusted to committees in every village, neighbourhood, factory and barracks. His ideas were reflected in the MFA's institutionalization debate, in the concepts of revolutionary discipline, and ultimately in the *Guide Document of the People-MFA Alliance,* debated by the MFA Assembly on 8 July and which set out a blueprint for a direct MFA appeal to the people over the heads of the political parties.

COPCON support was concentrated almost exclusively in the Lisbon based military police, RALIS, the administrative school (EPAM), the first engineers, the supply school (EPSM) at Sacavém, the ordnance depot at Beirolas and the mixed detachment at Forte de Almada.[10] COPCON's strongest political backing came from the small Revolutionary Party of the Proletariat (PRP), whose leader Maria do Carmo exercised a strong influence over Carvalho. Unhappily for his subsequent military career, this Othello had no Iago to help him over his initial infatuation. Charged with keeping order in Lisbon, COPCON increasingly fell victim to its own ideology. COPCON troops spread over the capital to arbitrate illegal occupations of houses, factories and newspapers were instructed by Carvalho to act on the principle that 'the workers are always right'. Any act was permitted if it served the interests of the revolution.[11] COPCON increasingly wrote its own law, defying the orders of the Revolutionary Council to turn out those occupying *República,* a newspaper close to the socialist party and whose occupation led socialist ministers to walk out of the government on 15 July.

However, the spectacle of their commander bypassing the chain of command, forcing government officials and senior officers to negotiate rather than to issue instructions, was not lost on the soldiers who debated orders and challenged officers, gradually crippling COPCON's

The Resistance 195

operational potential until Carvalho was left with little more than a wheelchair command.

The concentration of dissident units in Lisbon contrasted sharply with the political disposition of most of the rest of the armed forces. Few units to the north of the capital had much time for the political antics in Lisbon. The left counted strong support only in the transportation school (CICAP) and the heavy artillery regiment (RASP) in Porto, and in the infantry regiment at Abrantes in central Portugal. Even in Lisbon, regiments who commanded much of the firepower — the commandos, the anti-aircraft regiment (CIAAC) at Cascais, the infantry school at Mafra, the cavalry school at Santarém — had so far refused to be seduced by revolutionary discipline. Even in the traditionally radical south, dissidents were unable to command a sure following, except at the Vendas Novas artillery school under the command of radical Captain Andrade e Silva. Units in the Azores, Madeira and Angola and the air force held aloof from the political excesses of COPCON. Only the paratroops whose discipline had been troubled by the left-wing national commission of sergeants remained a question-mark.

Moderate officers who hoped to organize resistance to the leftward march of the revolution could also look for political backing from the PS, PPD and CDS. But real weakness lay in their lack of press support, especially after the nationalization of banks on 11 March gave over large sections of the press to government control. *A Luta,* founded by refugee reporters from the occupied *República,* and the new *Jornal Novo* remained the only dailies which escaped the Gonçalvist press net. The weeklies *Expresso, O Jornal, Jornal de Notícias, Comércio do Porto* and Porto's *Rádio Renascença* virtually completed the list of independent viewpoints.

For the next six months, these groups fought for control of the MFA, a battle whose winner would command the country. Moderate officers aimed primarily to head off the Gonçalvist domination of the movement, which would assure strong communist presence in the government. Although numerically the weakest of the three factions, the strength of COPCON and the extreme left was massed around the strategically important capital. Moderate officers had so far offered a blanket opposition to a precipitous left-wing advance of the revolution, pushing Gonçalves and Carvalho into a progressive alliance. Clearly, a new strategy was needed to separate the Gonçalvists and COPCON forces and throw the balance of power in the moderates' favour.

The 19 June announcement by Vasco Lourenço that the

196　The Resistance

Revolutionary Council had approved a Plan of Political Action (PAP) rejecting both the Gonçalvist 'vanguard' thesis and the utopian structures supported by Carvalho was taken as a sign that the left's string of successes since 11 March had been cut short at last. PAP recognized that the revolution could move forward only with popular backing; any attempt to impose a radical solution on a reluctant country was a formula for disaster.

Hopes that the revolution might be confined to progressive limits acceptable to the nation, with a peaceful transition from Salazar to the future, were shaken badly on 8 July when the MFA Assembly voted the *Guide Document of the People-MFA Alliance* which set aside the laboriously negotiated PAP and elected to allow *República* to open under worker management. Both decisions brought the crisis long simmering in the army and in the corridors of government bubbling to the surface.

Even for seasoned observers of the Portuguese revolution, long accustomed to surprises, the approval of the *Guide Document* came as a surprise. Not only did the document sign the death warrant of the PAP, announced barely three weeks before, throwing the revolution off balance yet again, but was itself a baffling hybrid of Gonçalvist and COPCON philosophy. Carvalho's hand was most evident in the call for a new democracy based on 'popular committees' elected by a show of hands in assemblies in every factory and neighbourhood. These committees would be charged with 'social action in the domaines of health, assistance, culture, sports, literacy, housing, social organization (urbanism), transportation, etc.; an economic action. . .through control of production in nationalized and private sectors, supply prices, etc.' Under the watchful eye of the MFA, they were even allowed to organize their own defence. These local assemblies formed the base of a hierarchy of popular assemblies which would stretch through every commune, canton and district, capped by a national assembly. Every elected delegate could be recalled by his constituents at any time.

The call for a decentralized state 'permitting local initiative under the control, surveillance and the progressive actions of popular committees' aimed to destroy the machinery of the centralized state, which the extreme left denounced as 'bourgeois'. However, the support of Gonçalvist officers was assured for those portions of the text which called for the development of a 'large state sector' and stressed the need for discipline. 'I consider the *Guide Document* is the hinge of the revolutionary movement', said fifth division spokesman Captain Paulino. 'The state bureaucracy was installed by fascism to serve the interests of

The Resistance

capitalism, not of the Portuguese people. . .This organization, which will be constructed daily upon a solid foundation, will progressively come to replace the parallel organization of fascist power. It will be a popular democracy, a direct democracy.'[12] On 9 July the PCP issued a statement supporting the *Guide Document*, underlining the need for new purges in the administration and a larger role for progressive parties.

The decision taken on the same day to allow *República* to publish was geared to throw the socialist party into opposition and produce a government crisis. Founded in the early days of the First Republic, *República* quickly established a tradition of liberalism which it carried with it into the post-war world. In 1965, the socialists organized to save the newspaper from financial ruin, and although *República* was not a socialist party publication, under its editor Raúl Rego, it remained the most widely read exponent of centre-left views in Lisbon. The troubles affecting most of the Lisbon press had not spared *República*, and after the '1 May scandal', tensions between leftists and socialists on the paper broke into the open. Typographers refused to print articles denouncing the role of the communists and the Intersindical in the events of that day, and stopped the presses. A series of further skirmishes climaxed on 19 May when leftists called for the scrapping of two articles: one on the return from China of a delegation of the Maoist PCP-Marxist Leninist and another on a planned communist purge of Lisbon television journalists, several of whom were to be denounced as adulterers and homosexuals. The newspaper appeared with both of the articles – but that very night, *República* was occupied by some of its workers while hundreds of socialist militants kept an all-night vigil in front of the building demanding the return of 'their' newspaper. The effort failed as COPCON troops arrived and closed the paper down.[13]

The case of *República*, together with that of Rádio Renascença occupied after a similar sequence of events on 27 May, formed the nub of many debates in the Revolutionary Council over the next few weeks. On 10 July, following the decision of the MFA Assembly, pirate editions of *República* appeared under the control of its workers. The role of the communist party in the *República* seizure was hotly debated. Communists claimed that the workers' committee contained only two PCP members and that the views expressed in the newspaper after 10 July were closer to COPCON's anarchistic opinions than those of Cunhal.[14] Soares, however, placed the communists solidly behind the attempt to deprive their most serious political rivals of their last national voice:

198   *The Resistance*

The truth was clear. The communists, working through several typographers, took possession of the newspaper 'of the socialists': that is what we claimed to all those who would listen to us and were ready to defend us. . .I never denied the existence of non-communist elements in the affair. . .It is certain that these people were not all communists. There are subtleties. . .[But] the most responsible person is he who launched the operation and opened the conflict. The extreme left was not strong enough to take it on alone. . .I am convinced that the PCP is the primary instigator of this 'struggle'. . .They thought it possible to reedit *República* as they had done at *Diário de Notícias*. They thought that we would protest but did not imagine that we would fight to the finish for our liberty and for that of all of the Portuguese people. The communists had a plan, drawn up and approved at the highest level, to muzzle and destroy us, that is beyond doubt. The first director they named for *República* was Belo Marques, well-known for his communist sympathies.[15]

The *República* crisis broke the fourth provisional government. On 10 July, Soares announced that the socialists would quit the cabinet and pass into opposition following President Costa Gomes' refusal to intervene in the affair. 'The case of *República* is symptomatic of the vast crisis of state authority, eroded by demagogy', Soares told him. 'I, for my part, cannot continue to sit in a government which does not govern and which daily becomes less able to carry out its duties.'[16] The Revolutionary Council instructed the President to fill the cabinet vacancies, but four days later the PPD also pulled out, bringing the fourth provisional government crashing down like a house of cards.

With the collapse of the government, the Portuguese revolution now entered its most critical phase and the one which brought its closest brush with civil war. Political attitudes were hardening into immobile stances. Public hostility to the MFA increased immeasurably with the 26 July formation of a triumvirate of Costa Gomes, Otelo de Carvalho and Vasco Gonçalves 'to guarantee the authority of the government'. Riots in the north protesting the Prime Minister's attempt to impose a communist régime on the country were fuelled by revelations that Vasco Gonçalves had given the Soviet 'fishing fleet' harbourage in Madeira, once safe NATO water. Political parties and military factions seemed virtually to have abandoned negotiation to settle disputes, falling back instead on muscle-flexing street demonstrations and violent speeches as a prelude to a serious exchange of blows. Carvalho

The Resistance

199

told journalists that he had grown tired of the 'very humanist and pretty revolution of the carnations. . .It would have been better to eliminate hundreds and thousands of counter-revolutionaries after 25 April 1974.' His calls for 'popular vigilance' were backed by a 16 July march of 8,000 left-wing demonstrators led by RALIS soldiers sitting on tanks and armoured cars through the streets of Lisbon shouting for the dissolution of the Constituent Assembly. Mass socialist rallies in Lisbon and Porto on 18 and 19 July met a rerun of the 28 September call by Intersindical for 'popular barricades' to halt the 'reactionary march'. In Porto, however, communists were too few to halt the human wave of Soares' supporters which surged past their barricades to a 75,000 strong rally in the sports stadium. In Lisbon, COPCON troops broke up barricades before serious clashes could occur. Socialists paraded down the Avenida da Liberdade shouting: 'the people are not with the MFA', parodying the MFA's most popular slogan. On 13 July, the population of Rio Maior, a small town north of Lisbon, burned down the headquarters of the local PCP, lighting the signal for the widespread destruction of PCP and MDP headquarters and the sacking of the homes and offices of many of their local leaders throughout northern and central Portugal.

Equally serious was the indication that an important faction in the Church had abandoned its hitherto discreet attitude to the revolution and was prepared to feed the flames of anti-communism licking the north. The Bishop of Braga had been celebrated for his outspoken anti-communism in Salazar's time, but under the moderate influence of the young Cardinal-Archbishop of Lisbon, Monseigneur António Ribeiro, and the Bishop of Porto, Monseigneur Ferreira Gomes, exiled under Caetano, he bit his tongue while his fellow bishops espoused a supple diplomacy aiming to spare the Church a repetition of the First Republic's anti-clerical crusade. Monseigneur Gomes instructed priests in his dioceses not to attack the communists openly, but simply to stress the danger of the erosion of fundamental freedoms. Monseigneur Ribeiro received leaders of the MFA and political parties in his episcopal palace, judiciously feeling for a formula satisfactory both to the Church and the revolution on the thorny questions of divorce and the civil rights of bastards, an estimated 500,000 people. He tried to build a bridge between the substantial minority of progressive and left-wing Catholics concentrated in Lisbon, Coimbra and Porto, and the mass of the faithful: Father Agostinho Jardim Gonçalves, secretary of the Bishop's Congress, spoke of the 'profound affinity' between French theologian Teilhard de Chardin and Karl Marx, while a

200   *The Resistance*

progressive monk, Bento Domingues, wrote for the socialist party, stressing that socialism was acceptable as long as it was not 'dogmatic, totalitarian or bureaucratic'.[17]

The Church's more independent frame of mind began to emerge with the 25 April elections, when it warned its flock that under no circumstances were they to vote a blank ballot. At the same time, however, the Cardinal-Archbishop protected his flanks by declaring that the revolution had brought with it authentic evangelical values. COPCON's complicity in the occupation of Rádio Renascença on 27 May angered many Catholics, pushing the Church toward a final break with the revolution. Deprived of their radio station, attacked openly by cultural dynamizers in the north who saw the Church, not without some justification, as a force of reaction, the Bishop of Braga blasted the left-wing orientation of the revolution on 11 August. straining the already tense atmosphere in the north to breaking point.

The break-up of the fourth provisional government, the MFA Assembly's adoption of the *Guide Document,* and the increasing anarchy which threatened to bring the revolution to a bloody conclusion at last convinced several progressive officers to organize a resistance. The decision was crucial, for the course of Portuguese politics could only be altered peacefully by a well organized and skilfully directed campaign from within the armed forces itself. The initiative for the group which came to be known as the 'nine' or the 'Antunes group' after the author of the moderate manifesto backed by 80 per cent of professional army officers, was not Melo Antunes as much of the press claimed but Vasco Lourenço. As early as late June, Lourenço had been meeting with officers eager to capture control of the MFA and the revolution from the Gonçalvists and COPCONists.

A study of the political situation within the army was far from discouraging, but required a cautious strategy if a potentially bloody confrontation was to be averted. Dissidents controlled the Revolutionary Council and the MFA Assembly. Their influence in combat units was relatively weak, but in the event of a confrontation they could call on extremists, increasingly well provided with arms through the connivance of left-wing officers. At the top of the military hierarchy, President Costa Gomes, commander-in-chief since September 1974, remained largely a question-mark. Known simply as 'the General' his military prestige stemmed largely from the feeling widespread among the new constellation of young political generals and brigadiers that he was the only real general among them, the only one who had exercised an army command in wartime, the only one

The Resistance

whose promotion had not been the result solely of a political popularity contest. However, his influence was directed almost exclusively toward preventing bloodshed, which too often found him on the side of his prime minister, Vasco Gonçalves, rather than fighting to re-establish discipline or help moderate officers take the revolution in hand.

The youth of the service commanders bolstered Costa Gomes' prestige, but did little for discipline. Navy chief Admiral Pinheiro de Azevedo passed for a convinced leftist and, although he later defected to the moderates, for months he allowed his executive officer Martins Guerreiro to restructure and purge the navy, transforming it into a Gonçalvist stronghold. The air force was traditionally more moderate, despite the command substitution of Morais e Silva for Mendes Diás after 11 March. Morais e Silva hesitated to join the moderates, but finally sided with them to oppose Vasco Gonçalves' nomination as army chief on 31 August. The vast majority of air force officers kept the left at arm's length, but their operational potential was restricted. Of their four principal bases, only Sintra was relatively inaccessible to a pro-communist population or naval base, or free from paratroop battalions which had attracted the special attention of left-wing agitators after 11 March.

Control of the army was obviously a vital concern for all political groups, and here the moderates were hopeful. Army commander Fabião had proved increasingly unable to cope with the discipline crisis which left regional commanders with a large degree of autonomy. The north was stuffed with locally recruited combat units which largely reflected the conservative political bias of that region. Left-wing attempts to bring northern officers to heel by the appointment of Eurico Corvacho, an officer close to Prime Minister Gonçalves, to that command had not been successful and northern officers continued to provide the most consistent support for moderate initiatives. Franco Charais, commander of the centre military region, worked from the beginning to keep politics out of his command, and was largely successful except among units stationed in the university town of Coimbra. Moderate control of the centre was essential in isolating Corvacho from his Lisbon support base, and Charais obliged by becoming the first regional commander to condemn publicly the increasingly 'totalitarian' slant of the revolution.[18]

Military discipline in the Lisbon region suffered all the disadvantages of a large, politicized population and a left-leaning commander, Otelo de Carvalho. However, important combat units remained largely

202 *The Resistance*

untouched by disorder — the commandos, the infantry school at Mafra, the cavalry school at Santarém. Carvalho's eventual replacement as Lisbon commander by Vasco Lourenço pushed the paratroops into revolt on 25 November, but the remainder of the garrison refused to follow. In the south, Pezarat Correia also sided with the moderates, but was forced to remain discreet in a region known for its pro-communist sympathies.

Moderate officers meeting secretly from mid-July elected to follow a defensive strategy, calculating that an attempt to crush the left would lead to a dangerous military confrontation which could suck in well-organized civilian leftists. Moderates would also risk being stamped as 'reactionary' or 'counter-revolutionary', a sure formula for failure in a country permanently tensed for a military *coup*. They elected to work legally through government and MFA institutions, and to establish close links with the moderate political parties. Moderates would speak out in all MFA organizations, especially in the Revolutionary Council, to keep up a vigorous debate on the direction of the revolution and to denounce totalitarian tendencies. The authority of moderates in the government and the forces would be bolstered, but the initiative for military confrontation would be left to the extremists. Aided by the political parties, moderates began an active campaign to underwrite the activities of the constitutional government, in particular of the new Constituent Assembly. Soldiers launched a campaign to root out dissidents in the units and reaffirm the value of traditional military discipline.

Remembering their pre-25 April experiences, moderates split into political and military groups. The political group under Vasco Lourenço included five officers on the Revolutionary Council — Sousa e Castro, Alves, Antunes and Crespo — who set out to define a strategy to be followed in the Council and the MFA assemblies and were charged with contacting sympathetic politicians. The military group under Ramalho Eanes included Garcia dos Santos, Vasco Rocha Vieira, Loureiro dos Santos, Tomé Pinto and José Manuel Barrocco, who charged Costa Bras to draw up a plan to follow in the event of a military confrontation. A small information section was also set up to offset the propaganda monopoly of the left. Although the group was not disciplined in a formal sense, the good relations between Lourenço and Eanes assured close cooperation.[19]

At the head of the political committee, Vasco Lourenço cleverly directed a tactic which aimed to dislocate the Gonçalvist strong points. He calculated that an unqualified attack on the MFA's revolutionary

The Resistance 203

organs would be denounced as counter-revolutionary, so he sought to shift the centre of political decision-making away from the left-dominated Revolutionary Council and the MFA Assembly to the branch assemblies where, in the army and air force at least, moderates were in a majority. At the same time, he looked to use his personal influence with Carvalho gradually to pry apart the COPCON-Gonçalvist alliance, which he judged 'theoretically incompatible'. He also feared the growing influence of Gonçalvist officers within COPCON, which threatened to lend a much needed punch to the Prime Minister's power pretensions.

Vasco Lourenço's counter-attack began in the 23 July meeting of the Infantry Assembly. Sensing that the mood of the infantry unit delegates was favourable to a harsh reassessment of the MFA's political stance, he presented and had voted by a substantial margin motions calling for the dissolution of the fifth division, for reducing the MFA Assembly to a consultative organ with no legislative power, for a secret vote in all military assemblies, a reallocation of seats in the MFA Assembly based on proportional representation in each service – a motion which aimed to slice away the influence of the left-wing navy – and finally a call for the resignation of the Prime Minister. This first success, enthusiastically greeted by moderate officers, was not, however, repeated the next day in the Army Assembly, chaired by Carlos Fabião. Vasco Lourenço launched a stinging attack on the MFA Assembly's 8 July rejection of the Political Action Plan (PAP) and its adoption of the *Guide Document.* He told the army delegates that communist influence in the MFA had lost it much popular support: 'A revolution is a revolution only when it is made with the people and not against them', he said. 'If the revolution is made against the real interests of the people, they will abandon the movement.' He suggested to army officers that the revolution might flourish better without Vasco Gonçalves. Lourenço was immediately attacked as an agent of the socialist party, which he vigorously denied. But in the face of concerted opposition, he elected to withdraw the motions voted the day before by the Infantry Assembly.

The Army Assembly had produced no concrete results, but had allowed Lourenço to state his case and announce to those inside and outside the armed forces that resistance was organizing to the increasingly radical stance of the MFA. On the night of 24 July, moderate officers met to draw up a strategy to be followed in the MFA Assembly meeting scheduled for the following day. Melo Antunes, Vítor Crespo, Vítor Alves, Costa Neves and Canto e Castro signed a document

204 The Resistance

claiming that the Assembly was meeting illegally. Their claim was based on the 16 July instruction of the Revolutionary Council that the Assembly would next meet to discuss a plan to overcome Portugal's political crisis to be drawn up by Costa Gomes, Vasco Gonçalves and Otelo de Carvalho. The moderates held that this 25 July meeting had been called by Assembly radicals with a view to purging moderates on the Revolutionary Council. Alves and Aventino Teixeira met President Costa Gomes to inform him of their plans. At the same time, Alves phoned Carvalho who was visiting Cuba to gain his support against a possible renewal of Gonçalvist purges of moderate officers, especially those in the northern military region who were approving motions voted in the Infantry Assembly in defiance of Corvacho. On 25 July, Carvalho instructed his COPCON staff not to allow purges, driving the first wedge between himself and Gonçalves in the first step to the Prime Minister's eventual isolation.

On 25 July, Costa Gomes delivered a sobering warning to Assembly delegates that the speed of the revolution was rapidly losing the support of the Portuguese people. 'In Lisbon, we have a political microcosm which is able to absorb advanced political opinions, but its influence. . . stretches to a radius of perhaps 30 kilometres. We risk leaving the rest of the country behind. . .The revolution has picked up a speed which the people are not able to follow.' He also suggested that radicalism placed political and economic links with neighbouring countries at risk, and threatened Portugal's territorial integrity. An open door to the East and the Third World would not compensate for the fact that 80 per cent of Portugal's trade was with the West, or that Madeira and the Azores might go their own ways. 'It seems to me, sincerely, that national independence is not compatible in the short term with any strategy which involves hostility to the West', he said.

Vasco Gonçalves replied in a improvised speech that the rapid march of the revolution was made necessary by the hold of monopolistic capitalists on the Portuguese economy. He denied that the MFA left aimed to destroy the small and medium bourgeoisie. Europe was frightened by the spectre of a left-wing military, he said. Portugal must show a firm commitment to socialism and demonstrate that the government was well in control of the country. The outside world would not then be tempted to intervene.[20] Gonçalves then presented a plan for Portugal's political organization which reflected his group's desire for strong central organization with its men in key posts. Vasco Lourenço immediately objected that the plan had not been approved by the Revolutionary Council and so could not be

The Resistance   205

discussed by the Assembly. He accused Gonçalves of attempting to bypass the Revolutionary Council and threatened to walk out, taking most of the army delegates with him. Costa Gomes persuaded Gonçalves to withdraw his programme, and Lourenço remained.

July 25 found moderate officers in a strong position. Their unified opposition had prevented the Gonçalvist officers using the Revolutionary Council and MFA Assembly as rubber stamps for their political programme. They had also demonstrated that a majority of army delegates were prepared to back a moderate attempt to put the revolution back into touch. On the night of 25 July, moderate officers met to consider an appeal for support to the masses of the armed forces. Intoxicated with his success, Vasco Lourenço urged that they issue a 'cry of revolt', a quickly drawn up document denouncing Gonçalvist penetration of the MFA and the government and capitalizing on the growing spirit of revolt among professional officers. Antunes, however, urged caution, holding that a more carefully thought out document clearly stating commitment to a progressive Portugal might stop the moderates being denounced as reactionaries.

Any hesitation vanished with the news on 1 August that the commandos at Amadora, close to Lisbon, had voted to oust their commander Colonel Jaime Neves, eight other officers and four sergeants for their reactionary views. 'The need to reinforce the alliance between the people and the MFA implies a correct insertion of military units within the population and a discipline perfectly adapted to the will of the masses to construct socialism', said the COPCON communiqué announcing the dismissals – a serious setback to the moderates, who had counted on Neves' disciplined commandos to stand in the front ranks in any shootout with the left.

Life in the middle of Lisbon's industrial red belt had been difficult for the commandos, especially since 11 March. In April, General Fabião had suggested to Neves that he purge five regular officers, including the regiment's second in command, Major Pinho Bandeira. Neves called a meeting of all officers the following day to ask if there were any complaints against any of the five officers mentioned. As there were none, he promptly forgot the matter. In May, seven regulars backed by milicianos called for the removal from the regiment of the five officers 'for lack of political confidence'. In an officers' assembly, Neves demanded an explanation, and when none was forthcoming, the regular officers voted unanimously to exclude the seven who had made the proposal. 'We backed the five and purged the seven, but I noted a certain hesitation, due naturally to the climate of terror which reigned

206   *The Resistance*

during the Gonçalvist period', Neves said.

Toward the end of July, the appearance in the regiment of many political leaflets announced the beginning of a campaign directed against Neves and the commandos. On the night of 30 July, Major Lobato de Faria, one of the officers whose purge had been demanded, telephoned Neves to tell him that rumours, apparently believed by many troops, were circulating in the regiment claiming that their colonel was planning a *coup d'état* with CIA backing. Neves raced to the barracks and made the rounds to explain that the rumours were nonsense. All appeared calm and he went home, noting however, as he left, the presence of Captain Patrocínio, the officer who had called for the expulsion of the five 'reactionary' officers. At 04.00 on the morning of 31 July, he was awakened by a phone call claiming to be from the socialist party and warning him that the communists planned to take over his barracks. A call to the duty officer confirmed that all was well, but at 05.30 Major Lobato de Faria telephoned to say that several soldiers had occupied the arms room and blocked the door with three armoured cars. Neves arrived at the regiment to find Captain Patrocínio in command of the arms room with twenty mutinous soldiers. The Captain coolly informed Neves that he was no longer in command. Carvalho was called and arrived within twenty minutes. He went immediately into the arms room and talked with the insurgents for some fifteen minutes. When he walked out, he informed Neves that he had 'lost the confidence of his men' and directed him to report immediately to general staff headquarters, brushing aside the Colonel's demands for a unit assembly. 'As Otelo was leaving', Neves remembered, 'a VW appeared driven by João Valente, of the Amadora communist party, who greeted Otelo and said to him: "Have we won, Brigadier?" Otelo returned the greeting and smiled.'

Neves' exclusion from his regiment came as a body blow to moderate hopes of re-establishing a political equilibrium in the forces. But the obvious communist hand in the affair, its embarrassingly large press coverage, even abroad, and Lourenço's pressure on Carvalho to reinstate Neves, caused the COPCON Commander to reconsider his decision. 'On 3 August, Otelo ordered me to report to COPCON', Neves said. 'I had my doubts about going there, and before I went took the precaution of strapping on two pistols and a hand grenade.' On his arrival at the Alto do Duque, however, he was greeted warmly by Carvalho who told him that he had learned of a plot against him which he believed to be communist inspired. He accompanied Neves back to his regiment where he urged assembled troops to support their

The Resistance
207

commander. Neves was reinstated in his command by a show of hands; the twenty mutineers were purged.[21] A 4 August COPCON communiqué sent to all regiments pointed out the dangers of the 'interference of political groups and their divisive and pernicióus activities in a unit which until now has been cohesive, highly disciplined and faithful to the MFA'. The communiqué stressed that military democracy was expressed in unit assemblies, not in mutinous acts: 'This command cannot permit actions of this sort to continue.' Once again, Carvalho had intervened to help moderates over a rough spot.

Neves' reinstatement was not the only setback for the Prime Minister. Riots continued to rock the north, and in Lisbon the socialists, PPD and CDS were slamming his attempts to govern the country with a patchwork cabinet of communists, MDP and a few radical officers. Moderates judged the moment right to release their protest document. On the night of 6 August, the paper drawn up by Antunes was discussed and suggestions of Crespo and Costa Bras incorporated. At 21.00 it was printed and signed immediately by Lourenço, Antunes, Alves, Sousa e Castro, Costa Neves, Vítor Crespo and Canto e Castro. The group then split up, to disseminate the document in various regiments throughout Portugal and to escape arrest. The following day, Franco Charais signed in Coimbra and Pezarat Correia in Evora, giving the moderates the support of two regional commanders to complete the 'nine'. An attempt to involve COPCON failed when Marques Junior refused to sign unless Carvalho signed. Carvalho refused.

Reaction to the document was immediate. Costa Gomes suggested to Lourenço that the timing was 'inopportune', Gonçalvists attempted to prevent distribution and the fifth division was hysterical, threatening harsh punishments for any soldier who dared sign the Antunes document. The chiefs of the navy and air force, and of the Lisbon and northern military regions forbade its circulation — but did not prevent it accumulating the signatures and votes of more than 80 per cent of regular army officers. The Naval Assembly, politically so unrepresentative of that service, excluded Crespo, the only one of its members to sign. The chiefs of staff voted to suspend Revolutionary Council signatories, an action which succeeded only in drawing support to the moderates.

The 'Document of the Nine' was a harsh indictment of the influence of radicals on the revolution. The officers stressed that they were not attempting to divide the country, but merely exercising their civic duty to speak out against abuses of government. 'Since the elections for the Constituent Assembly, the march toward socialism has become

208   *The Resistance*

irreversible', read the document.

> However, in spite of the dynamization of the process and the
> support of the people, things have moved too fast to avoid tearing
> the existing social and cultural fabric. The social and economic
> organization of the small and medium bourgeoisie quickly
> disintegrated, without new structures being created to guarantee the
> management of production and distribution units and to maintain a
> minimum of morality in the relationships among all Portuguese.
> Hand in hand with this, we have witnessed a progressive deterioration
> of the state machinery. Wild and anarchistic forms of management
> have appeared everywhere, even within the MFA itself. Well-
> organized partisan organizations eager to seize the various power
> centres have tried to profit from the disorder. The MFA, which at
> first claimed to be above the parties, has become increasingly a
> prisoner of the manoeuvres of parties and popular organizations. It
> has finally compromised itself with a determined political programme
> out of step with its initial vocation and with the role which the
> people expected of it. The country is profoundly shaken. It feels
> that the great hopes to which the MFA gave birth have been betrayed.

The document continued that a 'revolutionary *avant-garde'* was trying
'brutally' to force through a programme supported only by a 'minority. .
of the proletariat around Lisbon and the Alentejo, not taking into
account the historical, social or cultural reality of the people'. For this
reason, the situation in Angola and in Portugal was getting out of hand
and threatening to compromise the gains of the revolution, the nine
maintained. Large sections of the press, the radio and television 'are
submitted to a rigid partisan control. As a result, we are confronted
with the degrading and shameful spectacle of a large part of our
population who listen to foreign news broadcasts for news about our
country.' They blasted plans to establish a 'news analysis committee —
why not call it the censorship committee?'

The officers rejected both the 'totalitarian, bureaucratic' model of
the states of eastern Europe which Vasco Gonçalves was attempting to
force on the country, and Western social democracy as unsuitable for
Portugal. They called instead for a socialist régime constructed
'gradually, without convulsions, peacefully. This objective will not be
reached until the Leninist theory of the "revolutionary *avant-garde*",
which imposes its doctrines in a violent and sectarian manner, is
superseded by solid social support for national transition toward

The Resistance

socialism. . .This socialistic model is inseparable from liberties, rights and fundamental guarantees.' The MFA must return to its original political neutrality, 'energetically rejecting anarchy and populism which lead inevitably to the catastrophic dissolution of the state'. The government must be reinforced to bring an end to

> . . .the arbitrary decisions of the 5th division, of the MFA Assembly, of *ad hoc* military assemblies, called suddenly and mysteriously, of the dynamization cabinets, of the Revolutionary Council, of COPCON, of the unions, etc. How can the government govern in these conditions? What authority can it have? No plan can be drawn up and applied without a government capable of executing the overall political plan defined by the MFA and backed by the necessary authority to be obeyed. . .The country risks being submerged in a wave of uncontrolled violence. . .It is ridiculous to suggest, as have certain political parties and news media, that it is a question of 'reactionary manoeuvres'. The discontent, the malaise, the agony are real and clear for all to see. Their profound causes lie in the errors of political decisions accumulated over the last months as well as in the practical policies of the MFA. We must reconquer the confidence of the Portuguese. Appeals to hate, incitements to violence, bitterness must cease. We must construct a society based on tolerance and peace, and not on new mechanisms of repression and exploitation. This is not possible with the present government, even if partially reshuffled. It lacks the credibility and the capacity to govern.

The 'Document of the Nine' was coupled with a fierce attack on Vasco Gonçalves by Mário Soares, in an open letter to the President of the Republic. The government, he pointed out, was based on barely 18 per cent of the electorate; 'a government, if not of communists, at least of crypto-communists or of elements closely associated with them.' He cited the 'tragedy of Angola', press censorship, separatism in the Azores, illegal occupations, the increasing divisions of the Portuguese, the increasing international isolation of the country, 'the prisons, more full than during fascism' as the result of a ruinous government policy which aimed to impose a 'socialism of misery' on the country. He appealed to the President to use his constitutional powers to dismiss the government.

In the north, violence continued and the army appeared increasingly unable, or unwilling, to control crowds who sacked local communist

210 The Resistance

headquarters. Regional recruitment meant that units in the northern command shared the political opinions of the conservative north, not those of the MFA left. 'Why don't we intervene?', said a captain in Braga whose unit looked on as a crowd swept through the PCP offices. 'We arrived too late. And besides, you don't seriously expect us to fire on our neighbours and friends.'[22] Large demonstrations greeted Fabião, Carvalho and Corvacho in Porto, crying 'the people are no longer with the MFA'. Northern military commanders meeting with the three generals declared that their troops were 'totally exhausted, physically and mentally, after trying to keep order day and night at hot points in the North'. MDP and communist headquarters were sacked in several towns, and in Fafe on 7 August young communists fired into an ugly crowd surrounding their headquarters, killing one and wounding five.

August 1975 became a month of political manoeuvrings, governmental crisis and growing popular violence which reduced foreign ministries in many western capitals to a pulp of apprehension. Having refused to sign the 'Document of the Nine', Carvalho replied with his own programme, 'COPCON's Revolutionary Autocritique and Proposal for a Political Programme' published on 13 August. The language betrayed the vague populism which had come to characterize COPCON communiqués, but joined with the nine in criticizing Gonçalvist attempts to capture the state machine as a prelude to a 'totalitarian' solution to Portugal's political crisis. The 'Revolutionary Autocritique' sealed Carvalho's break with the Gonçalvist faction, while claiming to be 'the only vital and realistic proposal which offers the Portuguese people a successful socialist society, and which constitutes a firm and total rejection of FASCISM, SOCIAL DEMOCRACY AND STATE CAPITALISM, forms of exploitation which negate the real emancipation of the working classes'.

Having split Carvalho and Gonçalves, moderate officers looked to seal at least a temporary alliance with COPCON as part of their plan to dump the Prime Minister. Meetings between the nine and Carvalho aiming to strike a short-term political strategy took place on 13, 14 and 17 August in the house of Gomes Mota, and on 16 August in Lourenço's office in the general staff headquarters. In a final meeting on 19 August in the presence of Costa Gomes, the COPCON commander told the President that Gonçalves must go, adding that if he did not then the soldiers would be forced to find a new chief of state. Meanwhile, on 18 August, Sousa e Castro and Ramalho Eanes left to visit military units in the north and south to test the solidity of moderate support. On the night of 20 August, Alves, Antunes and

The Resistance 211

Vasco Lourenço arranged to meet army chief Fabião to discuss the
possibility of his replacing Gonçalves as prime minister on 24 August.
The choice of Fabião reflected the clear tactical thinking of the
moderates, who hoped to substitute one of their own at the top of
the army with a prime minister they could control through the
nomination of Alves and Crespo as vice-premiers. Antunes would be
given the foreign ministry, Almeida Santos justice and Alves social
communications. Four portfolios would be handed to the socialists
and three to the PPD, while the communists would be offered the
choice of the labour ministry or a spell in opposition. Eanes would
take over the Military Academy. The plan collapsed, however, when
the enigmatic Fabião failed to appear. Officers sent to find him finally
traced him to his father-in-law's house at Trafaria near Lisbon, but
Fabião refused to come, claiming that he was under 'popular vigilance',
that agents in the pay of Gonçalves watched his every move. The
moderates concluded that perhaps a stronger character was needed
under the circumstances.

A meeting on 25 August brought together MFA leaders and the
chiefs of the general staff to hammer out a compromise. Fabião
renounced any intention of becoming prime minister and it was
decided to name left-wing naval chief Azevedo to chair the council
of ministers, while shifting Vasco Gonçalves to the armed forces chief
of staff position. In return, Costa Gomes proposed that the
Revolutionary Council reintegrate the five members of the 'nine'. The
compromise left moderates apprehensive: there was little in Azevedo's
record to suggest he was anything but a convinced Gonçalves supporter.
For more than a year he had presided over the service counted as the
Prime Minister's safest power bastion. But like many officers who saw
that the power balance was shifting in the moderates' favour, he
changed his political tack almost overnight.

But the pill which moderates refused to swallow was Vasco
Gonçalves' nomination as armed forces chief of staff. They argued
that from this powerful position, Gonçalves would be able to purge
the armed forces of moderate officers. As the Revolutionary Council
was scheduled to confirm the 25 August decisions in a meeting on 29
August — a meeting at which the five moderates would not be present
because they had been excluded for signing the 'Document of the
Nine' — they had to strike directly at Gonçalves. Vasco Lourenço
urged Carvalho to launch a tactical operation against Gonçalvist control
of the media, suggesting that the fifth division and *Diário de Notícias*
and *Século* be occupied. On 26 August, Carvalho agreed to break up

212   *The Resistance*

the fifth division, but objected that the closing of two newspapers by force of arms might shake public opinion. The action was handed to Jaime Neves' commandos who occupied the fifth division and its Centre of Military Sociology without resistance on 27 August. Costa Gomes was not consulted beforehand. On 29 August, the nine denounced that day's meeting of the Revolutionary Council as illegal, because the five ousted members were not present. 'As representatives of the feelings of 80 per cent of the armed forces in Portugal, its adjacent islands, in Macau, Timor and Angola', read their statement to the press,

> and believing to be interpreters of the proven desire of the overwhelming majority of the Portuguese people, we unequivocally inform the President of the Republic of our disassociation from all the decisions recently taken (by the Revolutionary Council), most especially the possible designation of General Vasco Gonçalves as chief of staff of the armed forces.

The moderate communiqué raised a storm of protest in the army and the country against the Revolutionary Council's nomination of Gonçalves. The left, however, hoped to confirm it in the MFA Assembly scheduled for 5 September. Moderate tactics called for persuading the preliminary Army and Air Force Assemblies to boycott the 5 September meeting. The 2 September Army Assembly was moved from Lisbon to Tancos to discourage left-wing attempts to influence its decisions. Fabião opened the meeting with a warning that increasing divisions in the MFA could lead to civil war, and denounced the 'café programmes' which passed for serious political thinking. However, Fabião's grip on his command had long since grown weak, and Vasco Lourenço got an enthusiastic majority for a proposal that army delegates boycott the MFA Assembly until its representation was more equally distributed. Soldiers voted 190 to 47 with 40 abstentions against the nomination of Vasco Gonçalves as commander-in-chief. A similar vote was recorded the next day in the Air Force Assembly. Costa Gomes ordered Fabião to call a new Army Assembly to reconsider the 2 September decision, which Fabião scheduled for 5 September. Costa Gomes appeared to hear an appeal from Vasco Gonçalves to the army delegates to support his nomination. Antunes then stood up to denounce the abuses of Gonçalves' ministry and his political designs on the country's future, interrupted on several occations by Gonçalves crying 'lies, lies, all lies'. Gonçalves' reply was

The Resistance 213

cut short by a stinging attack by Vasco Lourenço which sent the ex-Prime Minister storming from the Assembly. The army, joined by the air force, voted once again to boycott the MFA Assembly. Costa Gomes held the MFA Assembly anyway, with only navy delegates and the rump of the other two services, but Gonçalves realized that he had lost and withdrew his name from consideration.

The moderates' victory was sealed by a restructuring of the Revolutionary Council, judged to have become too large. Voting in each service assembly returned Rosa Coutinho, Almada Contreiras and Martins Guerreiro for the navy, but excluded left-wingers Ramiro Correia and Miguel Judas. The air force voted in Pinho Freire, Canto e Castro and Costa Neves, sending home leftists Graça e Cunha, Costa Martins and Pereira Pinto. In the army, moderates led by Vasco Lourenço, Pezarat Correia, Melo Antunes, Franco Charais and Sousa e Castro were elected. Marques Junior, close to Carvalho, was also returned, but radicals Vasco Gonçalves, Ferreira de Sousa, Ferreira de Macedo and Eurico Corvacho were voted out. The only moderate casualty was Vítor Alves.

Having eased Corvacho out of the Revolutionary Council, moderates looked to take him out of the northern command to which he had been named in the aftermath of 11 March. Lourenço asked Fabião to remove Corvacho, on the grounds that his political views had seriously compromised his ability to command the north. Fabião refused, pushing Lourenço to dramatize his case. Sousa e Castro arranged for several northern unit commanders to refuse to recognize Corvacho, informing Fabião that they henceforth took orders from Franco Charais at Coimbra. After negotiations at Alto da Serra on the Lisbon-Porto road, Fabião agreed to substitute Pires Veloso, giving moderates command of another military region and reducing left-wing influence almost exclusively to Lisbon. Franco Charais announced that the left would be committing suicide if it attempted to take power by force.

Azevedo's sixth provisional government took office on 19 September with only five soldiers, including Azevedo, in a moderate cabinet dominated by socialists and popular democrats and including Antunes and Alves. The communists had to be content with the public works ministry. Costa Gomes charged the new prime minister to win 'the economic battle. . .and consolidate the gains of the revolution'. 'The cohesion of the MFA and armed forces discipline are the basic factors for the success or failure of the revolution', Azevedo replied.

Military discipline seemed on the point of collapse, especially after

214   *The Resistance*

the September appearance of Soldados Unidos Vencerão (SUV) —
Soldiers United will Win — an attempt by the extreme left to reverse
at the base of the armed forces the victory the moderates had won so
laboriously at the top. Many suspected that the communists had a
heavy hand in the SUV. Soares said:

> Dispossessed by the MFA, rejected by a very large majority of the
> people, often hated and feared, the communists did not want to let
> go. Short of munitions in other fields, they brought out the
> unbelievable SUV: from then, I was sure that they planned to
> create havoc. Perhaps they had begun the last round. The
> communists played a primary role [in SUV]. But, above all, it was
> they who would benefit from the indiscipline and demoralization.[23]

Hooded SUV leaders told the press on 7 September that they intended
to disrupt military regiments so that the army would never turn against
the revolution in Portugal as it had done in Chile. SUV propaganda
called for:

> the free circulation of the workers' press and propaganda, [soldiers'
> assemblies], the constitution of soldiers' committees, organs of the
> workers in uniform within the barracks, elected and subject to
> recall at any moment by a plenary assembly, the expulsion of
> reactionary officers, free transportation, a common mess, against
> militarist discipline.

They told a Porto press conference on 21 September, 'We side on the
barricades with the oppressed and the exploited.'[24]

> One might have understood had the SUV appeared in April 1974,
> when we did not really know what the captains wanted. One could
> have had doubts then. But 18 months later it was nonsensical and I
> criminal. In all this time, the founders of the SUV had been
> flattering the armed forces movement, praising its role of
> revolutionary *avant-garde*, rattling on about the miracle alliance of
> the people and the MFA. . .and suddenly, when the top organs of
> the movement escaped PC control, we saw the barrack soviets
> flourish: a troubling coincidence. In an instant, this army that we
> venerated and flattered became an instrument of counter-
> revolution, an enemy of the people. . .What were soldiers' and sailors'

The Resistance   215

soviets taken straight out of Petrograd and Cronstadt, hardly dusted
off and carrying instructions dating from 1917, doing in the Portugal
of 1975?. . .How can one not see, not understand the rage of most
officers before these untidy troops saluting with clenched fists?[25]

SUV's first appearance was in Porto on 10 September, when an
estimated 1,500 troops marched through the city crying: 'Down with
Fabião'. On 23 September, three hooded men in uniform told reporters
that the success of SUV in Porto had encouraged the revolutionaries to
try their luck further south, to 'oppose a return of the bourgeois order'.
'SUV wants to prepare the conditions for the destruction of the
bourgeois army and the creation of the military arm of the workers'
power — the popular revolutionary army'.[26] This was followed by a
large demonstration in Lisbon in which soldiers, sailors and civilian
supporters marched to the Trafaria prison to demand — and obtain —
the release of two soldiers arrested at Mafra. COPCON soldiers were
noticeably reluctant to defend the prison.

In the wake of the 25 September Lisbon demonstration, the
government voted to establish a Military Intervention Group (AMI)
'to give the government an indispensable means of exercising authority'.
Antunes complained that COPCON had 'gone beyond its orders' and
that a new force under the direct orders of the President was needed to
cool the political violence which was fast growing uncontrollable. The
infantry regiment at Setúbal, the infantry school at Mafra and the
commandos were designated to lead the AMI, placed under Brigadier
Melo Egidio. The government also added regiments from the north and
Angola, and recalled reservists who could bolster the government's
authority. Fourteen officers and 45 sergeants, all ex-commandos, were
put back in uniform in the first week of October in response to Fabião's
call for soldiers who 'offer guarantees of a disciplined conscience and
a spirit of abnegation'.

But the AMI, designed to act as a COPCON in the hands of
moderation and perhaps eventually as the nucleus for a professional
force, never really operated as a unified command. On 9 October, the
PCP denounced AMI as part of the government's campaign against
'popular forces'. On 29 September, after a weekend of riots which saw
the sacking of the Spanish embassy with COPCON troops looking on,
a passive accomplice to the protest against Spain's 27 September
executions of five young anti-government terrorists, Prime Minister
Azevedo ordered the military occupation of several radio and television
stations whose 'workers' were inciting the left to further violence on

216   *The Resistance*

the air. COPCON troops, given the task, predictably fraternized with the occupiers. Carvalho withdrew his soldiers, and then gave a press conference which announced his reservations about the increasing disorder provoked by the left. He also admitted, in effect, his declining influence on Portuguese politics, which was now a straight struggle between order and anarchy. 'I lack a political education', he told reporters. 'If I had this background, I could have been the Fidel Castro of Europe.' He pleaded that he was a true revolutionary: 'I will always struggle against the exploitation of man by man. I made many mistakes because I lacked a political education, but I always succeeded in avoiding civil war. . .' He had never fought for power, only for his ideas. 'The revolutionary left does not have a vocation to govern', he continued, 'only to remain in opposition.' The left's insistence on pushing through 'an extremely violent revolution' was pushing the country toward reaction. If 'the people' were looking to Carvalho as their Napoleon, all they got was Boulanger.

The next two months were the most turbulent in the history of the revolution. October began with a massive rally of socialists, popular democrats and Angolan refugees in support of firm government. SUV-inspired disorder disturbed Lisbon and Queluz, and in Beja paratroops were flown in to control airmen rioting over the arrest of four comrades after an SUV march. Dinís de Almeida claimed that the government planned to shut down RALIS, but that he and his men were prepared to defend the barracks. Left-wing demonstrators shouted their support in front of RALIS, while an estimated 30,000 people led by 2,000 men in uniform marched through Porto crying 'up with our miserable pay! Free transportation! Revolutionary unity between workers, peasants, soldiers and sailors!'

Opposition in Porto centred on the transportation school (CICAP). When Pires Veloso closed it down on 6 October, soldiers immediately occupied the barracks of the heavy artillery regiment (RASP) and established a 'coordinating committee for the reopening of CICAP' which denounced the sixth government as 'the guard dog of the bourgeoisie', demanded the replacement of Veloso, the reopening of CICAP, and the reintegration in the regiment of five soldiers and two officers transferred for their political views.

The closing of CICAP and the occupation of the heavy artillery barracks were interpreted by many as a sign that the revolution at last was spreading beyond the 'Lisbon commune' to paralyze the northern regiments to which the government looked for support. Revolutionary soldiers in Porto claimed the support of soldiers in

The Resistance   217

eighteen northern regiments. 'Minority groups. . .today have managed to lock up the entire country by the systematic intoxication of the army', declared Porto's Rádio Renascença, still in the hands of the Church, in an observation which seemed confirmed by a demonstration of 2,000 soldiers in Charais' Coimbra.

However, the Porto occupations showed up a lack of support for revolutionaries in the northern regiments, and pitted moderate officers in a power struggle with Costa Gomes and Fabião in which they eventually came out on top. While a small minority of militants existed in many regiments, few regiments outside Lisbon could claim to be dominated by the left. CICAP had become a dumping ground for troublesome soldiers from several northern regiments. Moderate officers hoped to maintain the 'operational' potential of their combat units by ridding themselves of discipline problems, whether politically inspired or otherwise. Grouped together at the transportation school, the ability of these soldiers to add substantial muscle to any left-wing revolt would be limited. When the school was closed and the inmates bolted for the heavy artillery regiment, few artillerymen remained to back them up. Their claims of support in eighteen northern regiments were based on the unit origins of the soldiers originally sent to CICAP. Likewise, the demonstrations in Coimbra, Porto and elsewhere were swelled by soldiers from Lisbon — with civilian supporters often dressed in uniforms — who were ferried around Portugal as a mobile revolutionary mob.

As a revolutionary organization, SUV was a total failure. When the left-wing military revolt came on 25 November, SUV was unable to move a man to support it. Its importance lay not in the clandestine web of subversion which it claimed to be weaving in the regiments, but in the illusion of instability and indiscipline which it created, aided by a manipulated press. Faced with a weak and politically compromised high command, and a president who appeared ready to sacrifice even military discipline if it postponed civil war for a few hours, officers were often forced to negotiate with their men rather than give orders to them. The background of political upheaval created by SUV and their civilian allies meant that soldiers often held the whip hand. A naval captain recalled:

One day as we were anchored off a small town in the South [of Angola], a small boat arrived with a refrigerator bought by one of the sailors. Most of the merchants were selling their goods for next to nothing just to get rid of them before leaving. I had forbidden

218   *The Resistance*

the sailors to buy them, not only because we had no room on the
ship, but also because I felt it was too much like plundering. So I
refused to allow it on board. A couple of his friends immediately
joined him, saying that the ratings would refuse to follow orders if
I did not allow it on board. So I met with them and was forced to
compromise. I took him and his refrigerator as far as Luanda, and
then I had them both transferred to another ship. I had more or less
decided to quit the navy when I returned to Portugal. I had no real
discipline problems, but it was the compromises I did not like;
they went against the grain.[27]

Most military indiscipline during this period had little political content,
and quickly evaporated when order was restored after 25 November.
   Moderate officers sensing this urged firm action against dissident
soldiers occupying the RASP barracks. Pires Veloso refused to
negotiate, and was backed up by the army staff and 10,000 socialists
who demonstrated their support in a Porto rally. But on 14 October,
Fabião turned up in Porto to talk to the left-wing troops. His decision
to reopen CICAP for 'sentimental reasons' angered many officers: the
Prime Minister told Costa Gomes that Charais should replace Fabião as
army chief. Already in the first week of October, Costa Gomes had
appeared on national television to appeal to soldiers for discipline: 'If
a soldier places his weapon in the service of his own political ideas, if
he does not have the revolutionary courage to accept the defeat of his
ideas in the face of positions which better serve the interests of the
people, if he does not rally, within the MFA, to the collective opinions
of the people whom he defends, then he is betraying his uniform, the
MFA and the country', the President said, warning soldiers not to let
themselves be manipulated by clandestine organizations who might
prepare the way for reaction. Azevedo lamented that 'soldiers who
carry out my orders are denounced as fascists, as reactionaries', and
underlined the importance of a disciplined army to the success of the
government: 'The re-establishment of military discipline is of
fundamental importance to Portugal if it wants the government to
have any authority', he said. 'If we wait another week, military
discipline could collapse all at once. If our army collapses. . .we will
not have any force, and after that there will be no more authority, no
more government.' The Revolutionary Council charged Fabião to
draw up suggestions to re-establish discipline with his four regional
commanders. But as disorder grew, capped by the left-wing break-in
on 21 October at Lisbon's Rádio Renascença to begin transmitting

The Resistance

calls for renewed revolution, Jaime Neves hinted darkly that 'armed conflict' was inevitable.

In November, Lisbon was virtually ungovernable and the Portuguese republic appeared headed for complete collapse. SUV meetings and demonstrations continued, especially around the capital. On 5 November, workers in the ministry of social communications attempted to kick out Ferreira da Cunha, a moderate army officer serving as secretary of state, claiming that he had run a 'counter-information service' under Caetano, a charge he vehemently denied. On 11 November, left-wing military police fired over the heads of socialist demonstrators, causing panic and redoubling demands for the dissolution of that increasingly indisciplined unit. But government impotence was underlined forcefully on 12 November when building workers led by a 'para-military militia' arrived at the National Assembly, sealed off all exits and blocked the newly elected deputies inside until the government agreed to grant them substantial wage increases. Azevedo phoned President Costa Gomes and demanded that he send troops to raise the siege. Costa Gomes replied that the police were too few, the Republican National Guard had been disarmed and the military police could not be counted upon. 'The President of the Republic, called on to act, replied that he did not have the force to make himself obeyed', Soares said. 'Power had fallen into the streets into the hands of a few agitators.'[28] Azevedo called on Jaime Neves to lift the siege. 'I am ready to do it', he told the Prime Minister, 'but I will not stop at São Bento. After that, I will make the rounds of the newspapers and the radio and television stations because I am not prepared to be treated yet again as a dirty fascist by a press under the orders of the communists. If you let me clean up all that, it's a deal. Otherwise, I'm not moving.'[29] Azevedo elected to give in to the building workers rather than the commando chief. Soares noted sourly that throughout the siege communist deputies were well supplied with chicken and sandwiches while moderates were forced to go hungry.

Since early October, the possibility of a 'Lisbon commune' had been seriously discussed by soldiers and politicians. When on 16 November, the PCP massed 70,000 demonstrators in Lisbon many believed the day had arrived at last. Soares, however, calculated from documents produced by officers in the fifth division that the final left-wing push was scheduled for January. '16 November was an important stage which permitted them to show their force and prepare new offensives which would modify little by little the differences in strength', Soares said. 'They wanted to regain control of the

220   *The Resistance*

revolutionary organs and then use them in a decisive manner.'[30] On 20 November, demonstrators calling for 'popular power' and a 'revolutionary government' marched on Belem, where they were told by Costa Gomes that: 'It is easier to launch an idea than to defend determined principles, which we judge better and which better serve the people. A civil war will not solve our problems.' The government appeared to be moving toward total paralysis and moderate officers and politicians looked helpless to prevent anarchy. French journalist Pierre Georges wrote a series of articles in *Le Monde* entitled 'The Soldiers of the Year II' and suggesting that the class war fanned by the SUV was spreading like wildfire in the barracks. Kenneth Maxwell predicted that civil war was 'impending' and could be avoided only by a 'miracle'.[31]

Notes

1. Soares, *Portugal, Quelle Revolution?* Paris, 1976, p.127.
2. Gomes Mota, *Expresso*, 23 April 1976.
3. Ibid.
4. Fremontier, *Portugal, Les Points sur les i*, Paris, 1976.
5. *O Jornal*, 28 November 1975.
6. Frémontier. op.cit., p.155.
7. Mota, *A Resistência*, Lisbon, 1976, p.30.
8. *Financial Times*, 20 June 1975.
9. Frémontier, op.cit., p.29.
10. Mota, op.cit., p.39.
11. Alleman, 'Withered Carnations', *Encounter*, December, 1975, p.86.
12. Frémontier, op.cit., pp.38-9.
13. Soares, op.cit., chap.10.
14. Frémontier, op.cit., pp.165-7.
15. Soares, op.cit., pp.143-5.
16. Mota, op.cit., p.55.
17. Harsgor, *Naissance d'un nouveau Portugal*, Portugal, Paris, 1975, p.174.
18. Mota, op.cit., pp.84-5.
19. Ibid., pp.98-9.
20. Ibid., pp.110-13.
21. For Neves affair, see Mota, ibid., pp.216-17, and *Le Monde*, 2, 3 & 8 August 1975.
22. *Le Monde*, 13 August 1975.
23. Soares, op.cit., p.184.
24. *Os SUV em Luta*, Lisbon, 1975, pp.19-10, 15.
25. Soares, op.cit., pp.183-5.
26. *Le Monde*, 23 September 1975.
27. Interview.
28. Soares, op.cit., p.190.
29. Ibid., p.191.
30. Ibid., p.193.

The Resistance

31. Maxwell, 'The Thorns of the Portuguese Revolution', *Foreign Affairs*, January 1976, pp.268-9.

8 25 NOVEMBER

Demonstrations, strikes, meetings, speeches, all-night sittings of the Revolutionary Council are the bread and butter of journalists and historians writing about the revolution. But a chronicle of these political events hardly conveys the reality of Portuguese life in the late summer and autumn of 1975. The revolution's short, sharp actions were separated by long periods of inactivity. The political graffiti decorating every available centimetre of wall, the peeling layers of party posters, the men grouped in front of newsagents' stalls to read the latest headlines announced to even the most casual tourist that Portugal was a country in turmoil. Lisbon was the front, the Verdun of the revolution, where politicians and soldiers fought tooth and nail for control of the government and the armed forces. But even there, shops kept regular hours, cafés and restaurants were full and queues formed in front of the cinemas for the eight o'clock film. Political beanos were conveniently scheduled for the early evening so that bank clerks, shop assistants and civil servants could march down the Avenida da Liberdade shouting the day's political watchword before returning home to their wives.

Thirty kilometres to the north or south of Lisbon the home front began, where discussions of the latest local gossip or the football fortunes of Benfica were only rarely interrupted by a visit of cultural dynamizers or by the sacking of the local PCP headquarters. And even then, only a few hundred yards from the crackle of gunfire, families paraded arm in arm, non-combatants praying for a quick peace.

The political demonstrations organized by the SUV, the leftists and communists aimed to create an illusion of instability, a revolutionary mirage for parched militants in a conservative desert. It was a tactic favoured by Foch, who had argued that to convince the enemy that you had won the battle was more important than the actual occupation of the terrain. 'The communist tactic is founded totally on blackmail', Soares claimed. 'They launch a campaign, intoxicate opinion, sow panic and look to make the adversary retreat. They think that the "enemy" will withdraw without their ever having to advance and deploy their forces. This is how they have worked — and scored many points — since 25 April, 1974, why should they not continue to be successful?'[1] The task of the moderates lay in exposing the weakness

25 November

of left-wing support, exploding their pretensions as the South Sea Bubble of revolutions. The problem was when and where to stick in the pin, to avoid deafening too many people with the pop.

In the face of growing anarchy provoked by the left, the moderates worked quietly to consolidate their control of key positions in the armed forces while waiting for the left to make a mistake. In late October, the government decided belatedly to exclude dissident soldiers from the forces, and in early November, air force chief Morais e Silva sent three captains and forty-nine airmen home after SUV disturbances in Beja. As Angolan independence neared on 11 November and units were ferried back to Portugal, the government terminated the service of several thousand milicianos and conscripts.[2] Moderate naval officers were in a state of near mutiny over the left-wing domination of their service. Already in September, 300 moderates had met at the Lisbon Naval Club to protest left-wing control of the Naval Assembly. Judas denounced them as 'reactionary' and the Naval Assembly threatened to suspend all officers present at the 'unauthorized meeting'. But *Expresso* reckoned that the split between the moderate majority of sailors and the Gonçalves-dominated leadership was beyond repair.[3]

In an early November meeting of the government and the Revolutionary Council, Prime Minister Azevedo criticized the weakness of several military chiefs, echoing the exasperation of many officers with the politics of Fabião and Carvalho.[4] The meeting decided to silence Rádio Renascença, and on 7 November paratroops blew up the transmitters. On 9 November, Azevedo denounced the communists and extreme left in a rally organized by the socialists, popular democrats and CDS. An important meeting of 25 moderate officers on 15 November at Laranjeiras chaired by Pinho Freire, on the eve of the large communist demonstration in Lisbon, discussed ways to discipline the news media, reinforce moderate military potential by arming the Republican National Guard and consolidate the sixth government. The officers present, who included the commanders of all of Portugal's air bases, then mapped out plans to organize resistance in the north and south if Lisbon fell to a left-wing revolt. Soares reckoned that awareness of this counter-strategy dissuaded Cunhal from taking the revolutionary plunge.[5] Lastly, they decided that Vasco Lourenço would replace Carvalho as Lisbon regional commander.[6]

On 18 November, Soares met with Vítor Crespo, Vítor Alves, Costa Bras, Vasco Lourenço and Melo Antunes to discuss a political strategy. All were aware that increasing anarchy had paralyzed the government, and that a 'psychological shock' was needed to jolt the country into

224   *25 November*

action. Several proposed that the government resign, but Soares objected that this was exactly what the communists hoped for. He proposed that ministers go on strike, an idea which appealed to all present except Antunes who argued that it was 'illegal' and would turn the political initiative over to the left. Azevedo called the cabinet which with the exception of the one communist minister voted to strike until the Revolutionary Council could guarantee its safety. Socialists backed the strike up with simultaneous popular demonstrations in twelve towns, and Soares had difficulty restraining many provincial party members keen to shoot it out with the communists. Costa Gomes pleaded with Soares to form a PS-PCP coalition, but the socialist leader refused, claiming that such a government would simply help Cunhal on his way to total power.[7]

The pretext for the 25 November revolt of the paratroops at Tancos lay in the Revolutionary Council's 20 November decision to name Vasco Lourenço to the Lisbon command, reviving the post of vice-chief of the armed forces for Carvalho, ironically the position held by Spinola before 25 April 1974. Some suggested that Lourenço's nomination was calculated to force left-wing soldiers to take up arms.[8] However, the moderates' strategy calling for diplomacy before confrontation and Lourenço's eagerness to strike an acceptable compromise with Carvalho indicate that they saw Lourenço's nomination as the prelude to a gradual purge of left-wing officers and the re-establishment of military discipline in the capital. Carvalho objected vigorously to the change of command when it was discussed on 20 November, to which Lourenço replied that he saw no reason why Carvalho should not continue as COPCON chief. As no acceptable solution could be struck immediately, Costa Gomes agreed to postpone a decision until 24 November.

On 21 November, Vasco Lourenço met at Belém with Carvalho, several COPCON officers and Costa Gomes. Carvalho said that he had complete personal confidence in Lourenço, but that this confidence was not shared by his subordinates. He also pointed out that Lourenço's nomination to the Lisbon command would mean his immediate and highly irregular promotion from major to brigadier, a strange objection given that Carvalho too had jumped two colonel ranks in his meteoric rise to brigadier. Lourenço repeated quietly that as regional commander he would never pretend to command Carvalho, but concluded that if his promotion were unacceptable to COPCON, then he would decline it. Costa Gomes repeated that the final decision rested with the Revolutionary Council. On the night of 23 November,

25 November

moderate officers met and decided that Vasco Lourenço's appointment was vital, not only to purge Lisbon regiments of leftists, but also to close down Contreiras' SDIC which guaranteed Gonçalvist control over a large section of the press.

November 25 became the left's 11 March and, like 11 March, the background to the events will probably never be fully known. The paratroops, part of the air force, had been counted among the moderate forces since the beginning of the new republic. Paratroops had surrounded the RALIS barracks on 11 March and on 7 November had carried out the Revolutionary Council's orders to blow up the Lisbon Rádio Renascença transmitters. Realizing that the paratroops substantially bolstered the moderates' operational potential, the left launched a campaign to win over the paratroop school at Tancos.

The campaign was led by the left-wing National Sergeants Committee and proved their most successful operation. Some officers had rallied to the MFA's left wing through a mixture of idealism and opportunism. The climate of indiscipline which grew in the late summer in many garrisons meant that soldiers were not infrequently led astray by left-wing militants. NCOs, however, remained the least affected by the revolution. Few had anything to gain through indiscipline. The shortage of officers before the revolution meant that qualified NCOs found it relatively easy to gain a commission, so that revolution offered them no greater opportunities for personal advancement. Indiscipline challenged their status and complicated their regimental tasks. The failure of the left to gain adherents among NCOs was one of the major stumbling blocks to its plans to control the forces. Left-wing converts were limited almost exclusively to conscript sergeants.

The National Sergeants Committee calculated that the recruitment of NCOs to their camp would break the command link between officers and men which guaranteed discipline. Several observers argued that the Tancos revolt was the work of soldiers aided by a few revolutionary sergeants. But paratroop officers claimed that plans to disrupt discipline in the battalion dated from mid-September, when the Central Coordinating Committee of Air Force Sergeants began to infiltrate Tancos with left-wing NCOs who gradually won over many soldiers in meetings and 'enlightenment sessions'.[9] These NCOs seized on the destruction of the Rádio Renascença transmitters and low morale following press diatribes against 'reactionary' paratroops to crack discipline in the battalion. A sergeants' meeting condemned the action and voted to ignore any future orders which went against the interests of the workers. They released a press communiqué stating

226   *25 November*

their position.

When Morais e Silva read of the decision, he immediately travelled to Tancos and called a meeting of the 1,600 men stationed there. Virtually all NCOs, however, boycotted the meeting attended by most of the officers and men. The air force chief explained that the destruction of Rádio Renascença had been ordered by the Revolutionary Council, and as such had to be carried out. Meanwhile, two left-wing sergeants had mobilized a small group of privates in the soldiers' club and surrounded the General as he left the meeting. One of the soldiers, who had participated in the Rádio Renascença operation, told Morais e Silva: 'The General is a bourgeois who has already made his class option! We have no business here!' He then shouted to the other soldiers: 'Comrades! Let's get out of here and go to the meeting of sergeants and soldiers!' Most of the soldiers promptly left to vote the sergeants' motion. Confronted with a revolt, the officers then held their own meeting. After deciding that they had been 'marginalized' and no longer effectively commanded their troops, 123 of 150 officers walked out of the barracks gates.[10]

When the Revolutionary Council met on 24 November, the decision of moderate officers to press Vasco Lourenço's nomination was reinforced by a revolt in Rio Maior of farmers — estimated by some to number 35,000 — protesting agricultural reform. The barricades they threw over the highway and railways effectively cutting communications between Lisbon and the north confirmed the fears of many officers that the population in the north needed little prodding to lay siege to the capital. When Lourenço's nomination was announced, Major Pessoa, who had assumed command of Tancos, called together NCOs and soldiers in two separate meetings: 'I am in this to the end', he told them. 'It is already too late to pull out. Now, everyone must accept his responsibility. For my part, I am ready to fight.'[11] Rather than get down to hard planning, however, a highly theoretical debate followed with Pessoa suggesting that the regiment must decide upon a political line and then appoint a 'hierarchy of competence' to give orders. A large number of sergeants argued that to adopt a political line was to admit political party influence within the armed forces. Repeating arguments lifted straight out of the SUV pamphlets, they claimed that hierarchies created anomalies which led to class struggle. Soldiers must have the right of all citizens to refuse to carry out orders which went against their conscience. This sterile debate only finished when Pessoa was called away to answer the telephone.[12]

Throughout the night of 24-25 November, officers in various

25 November

left-wing Lisbon units and representatives of the Soldiers' and Sailors' Committee which aimed to become an efficient alternative to the SUV met at COPCON headquarters to tell Carvalho that they acknowledged only him as the legitimate commander. Carvalho refused to commit himself to revolt preferring the limited objective of bringing down the government.[13] He eventually went home to bed, leaving Valera Gomes to cobble together a plan of action. It was decided that the paratroops would occupy the air bases, the administration school (EPAM) would take over radio and television stations protected by the military police, and RALIS was left to block the motorway leading north out of the city. The 2,000 marines at the Alfeite naval base on the left bank of the Tagus would also be brought into the city, and left-wing civilians armed.

Throughout the night, left-wing militants arrived at the air bases of Tancos and Montijo[14] and at 08.00 on the morning of 25 November, General Pinho Freire, commander of the first air region, found his mess at Monsanto surrounded by paratroops who told him that he could not leave. Incredibly, they did allow him the free use of his telephone, and under the very nose of the putschists, Freire began to put the prearranged counter-*coup* plan into action. He first telephoned Morais e Silva to inform him that the paratroops had revolted and that he was held by a mere forty or fifty soldiers who should be easy to overcome. He then ordered pilots to fly their planes north, depriving the left of air support and the paratroops of air mobility. As only three air bases were occupied, he placed all others on alert.

By the time *Rádio Clube Português* broadcast the paratroop communiqué claiming that 'the majority of paratroops and air force personnel' had revolted and were calling for the resignations of Morais e Silva and Pinho Freire from their commands, and of Costa Neves and Canto e Castro from the Revolutionary Council, the moderates had moved into action. In line with their previous strategy, they sought to avoid a potentially bloody confrontation and instead moved into blocking positions from which they could persuade the rebels that resistance was futile. Eanes established a command post in the commando barracks at Amadora with Firmino Miguel and Costa Bras, while Lourenço moved to Belém to coordinate plans with the government. They quickly established contact with commanders loyal to the government. Although the firepower of the insurgent regiments was limited, large-scale intervention by well-armed civilians or by the 2,000 marines led primarily by Gonçalvist officers could have tipped the Lisbon military balance in their favour.

228 *25 November*

Tanks from the cavalry regiment at Estremoz were sent to Setúbal to handle any trouble in that strongly left-wing industrial town. Tanks moved from Santarém to take up positions in front of RALIS, which so far had done little more than beef up its sentries. The commandos formed the moderate spearhead, backed by infantrymen from Mafra. At dawn on 25 November, Chaimite armoured cars sealed off the military police barracks, locking inside much Angolan war matériel destined for the paratroops. Jaime Neves called in his NCOs to explain the situation and then convened a regimental assembly, telling his men that they must obey orders. At 17.00, Neves arrived at Monsanto and through a megaphone ordered the paratroops to surrender, which they did. At Monte Real, insurgents were surrounded by a hostile crowd and quickly turned over their weapons to loyal troops. At 18.00, barely thirty minutes after Costa Gomes had declared a state of siege, paratroop Captain Durand Clemente stormed into the Lisbon television station and briefly lectured stunned Portuguese on the need for popular power and truly revolutionary leaders before a quick-thinking technician replaced him with an American film.

By the morning of 26 November, the rebellion had been confined to the air base at Tancos, RALIS and the military police barracks. Carvalho had been called to Belem by Costa Gomes and, although he refused to aid the conspirators, moderates thought it best to refuse his demands to be allowed into COPCON headquarters. At 04.00 on the morning of 26 November, a very nervous Dinís de Almeida arrived to confront Costa Gomes, Admiral Azevedo, the three service chiefs, the commanders of the four military regions, the members of the Revolutionary Council minus Contreiras and the commanders of several units. Almeida confessed that a *coup* attempt had been planned but said it had been betrayed by 'social fascists', the extremist term for the communists. The PCP limited support for the *coup* to the 24 November strike call which fell flat. Almeida was placed under arrest. RALIS commander Colonel Leal de Almeida called a regimental assembly which voted to surrender after professionals told die-hard milicianos to fight on alone.[15] The only deaths in the short-lived revolt occurred when Jaime Neves was despatched to look for the three senior officers of the military police who refused to obey Gomes' summons to Belém. Military police opened fire on the commandos, killing two of them. When the commandos returned the fire, killing a soldier, the military policemen quickly turned their commanders over. Realizing the game was up, Major Pessoa and Durand Clemente slipped quietly away. Their command played football until loyal troops arrived to

25 November 229

lock up a few ringleaders and send the rest home. Valera Gomes also disappeared to surface eventually in Lusaka. Porto radio stations began to play *fado* songs which had not been heard in over a year, announcing that the *coup*, and the revolution, were over.

November 25, like 11 March, was characterized by a lack of planning and the belief that a symbolic action was enough to rally a vast groundswell of support. Both were based on bluff, on the hope that a show of force would head off a serious punch up, professional solidarity proving stronger than politics in regulating disputes among brother officers. The luckless paratroops catalyzed events on both days.

However, the left-wing military revolt faced serious handicaps from the beginning. Left-wing soldiers were more split by ideologies and personalities than were most of their more moderate colleagues. The COPCON-Gonçalvist duel was only a blanket disagreement under which squirmed a thousand disputes and ideological nuances. Valera Gomes' 25 November attempt to take the command at the Alto do Duque was a sure guarantee than any number of potential rebels would sit at home. Politics were the petrol of left-wing Portuguese units. But internal combustion is a poor principle upon which to base military organization, and rebel units quickly fell victim to the discipline and determination of the commandos and cavalry who spent more time in training than in political debate. 'If the left was united, it would have won already', Dinís de Almeida said from prison:

> The disputes of the left abused and exhausted the spirit of sacrifice of the rare professional officers who stayed at their posts until the end, enduring difficulties no civilian can understand. Several times and for a long time, we had total victory within our grasp. A thousand Maos and Lenins betrayed us. Now we can only choose what form our defeat will take. You make an omelette with eggs, not with sardines. To make a revolution with professional officers is like making an omelette with sardines.[16]

However, few officers on 25 November could have had many illusions about the revolt's chances of success. 'If the crazy adventure of the communists and leftists had succeeded', Soares said, 'Portuguese history would have been enriched with a "Lisbon Commune", but also with a civil war: the insurgents would have held out for perhaps a month before being massacred.'[17] Despite the 'artificial atmosphere'[18] created in Lisbon by the media, a reluctance to confront fellow officers combined with a professional appreciation of the enormous disparity

230   *25 November*

of firepower available to the two camps convinced most left-wing officers that their lives and their careers were simply not worth the sacrifice. 'Opportunism, personal motivations, lack of conviction or courage in some are important [in a revolutionary situation]', Soares claimed.

> It is much easier to draw up a plan than to apply it with men who, when the time comes to act, sometimes hesitate to take the step. A large number must have reconsidered after seeing the peoples' unenthusiastic response to the pathetic appeals on radio and television. 25 November was not 25 April: there was neither joy, nor celebration, nor carnations. It was therefore better to stay at home and wait. What was the point of an adventure if one risked losing everything? I know from experience the hesitations, the contradictory ideas, the agony which grips you before the final plunge. On that day, there were many reasons for hesitating. This is what officers like Rosa Coutinho and Martins Guerreiro understood. They had been at Belem for a long time in the entourage of the President of the Republic: they understood the situation, realizing what was taking place on the other side to defend the state. They felt very quickly that this was not a joke, but that a very serious confrontation was risked if the marines joined the rebellion. They were afraid of a bloody battle, of the possibility of thousands of deaths, of the civil war which would surely follow.[19]

Moderate officers moved quickly to consolidate their victory. Jails were emptied to make way for left-wing officers like Carvalho, Dinís de Almeida, Costa Martins, the ex-Minister of Labour, Captain Paulino of the fifth division and a number of military policemen. COPCON and the military police were disbanded. Fabião resigned as army chief to be replaced by Eanes, while Admiral Souto Cruz took over the navy. Coutinho and Contreiras lost their places on the Revolutionary Council. Antunes, however, was especially keen that the change in the moderates' fortunes should not degenerate into a witch hunt forcing the communists underground. 'The control of the military situation gives us guarantees to clarify the political situation and continue with a left-wing government', he said in a television speech which shocked many. 'Communist participation in the construction of socialism is indispensable. . . The MFA has again found its unity and capacity for direction' of the political process.

However, Soares saw 25 November not as the MFA's rebirth but as

25 November   231

the 'crowning of the death of the MFA'.[20] As politicians dreamed of running a government, he reasoned, so most soldiers longed for the quiet of the barracks square: 'The MFA, motor of the revolution, is an outmoded concept', Sousa e Castro said. Although the new Portuguese constitution promulgated on 2 April 1976 allowed for an almost exclusively military Revolutionary Council with complete control over military affairs and the task of guaranteeing the 'fidelity' of the government and constitution to the 'spirit and principles of the Portuguese Revolution of 25 April, 1974',[21] and allowed for a military presence in parliament, Eanes made it clear that politics were out of place in the barracks: 'Partisan activities will not be permitted in the army', read his December orders abolishing 'soldiers' committees and committees of revolutionary vigilance'. 'The principal factor of cohesion in the forces is discipline.'

The military *coup* has become one of the bad jokes of modern politics. Not that the *coup* is always unjustified or municipal councils loath to alter a few street names. But as in most sports, those who enjoy the rough and tumble of a military takeover are often beaten to the bar by others who only come for the *après-coup*. However, the origins and political consequences of each military insurrection mean that journalists catch the first plane out to the dusty capitals to flatter the new military leaders with interviews and flashbulbs, satisfied social scientists tick another country off their lists, and the left, increasingly, announces the birth of a new régime more beautiful than the last.

Portugal's 1974 revolution was hailed as a break with the European past of right-wing soldiers in politics, a sign that the phenomenon of leftist military revolutions hitherto confined to underdeveloped nations was spreading into Western Europe. Portuguese soldiers were left wing, Portugal was an underdeveloped nation both economically and politically, and Portugal had a 'Third World vocation', as the revolutionaries themselves claimed. 'The weight of our history, the long Arab presence on the Iberian Peninsula, has marked us profoundly', wrote Melo Antunes. 'Incidents of colonialism in the home country made "European" Portugal a case different from the rest of the continent.'[22] Portugal's Third World vocation was a theme which ran through the radical phase of the revolution, inspiring cultural dynamization teams and military leaders alike with the idea that the MFA must become the country's liberation movement, educating the nation to socialism and absorbing political groups and factions like a sponge. Soldiers looked for models, first in Peru, then in Algeria or Cuba, debating the advantages and drawbacks of each as if they were

232   *25 November*

different brands of soup, but never in doubt that the choice lay with the armed forces. 'The MFA never created anything by itself, either politically or ideologically', Soares said. 'All of its ideas came from outside.'[23] It was exciting stuff, and what is more, it was close to home, guaranteeing Portugal a wide audience, both of political pundits and apolitical curious.

Once the glamour of the first hours began to wear thin, however, the Portuguese revolution began to reflect the dull lustre of every previous military intervention in politics, the dreary story of ambition, incompetence and institutional breakdown. Many soon realized that the 'Third World' talk was nothing more than a fig leaf to cover, however thinly, a desire to stampede Portugal into military dictatorship or an ill-conceived government based on 'popular power'. Portugal did not lack political traditions, it lacked politicians. The efforts of some left-wing officers to manoeuvre into power before a new generation of politicians could instruct themselves in the subtleties and hazards of their profession was neither the calamity Kissinger imagined nor the rebirth hailed by many idealists. It was simply a hurried improvisation.

In Portugal, as in France, the circumstances for the military *coup* were provided by a long and exhausting colonial war. The differences were crucial, however, for French soldiers felt that they were within spitting distance of victory and reacted against what they believed to be governmental betrayal. Portuguese officers were locked in a pointless struggle to maintain a burdensome empire. Portugal's colonial wars sapped the country's strength, made her appear ridiculous in the eyes of the world and ruined the army by flooding it with half-trained conscripts whom the government attempted to promote over the heads of long-serving regulars. The latent resentment which gradually built up to the boiling point in the officer corps was a combination of bruised national pride and wounded professional vanity, an explosive mixture of sentiments which Portuguese officers shared with revolutionary soldiers in Egypt and other Third World countries. The Portuguese experience proves that the increasing professionalism of the armed forces can hasten its entry into the political arena rather than discourage it as American historian Samuel Huntington has argued.[24] Professional discontent creates shop floor militancy and the *coup* substitutes for the strike.

The social origins of officers are not as important in explaining their decision to revolt as are the phenomena of increasing recruitment from within the armed forces, common education and experience

25 November 233

which focused resentment on the government. In these conditions, a few politically conscious officers rose like corks to the top, to give a firm political direction to what was basically – but by no means exclusively – professional discontent. They were joined by civilian political designers and architects in what became a squabbling mass of political planners.

The successful conversion of a military *coup* into a functioning government is a second fence at which soldiers often fall. The most successful soldier régimes, usually the only ones which survive for any length of time, are those in which the soldiers slip quickly out of uniform and into something more ministerial. Here, one must distinguish between military régimes run by a junta of officers and governments founded by soldiers. France had a soldier president for the first eleven years of the Fifth Republic, one who enjoyed dressing up in his kepi on state occasions, but France did not have a military régime any more than did America under Eisenhower. Nasser, Atatürk and others also proved masters of the art of quick change.

In common with many military takeovers, the MFA called its *coup* a revolution to emphasize the scope of the changes which it planned to introduce. But the long-term success or failure of soldiers in government usually has less to do with their politics than with the strength of civilian institutions within that country. In Great Britain and the United States, the question of active military intervention in politics is usually relegated to the realm of fantasy. In France, soldiers stepped in to overthrow the Fourth Republic, but no one, least of all themselves, seriously suggested that they take over the running of the government. Even in countries where political traditions are weak, if they exist at all, rebel officers feel the need for a front man to lend an air of respectability to their 'revolution'. In the Arab world, this has usually proved to be a general known for his liberal opinions and constantly in trouble with the régime, like Naguib in Egypt or Zaim in Syria. It is a man who can be comfortably discarded when officers feel strong enough to exert their leadership of the revolution.[25]

Portuguese officers fulfilled this basic requirement with Spínola, whose tactical skill and inspired leadership in Guinea was not repeated in Belém. It was perhaps bad luck on the left-wing officers of the MFA that Spínola proved such a single-minded but incompetent politician. For had he been allowed the occasional political victory, he might have held his ground longer, providing a cover for them to better think out and plan their takeover. As it was, the Portuguese revolution produced its Naguib, but not its Nasser.

234   25 November

This might not have been so important had the officers been bound by a common ideology, but their views on Portugal's future were as diverse as the branches and services from which they came. Their only point of agreement was resentment – resentment over the degradation of the armed forces and Portugal's low world status. It was easy enough to harness this anger to the task of overthrowing the Caetano government, especially as for many army and air force officers it was a question of life or death. Beyond that, officers were united only in their desire to end the war and re-establish Portugal's prestige. This of course implied a desire to modernize, which Morris Janowitz points out most military régimes place above even the desire to establish their own legitimacy.[26] However, this statement must be treated cautiously: many military régimes may aim to raise the living standards of the people they govern, and soldier ministers may be convinced that socialism and the abolition of privilege is the best way of achieving this. However, in Arab countries especially, this drive for modernization is usually tempered by a reaffirmation of traditional religious or tribal culture. Tradition provides a bedrock of social stability and political support, allowing a country and its 'intellectuals in uniform' to rediscover cultural and historical roots buried under years of colonial rule or national oppression.

A refusal to recognize Portuguese traditions, her political and social realities, led the Portuguese left down the road to utter failure. They treated Portugal as a *tabula rasa* and her people as a simple peasantry before whom they could wave a magic wand, produce a little smoke and, to worldwide applause, pull out of the hat a socialist régime the likes of which had never been seen before in the West. Many left-wing soldiers and politicians were ignorant of Portuguese conditions, either because they were naïve, had spent too much of their adult lives outside Portugal, in Africa or Eastern Europe, or both. While Arab officers have fashioned progressive régimes which respected Arab culture and tradition, Portuguese officers called for a complete break with the past, condemning outright many features of Portuguese society and culture – the Church, the northern peasantry, even *fado* – as reactionary.

The ignorance of officers of conditions in their own country enticed them to apply often badly digested Marxist equations at home. The result was that the political debate in Portugal seldom rose above the level of a confused babble of Marxism, from the top down. 'Vasco Gonçalves never had a solid political education', Soares said. 'His Marxist phraseology was taken straight out of the cheap little books

25 November 235

written by Politzer.'[27] Every cafe orator and half-educated NCO added a few essential words to his vocabulary – words like bourgeoisie, workers, reaction and fascism – then used them as ciphers to work a crude Marxist equation. Every situation was bent to fit into omnibus class categories, even if this meant flying in the face of reality: the populations of the north had to be made to recognize their class interests, even at the point of a gun. SUV recruits could easily extrapolate from the class analogy, concluding that soldiers represented the workers and officers the bourgeoisie. The result was not 'revolutionary discipline', but anarchy: 'The unit delegate assemblies were like stones in the shoes of the army', said one left-wing sub-lieutenant. '[They were] something which sharpened the contradictions of the system. . .The first step was to bring the soldiers and the officers into conflict: all soldiers are oppressed. If the officers are not all oppressors, at least they are privileged.'[28] Without discipline, left-wing units sloped from strike to illegal occupation, debating orders and sinking left-wing power hopes as surely as if they had capsized in Lisbon harbour. Melo Antunes, probably the only real intellectual in the military camp, condemned the disastrous effect of this Marxist mumbo jumbo upon the course of the revolution.

> Marxism is a method of analysis, a 'historical dialectic'. . .a 'guide of action', not a catechism in the service of an infallible and dogmatic church. Open the way with an accord which will make possible the elaboration of a national plan for a peaceful transition to socialism. . .build up this country starting from the basic reality of the people. Everywhere I see a delirium, the ideological delirium of those incapable of standing on their own feet; of those who submit all reason to a public conscience, a tenacious scholastic inspiration; who transform ideology into absolute reason. The political delirium of the revolutionaries is vulnerable to all the impulses of facile rhetoric and triumphant demagogy.[29]

While extreme left-wing groups defined their ideological positions on the basis of such crucial issues as whether or not the Communist Chinese were right in banning Beethoven as bourgeois music and while the communists fought with the socialists and popular democrats over the more fundamental questions of democracy, cracks began to appear in the MFA façade. This resulted in part from the soldiers' inability to produce a strong man, a *caudilho* behind whom most officers were prepared to unite. Regardless of whether officers were affiliated to a

236   25 November

political party or had contacts with politicians, party debates impinged upon the closed world of the MFA, defining issues, forcing officers to take decisions and eventually blowing MFA unity sky high. Instability became yet another characteristic which the MFA shared with other military régimes.

The political distance between the left-wing MFA leadership and the mass of its members added to that instability. As in many military régimes, the most politicized officers seized the bulk of the top positions, creating a gulf of suspicion between themselves and most of the armed forces.[30] In Portugal, officers held almost 40 per cent of ministerial portfolios and 16 per cent of the under-secretaryships in six provisional governments.[31] The scepticism of most officers at the sight of their colleagues taking government positions grew with the realization that many were bent on imposing a totalitarian régime on the country. The result inevitably was a call for a return to the barracks.

Even politicized officers were forced to admit that politics should be kept separate from command. On 12 August 1976, the Revolutionary Council decided that its members must choose betwen the government and the army. Franco Charais and Pedro Pezarat resigned their centre and southern regions to retain their seats on the Revolutionary Council, and were replaced by moderates Pires Veloso and Pinho Freire. Vasco Lourenço also opted to leave the Lisbon region command, although he was kept on as military governor of the capital because of its 'political-military importance'.[32] In this way, commanding officers no longer represented a political opinion, and the authority of new President Eanes over the armed forces was strengthened.

Left-wing Portuguese officers had realized that the armed forces could never serve as a power base, and so attempted to purge and reorganize them to counteract conservative influence. But *esprit de corps* intervened to act as a safety net. Each time an officer out of favour with the left was transferred or even jailed temporarily, his influence was not eliminated: arbitrary actions of this sort increased the resentment of moderate officers and swelled the numbers of those prepared to do something about it. To this was added the growing apprehension over the corrosive effect which the revolution was having on military discipline.

But divisions among soldiers are not confined to politics. Military régimes also fall victim to professional rivalries and personal jealousies between officers eager to get ahead in the promotion race. The success of an officer considered not too bright at military academy is guaranteed to make him enemies later in the mess, especially if his

25 November 237

promotion is the result of a show of hands in a 'revolutionary elected' promotion committee, as was the case in Portugal. The ambitious and unprincipled quickly slip into the revolutionary jargon and political stances necessary to attract the attention of the new élite of political officers. The rest simply plot their revenge. Opposition among officers to Carvalho and Fabião resulted as much from the fact that they had jumped the promotion queue as from their political views.

Portugal's experience with a military-led revolution proved once again that soldiers make poor tutors for democracy. The astute politician in khaki, the Napoleons, de Gaulles, Francos and Nassers emerge by accident, overcoming the limitations of a military education to sense the needs and desires of their peoples and manipulate the national situation to their advantage. The success which some army-educated men have enjoyed as politicians is not a blanket endorsement for the entrance of the army into politics. Soldiers are paid to defend their country, and as such are educated in the fundamentals of patriotism and civic duty. They may quiver with anger at policies they regard as detrimental to national interests, and may even change them by force. But when they attempt to stretch this indignation into a lengthy seminar on how the country should be run, they display their limited vision, their naïve platitudes, clumsy public relations and incompetence. 'We know what army intervention in politics means', wrote Mário Soares in 1972,' even when it acts with the best of intentions and how, consequently, problems build up and become very complex.'[33]

Notes

1. Soares, *Portugal, Quelle Revolution*, Paris, 1976, p.204.
2. *Expresso*, 31 October and 5 November.
3. Ibid., 20 September and 31 October.
4. See *Le Monde*, 29 October.
5. Soares, op.cit., p.192.
6. Gomes Mota, *A Resistência*, Lisbon, 1976, pp.176-81.
7. Soares, op.cit., pp.194-5.
8. See Soares, ibid., p.205.
9. See *Expresso*, 22 November 1975.
10. Ibid.
11. L.P. Gil, *Novembre 25, Anatomia de um Golpe*, Lisbon, 1976, p.221.
12. Ibid., p.222.
13. Soares, op.cit., p.200.
14. See official report, 'Relatório do 25 Novembre', *Jornal Novo*, 20 January 1976, p.3.
15. See *Le Monde*, 28 November 1976.

238   *25 November*

16. Frémontier, *Portugal, les points sur les i,* Paris, 1976, p.37.
17. Soares. op.cit., p.211.
18. Ibid., p.198.
19. Ibid., pp.204-5.
20. Ibid., p.214.
21. *Constituição da República Portuguesa,* Lisbon, 1976, p.71.
22. Manuel de Rama and Carlos Plantier, *Melo Antunes,* Lisbon, 1976, p.46.
23. Soares, op.cit., p.127.
24. See Ambler, *The French Army in Politics,* Ohio State University, 1966, pp.370-1.
25. Haddad, *Revolutions and Military Rule in the Middle East,* Part III, New York, 1973, p.371.
26. Wilson McWilliams, *Garrisons and Governments,* San Francisco, 1967, p.756.
27. Soares, op.cit., p.127.
28. Frémontier, op.cit., pp.48-9.
29. Quoted in Mota, op.cit., p.224.
30. See Edwin Lieuwen, 'Militarism and Politics in Latin America', in J.J. Johnson (ed.), *The Role of the Military in Underdeveloped Countries,* Princeton, 1962, p.156.
31. 41 of 104 ministries and 27 of 163 secretaries of state. *Expresso,* 10 October 1975.
32. *Le Monde,* 14 August 1976.
33. Soares, op.cit., p.121.

APPENDIX I TELEGRAM TO PORTO COMBATANTS' CONGRESS

Around 400 regular army officers fighting overseas. . .certain that they interpret the feelings of hundreds of their comrades who, for various reasons, are truly unaware of the congress, would like to inform Your Excellency and the nation of the following:

1. Not accepting other values nor defending other interests but those of the nation.
2. Not recognizing the organizers of the '1st Congress of Overseas Combatants', and consequently this congress as representative.
3. Not participating in the work of the congress, nor admitting that because of their non-participation the final attitudes or conclusions (of the congress) are representative of the mass of combatants.
4. For all of these reasons they declare themselves totally opposed to the conclusions of the congress, independent of its contents or its views.

They sign the present telegram in symbolic representation of 400 soldiers. . .

APPENDIX II   THE ARMED FORCES AND THE NATION

As is generally known, for the past several months an 'officers movement' has grown up in the Armed Forces, whose origins have been surpassed and today has taken on the characteristics and directions that it is now time to clarify and define. This document, to be read by all soldiers, aims essentially to make them reflect critically on the fundamental aspects of the problems which the Armed Forces face — feeling that a comprehensive consideration is vital, and one which does not dissociate the Armed Forces from the nation at this critical moment which the country is going through — and, following from this, to consolidate support and arrive at a coherent policy which our analysis will show to be imperative, necessary and urgent.

Everyone knows and feels that the Armed Forces are considered as the support for a complex political-economic global structure, in the orientation of which. . .most citizens do not have any direct voice. They are aware that such a system cannot continue indefinitely. . .if its leaders do not have guarantees of unquestioning obedience for their goals from the Armed Forces. The general practice calls for the government to define the great national objectives and the Armed Forces to execute them. The myth of an 'apolitical' army transformed soldiers into the guardians of a legitimate constitution, into the mere executors of a policy defined from above. . .

If, prior to 1961, the Armed Forces were not openly touched in their prestige, or not in a violent way, it is because the régime's internal crises had not yet reached an excessively critical stage. Beginning, however, with the loss of India and above all as the African wars dragged on, the Armed Forces discovered not without surprise for many soldiers who for the first time saw things as they are, their real separation from the nation. The Armed Forces are humiliated, stripped of prestige and presented to the nation as responsible for the disaster.

Having invented a 'sacrificial lamb' and created the conditions in which the nation abandoned confidence in its armed forces, it followed that the prestige of the Armed Forces continued to sink. The Angolan war caused many soldiers to question its justice. However, as time passed and the situation worsened. . .as other armed rebellions grew (Guinea and Mozambique). . .the inability of the Armed Forces to

240

Appendix II 241

realize the objectives imposed upon them by a government which could not even accept the evidence that its policies were leading to a repetition of the fall of India became evident. Incapable of internal reform which would have killed it, the régime took an intransigent position on the overseas problem. As the shortcomings of this policy became more evident daily, the Armed Forces appeared increasingly responsible in the eyes of the nation, not only for the African *impasse,* but for the general crisis in the country, which is not only a political crisis but also economic, social and moral.

The gulf between the Armed Forces and the nation grew, lowering the prestige of the soldiers (the recent events of Beira, Mozambique, confirm this reality for everyone), a falling prestige which no measures taken can bolster.

It is not with a pay rise (this document demonstrates that the conscience of soldiers is not for sale), nor with the various rights and privileges, not even with the plans to re-equip the Armed Forces to carry on the war more efficiently (one doubts if this could be done in time), not with hasty measures designed to hush up criticism and quiet the growing discontent in the Armed Forces, that the government can heal the deep and sad wounds in the consciences of the majority of soldiers. Nor will these measures re-establish the already shaken prestige of the Armed Forces, because the problem is not confined to a socio-professional group: the prestige of the military institutions will be re-established only when the Armed Forces identify with the nation, when the Armed Forces and the people are in fundamental agreement on their objectives.

The major problem of the Portuguese people, which in large measure conditions the others, is at this moment the war in the African territories: Angola, Mozambique, Guinea. The question is very serious and is at the base of the general crisis which affects the régime [which is] already out of control. Despite the realization in the Armed Forces as well as in society that a military victory is not possible, all is done to promote the view that the government has defined an adequate strategy and that the Armed Forces have only to follow it to guarantee the integrity of the territories. Consequently, the situation worsens. . .

However, conscientious soldiers know that the solution to the overseas problem is political and not military, and work to denounce the errors of which they are the victims and which will transform the Armed Forces into the scapegoat for an impossible strategy: a political solution which will safeguard national honour and dignity, as well as all of the legitimate interests of the Portuguese living in Africa, but

242   *Appendix II*

which takes into account the fundamental and irreversible aspiration of all the African peoples for self-government. . .This solution must be carried out with realism and courage, because we believe that it not only corresponds to the true interests of the Portuguese people but also their authentic historic destiny and their highest sense of justice and peace. They know, as do conscientious soldiers, that such a solution will never be considered by the government, which claims exclusive rights on patriotism and pretends to have the support of the nation. We believe it does not have the support it claims.

And for this reason we believe that as a primary condition for the solution of the African problem, the crisis of the Armed Forces and the general crisis of the country, that the government has the maximum legitimacy, that its institutions be truly representative of the aspirations and interests of the people. In other words, without democratization of the country it is impossible to find a valid solution to our increasingly grave problems.

Therefore, above all we must obtain in the short term a solution to the problem of our institutions in the context of a political democracy.

In this context, we consider it indispensable and urgent that:

- Definite and clear national objectives acceptable to the nation should be spelled out.
- The role of the Armed Forces in achieving these objectives should be clearly stated to the nation.
- Permanent guarantees should be given (to the Armed Forces) that they will have the finances and means to carry out their mission.
- The restructuring of the Armed Forces with a view to promoting qualified men to the top positions, improving efficiency, respecting individual rights and justice should be carried out.
- The Armed Forces feel that their prestige is guaranteed and that they should not be assigned duties which are not within their competence.

Only when these conditions are met can the Armed Forces guarantee the will of the nation and not be in the service of a particular group. . . Only when these conditions are met can the Armed Forces have the necessary guarantees for the prestige which it claims: the army will be the 'people in arms' only when the barriers are removed between the people and the army, when the army is truly the incarnation of a collective will for defence, of an unequivocal affirmation, made by its

Appendix II 243

own people, of security and national defence.

APPENDIX III THE MFA PROGRAMME, APRIL 1974

As after thirteen years of fighting overseas, the existing political system
has failed to define an overseas policy which will lead to peace among
Portuguese of all races and creeds.

As this policy will be defined only after the purging of the internal
policies and institutions, transforming them by democratic means into
institutions truly representative of the Portuguese people.

As the present political system must be replaced without adversely
affecting the nation's peace, progress or well-being.

The Portuguese Armed Forces Movement, believing that it speaks for
the interests of the overwhelming majority of Portuguese and that its
acion is fully justified by the need to save the Fatherland, using the
force given it by the nation through its soldiers, proclaims and undertakes
to guarantee the adoption of the following measures, the platform which
it believes necessary to resolve Portugal's great national crisis:

A. Immediate Measures

1. Political power will be exercised by a Junta of National Salvation
until the rapid formation of a provisional civil government.

The Junta of National Salvation will order:

a) The dismissal of the President of the Republic and the present
government, the dissolution of the National Assembly and the Council
of State, measures which will be accompanied by the public announcement
of the convocation within twelve months of a National Constituent
Assembly elected by direct universal suffrage and secret ballot
according to an electoral law to be drafted by the future provisional
government.

b) The dismissal of all prefects in Portugal, in the autonomous
districts of the adjacent islands and the governors general of the overseas
provinces and the immediate dissolution of the National Popular Action.

— The government of the overseas provinces will be taken over
immediately by the respective general secretaries until the naming of
new governors general by the provisional government.

c) The immediate suspension of the DGS, the Portuguese Legion and
youth organizations.

Overseas the DGS will be restructured and purged, and reorganized
as a military intelligence as long as military operations require.

244

Appendix III 245

d) The delivery of the armed forces of those guilty of crimes against the new political order during the rule of the Junta of National Salvation, to try and sentence them.

e) Measures to permit rigorous inspection and control of all foreign economic and financial transactions.

f) The immediate amnesty of all political prisoners with the exception of those guilty of a criminal offence, who will be given to the proper authority, and the voluntary reintegration of civil servants dismissed for political reasons.

g) The abolition of censorship.

— Recognizing the need to protect military secrets and to prevent public opinion from being troubled by reactionary ideological aggression, a temporary *ad hoc* committee under the Junta of National Salvation will be created to oversee the press, radio, television, theatre and cinema, until the publication by the provisional government of new laws on the press, radio, television, theatre and cinema.

h) The reorganization and purging of the armed and militarized forces (Republican National Guard, Security Police, Customs Police, etc.).

i) The armed forces will police the frontier until the creation of a special service.

j) Measures to control corruption and speculation.

B. Short-Term Measures

1. Within three weeks of taking power, the Junta of National Salvation will designate from among its members a President of the Portuguese Republic, whose powers will be identical to those defined in the present constitution.

a) The remaining members of the Junta of National Salvation will assume the functions of Chief of the Armed Forces General Staff, Vice-Chief of the Armed Forces General Staff, and chiefs of staff of the navy, army and air force, and sit on the Council of State.

2. Upon taking office, the President of the Republic will name a provisional government composed of representatives of political groups and opinions and independent persons who accept the present programme.

3. During the exceptional period of provisional government, imposed by the historical necessity of political transformation, the Junta of National Salvation will be maintained to safeguard these stated objectives.

a) The exceptional period will end with the election, according to

246　*Appendix III*

the new constitution, of the President of the Republic and the legislative assembly.

4. The provisional government will govern by decree-laws which obey the spirit of this proclemation.

5. Aware that basic reforms will be the exclusive province of the future National Constituent Assembly, the provisional government immediately undertakes:

a) The application of measures to guarantee the functioning of the government and the study and application of preparatory measures of a material, economic, social and cultural character which will guarantee the future political liberties of citizens.

b) Freedom of assembly and association.

The application of this principle will permit the formation of 'political associations', the embryos of future political parties, and guarantee union freedom in keeping with a law which will regulate its functioning.

c) The freedom of expression and all forms of thought.

d) A new law for the press, radio, television, theatre and cinema.

e) Measures to insure the independence and dignity of the courts.

– An end to 'special courts' and the dignity of all phases of imprisonment.

– Crimes against the state in the new régime will be handled by the normal courts with the rights of the accused guaranteed. The judicial police will handle all investigations.

6. The provisional government will set out:

a) A new economic policy in the service of the Portuguese people, in particular the least favoured categories, which aims immediately to fight inflation and the rise in living costs, and which will require an antimonopolist strategy.

b) A new social policy in all areas which aims to defend the interests of the working classes and the progressive but rapid rise in living standards for all Portuguese.

7. The provisional government will follow a foreign policy based on the principles of independence and equality among states, the non-interference in the internal affairs of other states and the defence of peace, extending and diversifying international relations on the basis of friendship and cooperation.

8. The provisional government's overseas policy defined by the nation will be based on the following principles:

a) Recognition that the solution to the war is political, not military.

b) Create the conditions for a frank and open national debate on

Appendix III   247

the overseas problem.

c) Inaugurate an overseas policy leading to peace.

C. Final Conditions

1. As soon as the nation elects the legislative assembly and the new President of the Republic, the Junta of National Salvation will be dissolved and the armed forces limited to its specific mission of defending national sovereignty.

2. The Armed Forces Movement, confident that these principles and objectives constitute a pledge to the country and are necessary for the higher interests of the nation, earnestly call on all Portuguese for a sincere, enlightened and dedicated participation in national public life, and exhort them to guarantee, by their work and peaceful coexistence, whatever their social position, the conditions necessary to define quickly policies which will lead to a solution of the grave national problems and to harmony, progress and social justice indispensable for the purification of our public life and the obtaining by Portugal of the place she deserves in the concert of nations.

APPENDIX IV THE MFA: LIBERATION MOVEMENT JUNE 1975

1. Political definition

1.1　The MFA is the liberation movement of the Portuguese people; it stands above party and its essential aim is that of national independence. The MFA recognizes that this national independence involves a process of domestic decolonization, which can only be achieved by means of the construction of a socialist society.

1.2　By 'socialist society,' as the final aim to be attained, we understand a classless society, obtained through the collectivization of the means of production, eliminating all forms of exploitation of person by person, in which all individuals will be given equal opportunities of education, work and promotion, without distinction of birth, sex, religious beliefs or ideology.

The transition from our present society to a socialist society must necessarily entail several stages, the first of which will cover the period of transition laid down in the constitutional agreement platform, the stages of which will be determined by the socio-economic and political development of the Portuguese people.

But the MFA has already made it quite clear that this aim will be reached along a pluralist path.

1.3　Pluralism means freedom of expression and discussion of opinions, and also experiments in building the new society, by means of a permanent, open dialogue with the whole of the Portuguese people.

Socialist pluralism includes co-existence, both in theory and in practice, between various forms and concepts of the building of the socialist society. Thus the MFA repudiates the implantation of socialism by violent or dictatorial means.

Party pluralism, as laid down in the constitutional agreement, implies recognition of the existence of various political parties and currents of opinion, even though they do not necessarily defend socialist options. It thus makes allowance for an opposition, whose criticism may well be beneficial and constructive, provided that its activity is not opposed to the

Appendix IV 249

building of a socialist society by democratic means.

The MFA will enjoy the natural support and backing of those parties which, by their political programmes and practice, do show a real interest in adopting and realizing objective measures called for by the transition towards socialism, and with them it will establish the necessary alliances and coalitions.

1.4 During the period of transition to socialism, the political parties should play a very valuable role, not only through their pedagogical work in making the masses politically aware and ready to act, but also as vehicles to transmit the will of the people, by tuning in to their needs and aspirations in all possible ways, including elections.

But elections, to be held and developed through the transitional period, must be consciously integrated in the revolutionary process; they cannot in any sense be allowed to constitute an obstacle to it.

1.5 In accordance with the express vocation it has taken on itself as a national liberation movement, the MFA wants all the Portuguese people to play an active part in their own revolution, so that it will decisively support, and will establish links with, all base untis, whose aims form part of the realization and defence of the MFA Programme for the construction of the socialist society.

These people's organizations will form the embryo of an experimental system of direct democracy, through which we believe we can achieve the active participation of the whole nation in public administration and in national political life, in connection with the local and regional organs of the central power. They will also have the advantage of encouraging, starting at the base, concentration of the efforts of the various parties, through unity in realizing common aims.

But no armed civilian organizations, party-organized or not, will be allowed, although people's organizations may, on the initiative of the MFA itself and under its control and as an extension of its work, carry out, in cases of national emergency, tasks of self-defence of vital objectives.

Within the armed forces no politico-military organization will be permitted, whether party-based or not, outside the MFA, and all military personnel should be progressively integrated into this movement, which is theirs.

1.6 The MFA restates its determination to carry out, and ensure that

250   *Appendix IV*

others carry out, in their entirety, the terms of the constitutional agreement platform, freely laid down with Portuguese political parties, and solemnly states that it will denounce and will take action against all attitudes which, openly or covertly, seek to question and undermine that pact.

1.7   In accordance with the principles laid down, the MFA considers that it is its duty to make it publicly explicit that the sole power of the Constituent Assembly is to perform the patriotic mission of drawing up the political constitution of the Portuguese nation, and it is forbidden to indulge in any other form of official interference in national political or administrative life.

1.8   In foreign affairs the MFA will go on with a policy of national independence and of contribution to peace and cooperation in Europe and the world at large.

Within this context we shall respect already established alliances and undertakings, specifically Portugal's participation in NATO, so as not to endanger the political and military balance of Europe.

In the political field Portugal will follow a strategy of readiness to maintain relations with all countries of the world, without interfering in their domestic affairs, or allowing them interference in ours; she feels she possesses a historical vocation to serve as a link between the European peoples and those of the Third World, especially with the sister Portuguese-speaking countries.

In the economic sphere, our foreign policy will be oriented towards a progressive diversification of trade relations and we shall not permit any country or bloc to seek to impose on the Portuguese people, by means of economic relations, any form of domination.

2. The exercise of authority

2.1   Analysis of the present political situation and its likely development reveals the need to strengthen the revolutionary authority of the MFA, as an indispensable basis for a state power to allow a normal, pacific development of the path of transition to socialism.

There are in fact threats of counterrevolutionary activities encouraged from other countries and supported inside Portugal by agents of national capitalism and colonialism, now being uprooted, which, unless firmly and exemplarily eradicated, would represent a grave danger for disturbance of public order and the

Appendix IV 251

safety of persons and property, and could create a climate very propitious to the return of a right-wing fascistic régime.

On the other hand, certain manifestations of pseudorevolutionary leftism, even though sometimes well intentioned, tend to create situations of potential anarchy, which thoroughly disturb a coherent revolutionary process, the objective result being a strengthening of the declared aims of those whom they say, or whom they would have us believe, they are fighting.

We thus conclude that only the exercise of a firm, though not necessarily repressive, authority can guarantee the success of the revolution in which the MFA and the Portuguese people are engaged.

2.2 We thus re-affirm our intention of ensuring that all the laws that contribute to the aims of the Portuguese revolution shall be obeyed, until the process of history shows that they are unsuited to the concrete circumstances in which our society finds itself.

To further this firm exercise of authority, apart from the revolutionary legislation published, new laws will be published to bring about the desired aims.

2.3 The need to put down, with the necessary firmness, the possible activities of groups or clandestine armed organizations forces on us the publication of a special law, now being drafted, which will enable us to punish with severe penalties, those who participate in such counterrevolutionary organizations.

2.4 We consider that the struggle against leftism should be waged essentially in the ideological field, by seeking to recuperate its well-intentioned supporters for the aims and tasks of the revolution.

But different kinds of repression will be employed, including armed action if necessary, against those groups or organizations whose actions and practices systematically disburb law and order and which disregard the rules laid down for the construction of socialism by a pluralist means.

2.5 We recognize that one of the spheres in which manifestations of uncontrolled leftism have most disturbed public life in our country is that of education. Thus the MFA restates its determination to support the Ministry of Education in restoring a normal productive climate in which, within democratic rules of management, students and pupils can fulfil their duty towards our society by training themselves and making ready for their functions as the workers of the future.

252　*Appendix IV*

We must not forget that it is desirable that, in intellectual circles, there should be a strong revolutionary awareness. Intellectual workers – which includes students – have an obligation to prevent their political activities from so harming their specific forms of work that they become potential parasites on society.

3. Economic and financial policy

3.1　The current economic situation of our country is characterized by the following three basic critical factors.

    a)　Very marked imbalance of the balance of payments, the deficit on which is reckoned to be likely to reach, by the end of this year, a deficit far higher than that for 1974, which was about 17,000m escudos.

    b)　A high unemployment figure, about 250,000 workers, that is 8 per cent of the working population.

    c)　Falling internal production, endangering national independence; if present production trends are not altered, it is forecast that this year will show a fall of 6 per cent on the GNP for 1974.

3.2　All Portuguese people must, therefore, be quite clear about the economic and financial situation of our country, which can be summed up in the following facts:

3.2.1 Imports: These, mainly of foodstuffs, are far higher than exports, and the excess may well be as high as a figure of 50,000m escudos by the end of 1975. This figure is largely due to the high prices of foodstuffs and of oil in supplier countries.

3.2.2 This deficit is attenuated by foreign currency earned in Portugal by the remittances sent by emigrants and the sum spent here by tourists. (In the latter, as is well-known, there is a crisis at the moment.)

3.2.3 At the end of this year it is forecast that Portugal will be showing a deficit on the balance of payments of some 30,000m escudos, which will have to be met from the currency reserves of the Bank of Portugal, which will almost exhaust them, leaving only our gold reserves.

3.2.4 This financial situation is part of an economic context in which the wealth produced in the country will fall, unless the current trend is changed, this year by some 6 per cent in relation to 1974, even taking into account the rise in agricultural output.

3.2.5 This panorama is a very serious one, but not alarming, because it

Appendix IV   253

corresponds to a socio-political phase of the elimination of the
errors of capitalism, based on monopoly and major landowning,
which characterized our country and also the crisis of
international capitalism. But if this crisis is not to become
irremediable, the Portuguese people have no alternative but to
take upon themselves the construction of a new socialist
economic system and the working classes must take a conscious
decision to opt for either socialism, and the relative, temporary
sacrifices its construction entails, or capitalism, with all the
oppression and exploitation inherent to it.

3.2.6 The point is that if the destruction of capitalism calls for the
removal of the exploiting power of the rich monopolist
bourgeoisie, the big landowners and the major financiers, the
building-up of socialism calls for work, sacrifices and political
awareness from the working classes to create a future society
free of classes and of exploitation; but this does not mean, over
the short term, that all the forms of injustice permitted or
encouraged under the previous régime can be rectified and that,
all at once, we can start paying every Portuguese worker a wage
corresponding to his just desires and real needs.

3.2.7 This being the case, the policy of truth that has at all times been
put before the Portuguese people makes it imperative to adopt
certain realistic measures, if the working people do in fact wish
to build up a socialism. There are:

a) Reductions in imports, especially more superfluous goods, or
those which can be produced in our own country.

b) Policy of austerity in consumption.

c) Increase in home output, especially of such products as, for
example, foodstuffs, can replace those formerly imported,
or those which can increase the value of our exports.

3.3 In view of this grave economic situation, it is a matter of urgency
to adopt the following:

a) Immediate prompt measures.

b) A strategy of economic development, defined on the basis of
three critical areas: the balance of payments, unemployment,
and economic independence.

The future panorama of the politico-economic situation
and system, including discussion of the following aspects:
— organized control of output by the workers;
— local mobilization for development;
— organization of the planning system;

254 *Appendix IV*

     — qualitative and subsystems of the transitional economy (state sector and private sector).

     c) Policy of foreign economic cooperation.

3.4 The two basic topics, strategy of economic development and future layout of the economic system will be discussed as a matter of urgency by the economic team of the provisional government and by the four ministers without portfolio representing the parties of the coalition, in connection with the Council of the Revolution; the corresponding decisions should be taken by the end of July, thus making it possible to draw up a transitional plan for 1976-1978.

     The discussion of these topics and the immediate prompt measures will provide a far-reaching test of the political viability of the present coalition and its capability of carrying forward the united progress towards the real aims of socialism.

4. Government and administration

4.1 The Provisional Government: The provisional government will work in the present circumstances as a unified government, meeting rapidly and efficiently the national and patriotic aims of the construction of socialism, as defined above.

     The MFA considers that the grave economic and financial situation of the country calls for the present coalition government to set aside natural divergences and to achieve a common solution for the problem of economic development.

     The MFA believes that the Portuguese people, the overwhelming majority of whom are represented by the parties forming the coalition, have a right to demand that these parties shall prove to be up to their historic duty, on pain of being considered unsuitable in relation to the objective needs of the country.

     Thus the MFA thinks that the discussion of the strategy of economic development and of the economic model of society to be begun at once by the provisional government, and which should be concluded by the end of July 1975, will be an extremely important test that thé Portuguese people are entitled to see settled.

4.2 Inertia of the machinery of state. The present state machinery is extremely heavy and bureaucratic, and is clearly unsuitable to the dynamism of the present revolutionary process. It can only respond slowly and incompletely to the demands made of

Appendix IV 255

it. To meet this problem the MFA thinks it is essential to:

a) Decentralize the administration;

b) Gradually set up a new state apparatus, non-party, organized on dynamic patterns around basic programmed points, and endowed with staff sufficiently identified with the demands of revolutionary dynamism. As a parallel to this we shall start work to effect administrative reform in depth.

c) Lay down a correct policy of re-classification and recuperation of the work of civil servants, making use of the weapon of dismissal in cases where recovery is clearly out of the question.

d) Accept the pressure for dialogue between the organs of the state power, at the various levels, and the unitary popular organizations which correspond to the same scales and levels, and which will be progressively given powers to control the activities of such organs of the state machinery.

e) Eliminate excessively bureaucratic and complex procedures within the state machinery, replacing them by rapid, revolutionary methods able to meet the pressures of demand, attributing full responsibility to those who execute such a policy and such measures.

4.3 Administrative decentralization. Although this topic belongs to the domain of the future political constitution, the dynamism of the people in setting up associations to look after their common interests has made it necessary for the Ministry of Home Administration to adopt measures, which the MFA considers justified, for regional decentralization of various state services and departments, thus making possible, at the regional level, the drafting of plans more suited to local circumstances and to their execution, with the progressive participation of local people's organizations, although maintaining the necessary links and coordination with the central organs of the state.

The essentially pragmatic criterion adopted has consisted in the setting-up, at the level of a given region, of a planning bureau and a regional employment committee, to bring together representatives of the various ministries concerned, as well as a representative of the MFA. In collaboration with the planning bureau there are assemblies of the representatives of the various administrative committees of the local authorities, the latter, in their turn, in close contact with the already numerous committees of local inhabitants, trade unions, and other unitary organizations. This initiative has already been launched in the Algarve, with

256 *Appendix IV*

good results; it will soon be extended to the regions covered by the military zones of the north, centre and south so as to permit a better coverage and support by the MFA of local unitary people's organizations; it will be sufficiently flexible to permit a later adjustment to the decisions taken by the Constituent Assembly on the matter.

4.4 Link-up between the MFA and the unitary people s basic structures. The MFA considers that in the present phase of the revolution it is extremely important and perhaps decisive to strengthen and dynamize these structures as a determinant factor of popular unity and of the overcoming of the contradictions existing at the level of summit political structures.

This new power in the revolution does not seek to question the legitimacy of the existing political parties but rather to obtain an additional impulse towards unity and coherence through the dynamism of their basic structures based on the concrete everyday situation, thus causing an upsurge of energy from bottom to top. The future association of these unitary people's organs may set up the embryos of representative local organs or assemblies, reflecting the interests of the population, which gradually, through dialogue with the local organs of public administration, will dynamize them and identify themselves with the true local popular interests. The guidelines of this form of political orientation are now being studied by an MFA working-party appointed specially; their conclusions, formulated on the basis of real existing data, will shortly be publicized.

5. Dynamization and information

5.1 It is recognized that the desired construction of a socialist society by the pluralist path already defined cannot be done without a mobilization and indoctrination of the whole Portuguese people, to put them positively and consciously on the transitional path to socialism.

It should be noted that the implementation of a real socialism implies in essentials a development of mentalities so as to transform most of the almost purely materialist motivation, characteristic of capitalist societies, into a spiritual motivation to persuade individuals to leave a selfish, individualist attitude towards their fellows in favour of an altruistic, collectivist attitude, centring their attention and concern on the common weal.

Appendix IV   257

   This work will only be possible through a suitable policy of information which must be begun forthwith by a far-reaching transformation of the structures of the organs and services of social and mass communications. This does not mean that information and the media should be monolithic or propaganda-oriented, for this would not be, in our view, in accordance with the pluralist principles followed by the Portuguese revolution.

   But this information must be at once a form of true education, to inform and enlighten the people, instead of as hitherto, exciting and confusing them, as has so often been the case. The MFA sincerely believes that freedom and the socialist option are not incompatible, but the exercise of one must not limit the existence of the other.

5.2   One of the practices necessary to the attainment of the aims defined above is to transform one or more dailies, at present practically under state ownership, into official organs, whose presentation of news and comment will naturally reflect the positions of the MFA.

   It is hoped that by this step the Portuguese people will have at their disposal non-controversial dailies, without any party line or associations, following a general policy of truth and enlightenment of the people, the daily practice of which should make them eminently respected.

5.3   With the same aim it is necessary to control state radio and TV to bring to the public ear and eye, systematically, the position and views of the MFA on political events and the events of national life.

5.4   The mobilization of public opinion for aims of the national interest should be done through the rational use of publicity in the media, which will naturally imply the utilization of nationalized publicity organizations.

5.5   Free information has a right to exist in Portugal but very often it has been misused, giving rise to the diffusion through the press, on radio, and over the TV of news items deliberately distorted to cause confusion or alarm among public opinion. The same is true of certain foreign correspondents, who have misused the hospitality granted them and have sent to the papers for which they work false or biased news items, intentionally distorting and worsening the image of Portugal received in other countries. The Press Law does not permit any decisive rapid measures against these prevaricators, who abuse that Law to carry out — so far

258 *Appendix IV*

with impunity — activities perfectly well definable as counter-revolutionary; so the MFA is determined to proceed directly and effectively against them by publishing, if necessary, revolutionary legislation on this topic.

5.6 The major Portuguese communities spread about the world, whose feelings of nationality remain unchanged, have been the victims of systematic campaigns of defamation about events in Portugal, the intention being to estrange them from the feeling of national liberation and, sometimes, to make use of them as a weapon of the forces of reaction through friends or relatives living in Portugal.

The MFA hopes that all the Portuguese nation, including those who were forced to emigrate because of the lack of freedom or decent living conditions in their own country, will feel proud of their nationality, and to this end they must be informed truthfully and opportunely of the revolutionary process.

For this purpose the Foreign and Mass Communications Ministries will put into practice suitable systems and measures.

5.7 The mobilization of the Portuguese people for the socialist path demands not only a new policy of information but also a constant policy of dynamization which, by its presence and in practice, will make the recommendations and the programmes drafted by the central organs both visible and effective.

To this end there must be an intensive, effective campaign of dynamization by the military, in joint efforts with the people's basic structures, which can, better than anyone else, reflect and represent the most just hopes and needs of the population as a whole. To effect this work, the suitable human and material means should be made available, not forgetting that the revolution of April 25, 1974 was carried out for the people and that from the people will come its force, its continuity, and its justification.

APPENDIX V GOVERNMENTS

Last Caetano Government (12 August 1972)

Minister of State for Economic Planning: João Mota Pereira Campos
Defence: General Horacio José Sá Viana Rebelo
Interior: António Manuel Gonçalves Rapazote
Justice: Mário Júlio Brito de Almeida Costa
Finance: Manuel Cotta Diás
Navy: Rear Admiral Manuel Pereira Crespo
Foreign Affairs: Rui Patrício
Public Works and Communications: Ruy Alves da Silva Sanches
Colonies: Joaquim Moreira da Silva Cunha
Education: José Veiga Simão
Labour, Social Security and Health: Baltazar Rebelo de Sousa

First Provisional Government (16 May 1974)

Prime Minister: Adelino Palma Carlos (Independent, close to PPD)
Ministers of State without Portfolio: Alvaro Cunhal (PCP), Francisco
    Sá Carneiro (PPD), Francisco Pereira de Moura (MDP)
Interior: Magalhães Mota (PPD)
Foreign Affairs: Mário Soares (PS)
Justice: Salgado Zenha (PS)
Labour: Avelino Pacheco Gonçalves (PCP)
Defence: Lieutenant Colonel Firmino Miguel (Moderate)
Education and Culture: Eduardo Correia
Social Communication: Raúl Rego (PS)
Public Works: Pedro Nunes
Economic Coordination: Vasco Vieira de Almeida (Independent,
    close to PPD)
Industry and Environment: Manuel Rocha
Social Affairs: Mário Murteira (MDP)
Interterritorial Coordination (ex-Colonial Ministry): António de
    Almeida Santos (Independent, close to PS)

Second Provisional Government (19 July 1974)

Prime Minister: Colonel Vasco Gonçalves
Ministers of State: Major Vítor Alves, Major Melo Antunes,
    Alvaro Cunhal, Magalhães Mota

260 *Appendix V*

Interior: Colonel da Costa Bras
Foreign Affairs: Mário Soares
Justice: Salgado Zenha
Environment: José Augusto Fernandes
Labour: Captain Costa Martins (Gonçalvist, close to PCP)
Social Affairs: Maria de Lourdes Pintasilgo
Economy: Rui Vilar (Independent, close to PS)
Finances: José Silva Lopes
Information: Major Sanches Osório
Education: Magalhães Godinho (Independent, close to PS)
Defence: Lieutenant Colonel Firmino Miguel
Interterritorial Coordination: Almeida Santos

Third Provisional Government (1 October 1974)

Prime Minister: General Vasco Gonçalves
Ministers of State: Major Vítor Alves, Major Melo Antunes, Alvaro
  Cunhal, Magalhães Mota
Interior: Colonel da Costa Bras
Foreign Affairs: Mário Soares
Defence: General Vasco Gonçalves and Major Vítor Alves
Interterritorial Coordination: Almeida Santos
Justice: Salgado Zenha (PS)
Environment: José Augusto Fernandes
Labour: Captain Costa Martins
Social Affairs: Maria de Lourdes Pintasilgo
Economy: Rui Vilar
Education: Magalhães Godinho

Fourth Provisional Government (26 March 1975)

Prime Minister: General Vasco Gonçalves
Ministers without Portfolio: Alvaro Cunhal (PCP), Mário Soares (PS),
  Francisco Pereira de Moura (MDP), Joaquim Magalhães Mota (PPD)
Foreign Affairs: Major Melo Antunes
Economic Planning and Coordination: Mário Murteira (MDP)
Interior: Major António Metelo
Defence: Captain Silvano Ribeiro
Labour: Major Costa Martins
Education: Major José da Silva
Social Communications: Captain Jorge Jesuino
Finance: José Joaquim Fragoso (MDP)
Agriculture: Fernando Baptista

Appendix V 261

Foreign Commerce: José da Silva Lopes
Social Affairs: Jorge Carvalho Sá Borges (PPD)
Justice: Salgado Zenha (PS)
Social Infrastructure and Environment: Colonel José Augusto
  Fernandes
Transport and Communications: Alvaro Veiga de Oliveira (PCP)
Interterritorial Coordination: Almeida Santos

Fifth Provisional Government (8 August 1975)

Prime Minister: General Vasco Gonçalves, replaced on 29 August by
  Admiral Pinheiro de Azevedo
Vice-Prime Ministers: Lieutenant Colonel Arnão Metelo and
  Teixeira Ribeiro
Defence: Captain Silvano Ribeiro
Internal Administration: Major Cândido de Moura
Justice: Rocha e Cunha
Planning and Economic Coordination: Mário Murteira (MDP)
Finance: José Joaquim Fragoso (MDP)
Industry and Technology: Captain Quiterio de Brito
Agriculture and Fishing: Oliveira Baptista
External Commerece: Domingo Lopes
Foreign Affairs: Mário Ruivo
Navy: Admiral Pinheiro de Azevedo
Army: General Carlos Fabião
Industry and Environment: Henrique Oliveira e Sá
Education and Scientific Research: Major Emílio da Silva
Internal Commerce: Macaista Malheiros
Labour: Costa Martins
Social Affairs: Pereira de Moura
Social Communication and Culture: Commander Jorge Jesuino
Secretary of State for Decolonization: Jorge Ferro Ribeiro

Sixth Provisional Government (19 September 1975)

Prime Minister: Admiral Pinheiro de Azevedo
Foreign Affairs: Major Melo Antunes
Finances: Francisco Salgado Zenha (PS)
External Commerce: Jorge Campinos (PS)
Internal Commerce: Magalhães Mota (PPD)
Agriculture and Fishing: António Lopes Cardoso (PS)
Transport and Communications: Walter Rosa (PS)
Social Communications: Almeida Santos (close to PS)

262 *Appendix V*

Social Affairs: Jorge Sá Borges (PPD)
Industry: Alvaro Veiga de Oliveira (PC)
Industry and Technology: Marques do Carmo (Independent)
Internal Administration: Major Almeida Costa
Justice: Pinheiro Farinha (Independent)
Education and Scientific Research: Major Vítor Alves

APPENDIX VI NAVAL ACADEMY: PROFESSIONS OF FATHERS OF CADETS, 1975

1st Year

1 Industrial Worker
1 Proprietor
1 Printer
3 Civil Servant
1 Tailor
1 Station Master
1 Steel Worker
1 Teacher
1 Naval Officer
1 Naval Petty Officer
1 Army Officer
1 Salesman
1 Doctor
5 Clerk
1 Road Mender
1 Carpenter

2nd Year

1 Bill Collector
1 Teacher
1 Bank Employee
1 Pharmacist
2 Clerk
1 Bus Driver
1 Petrol Pump Attendant
1 Plumber
1 Farm Worker
1 Mechanic
1 Policeman
1 Customs Official
1 Air Traffic Controller
1 Judicial Clerk
3 Civil Servant
1 Proprietor
1 Industrial Manager

264　*Appendix VI*

3　Naval Officer
2　Army Officer
1　Naval Petty Officer

3rd Year

1　Policeman
1　Customs Official
1　Naval Rating
1　Salesman
1　Railway Worker
1　Worker
4　Civil Servant
1　Blacksmith
1　Watchman
1　Shop Keeper
2　Farm Worker
2　Clerk
2　Air Force Officer
2　Army Officer
1　Petty Officer
1　Army NCO
1　Air Force NCO
1　Proprietor
1　Doctor
1　Lycée Professor

4th Year

1　Bus Driver
1　Cabinet Maker
1　Watchman
2　Farmer
1　Chief Electrician
1　Bank Employee
1　Farm Worker
6　Civil Servant
4　Clerk
1　Marine Mechanic
1　Assurance Salesman
1　Policeman
2　Customs Official
3　Army Officer

Appendix VI

1 Air Force Officer
1 Naval Engineer
4 Salesman
2 Civil Engineer
1 Veterinary Surgeon
1 No Information

BIBLIOGRAPHY

Newspapers

Portuguese
A Capital
Boletim das Forças Armadas
Diário de Notícias
Expresso
Jornal Novo
O Século
República
Revista do Povo

French
Le Monde

English
Financial Times
The Times
Guardian

Journals
Revista Militar

Articles

Allemann, F.R., 'Withered Carnations', *Encounter,* December 1975.
Anderson, Perry, 'Portugal and the End of Ultra-Colonialism', *The New Left Review,* Nos.15, 16 & 17, London, 1962.
Blackburn, Robin, 'The Test in Portugal', *The New Left Review,* London, 1974.
de Figueiredo, António, 'The Portuguese Dilemma', *World Today,* February 1975.
Joxe, Alain, 'Le Mouvement des Forces Armées Portugaises', *Revue de politique étrangère,* Paris, June 1975.
Martins, Hermínio, 'Opposition in Portugal', *Government and Opposition,* Spring 1969.
Maxwell, Kenneth, 'The Hidden Revolution in Portugal', *The New York Review of Books,* April 17, 1975.

Bibliography

——, 'Portugal Under Pressure', *The New York Review of Books*, 29 May 1975.

——, 'The Thorns of the Portuguese Revolution', *Foreign Affairs*, January 1976.

Schmitter, Philippe, 'Liberation by Golpe', *Armed Forces and Society*, vol.2, No.1, February 1975.

——, 'Corporativism and Public Policy in Authoritarian Portugal', Sage Publications, London 1975.

Shercliff, Joseph, 'Portugal's Strategic Territories', *Foreign Affairs*, 1953.

Wheeler, Douglas, 'The Portuguese Army in Angola', *Journal of Modern African Studies*, October 1969.

——, 'The Portuguese Revolution of 1910', *Journal of Modern History*, June 1972.

——, 'Situation Obscure – The 28th of May Movement and the Fall of the Parliamentary Republic', Workshop on Modern Portugal, University of New Hampshire, October 1973.

Armed Forces Lists

Lista da Armada
Lista do Exército
Lista do Pessoal da Força Aérea

Books

Abshire, D.M. and Samuels, M.A., *Portuguese Africa: A Handbook*, London, 1969.

Alves, Marcio, *Les Soldats socialistes du Portugal*, Paris, 1975.

Ambler, John S., *The French Army in Politics*, Ohio State University Press, 1966.

Andrade, Mário and Ollivier, Marc, *A Guerra em Angola*, Lisbon, 1974.

Audibert, Pierre and Brignon, Daniel, *Portugal, les nouveaux centurions*, Paris, 1974.

Axelson, Eric, *Portugal and the Scramble for Africa*, Johannesburg, 1967.

Banazol, Luís Ataíde, *A Origem do Movimento das Forças Armadas*, Lisbon, 1974.

Bandeira, A.R., 'Military Intervention in Portuguese Politics', Unpublished paper, York University, Toronto, August 1975.

Baptista, Jacinto, *Caminhos para uma Revoluçao*, Lisbon, 1975.

Birmingham, David, *The Portuguese Conquest of Angola*, London, 1965.

Boxer, C.R., *The Portuguese Sea-borne Empire*, London, 1969.

268   *Bibliography*

Bruce, Niel, *Portugal, The Last Empire*, London, 1975.

Burchett, Wilfred, *Portugal depois da Revolução dos Capitães*, Lisbon, 1975.

Cabral, Amílcar, *Revolution in Guinea*, London, 1972; see also Cabral's other works.

Caetano, Marcelo, *O Depoimento*, Rio de Janeiro, 1974.

Calafate, Luís, *A Liberdade tem um Preço*, Lisbon, 1975.

Campinos, Jorge, *A Ditatura Militar, 1926-1933*, Lisbon, 1975.

Carvalhas, Carme, *48 Anos de Fascismo em Portugal*, Lisbon, 1974.

Carvalho, Otelo Saraiva de, *Cinco Meses Mudaram Portugal*, Lisbon, 1975.

Chilcote, Ronald H., *Emerging Nationalism in Portuguese Africa*, Stanford, 1969.

——, *Protest and Resistance in Angola and Brazil*, University of California, 1973.

Clemente, Duran, *Elementos para a Compreensão do 25 de Novembro*, Lisbon, 1976.

Constituição de República Portuguesa, Lisbon, 1976.

Cunha, Manuel Barão de, *No 23a Hora do MFA*, Lisbon, 1975.

——, *Radiografia Militar*, Lisbon, 1975.

Cunhal, Alvaro, *Discursos Politicos*, 2 vols., Lisbon, 1975.

Cutileiro, Jose, *A Portuguese Rural Society*, London, 1971.

Davidson, Basil, *The Liberation of Guinea*, London, 1969.

——, *In the Eye of the Storm, Angola's People*, New York, 1973.

Delgado, Humberto, *Memoirs*, London, 1964.

Duffy, James, *Portuguese Africa*, London, 1959.

——, *Portugal in Africa*, London, 1962.

Egerton, F.C., *Angola in Perspective*, London, 1973.

Ferreira, Eduardo Sousa, *Portuguese Colonialism from South Africa to Europe*, Freiburg, 1972.

Feio, J., Leitão, F. and Pinha, Carlos, *11 de Março, Autópsia de um Golpe*, Lisbon, 1975.

Ferro, António, *Salazar: Portugal and Her Leader*, London, 1939.

Fields, R.M., *The Portuguese Revolution and the Armed Forces Movement*, New York, 1976.

Figueiredo, António de, *Portugal and Its Empire: The Truth*, London, 1961.

——, *Angola: Views of a Revolt*, London, 1962.

——, *Portugal: Fifty Years of Dictatorship*, London, 1975.

Figueiredo, Martiniano de, *The Portuguese Armed Forces*, Lisbon, 1961.

Frémontier, Jacques, *Portugal: Les points sur les i*, Paris, 1976.

Bibliography 269

Foubert, Charles, *Portugal 1974-75: Les années de l'espoir,* Paris, 1976.

Freyer, Gilberto, *The Portuguese in the Tropics,* Lisbon, 1961.

Fryer, P. and Pinheiro, P., *Our Oldest Ally,* London, 1961.

Galvão, Henrique, *The Santa Maria – My Crusade for Portugal,* London, 1961.

Gil, L.P., *Novembro 25, Anatomia de um Golpe,* Lisbon, 1976.

Gomes, António Ferreira, *Paz em Portugal pela Reconciliação entre os Portugueses,* Porto, 1975.

Gonçalves, Orlando, *Ultimos Dias do Fascismo,* Lisbon, 1974.

Gonçalves, Vasco, *Discursos,* Lisbon, 1976.

Graham, L.S., *Portugal: Decline and Collapse of an Authoritarian Order,* London, 1975.

Harsgor, M., *Naissance d'un nouveau Portugal,* Paris, 1975.

Humbaraci, Arslan and Muchnik, N., *Portugal's African Wars,* London, 1974.

Insight, *The Year of the Captains,* London, 1975.

Kay, Hugh, *Salazar and Modern Portugal,* London, 1970.

Kuntz, J., *Les Fusils et les urnes,* Paris, 1975.

Livermore, H.V. (ed.), *Portugal and Brazil: An Introduction,* London, 1953.

Lourenço, Eduardo, *Os Militares e o Poder,* Lisbon, 1975.

Lourenço, Vasco, *MFA, Rosto do Povo,* Lisbon, 1975.

——, *No Regresso Vinham Todos,* Lisbon, 1974.

Machel, Samora, *Estabelecer o Poder Popular para Servir às Massas,* Lisbon, 1974.

Marcum, John, *The Angolan Revolution, Vol 1: The Anatomy of an Explosion,* Boston, 1969.

Marques, A.H. Oliveira, *History of Portugal,* 2 vols., New York, 1972.

Martins, Hermínio, *Portugal, Offprint from European Fascism,* London, 1968.

Melo, Galvão de, *M.F.A., Movimento Revolucionário,* Lisbon, 1975.

——, *Entrevistas,* Lisbon, 1976.

Mercadante, Paulo, *Portugal Ano Zero,* Rio de Janeiro, 1975.

Minter, William, *Portuguese Africa and the West,* London, 1972.

Mondlane, Eduardo, *The Struggle for Mozambique,* London, 1969.

Mota, Gomes, *A Resistência,* Lisbon, 1976.

MPLA Steering Committee, *Imperialist Powers are Supporting Portuguese Colonial Repression,* Brazzaville, 1965.

Naville, P., *Pouvoir militaire et socialisme au Portugal,* Paris, 1975.

Newitt, M.D.D., *Portuguese Settlement on the Zambesi,* New York, 1973.

270 Bibliography

Nogueira, A.F., *The Third World*, London, 1967.

Oliveria, César de, *O Operariado e a República Democrática*, Lisbon, 1974.

——, *M.F.A. e a Revolução Socialista*, Lisbon, 1975.

——, *A Crise da Revolução*, Lisbon, 1976.

Partido Comunista Português, *28 de Setembro, a Conspiração da Maioria Silenciosa*, Lisbon, 1975.

Poulantzas, Nicos, *La Crise des dictatures*, Paris, 1975.

Praça, Afonso, *25 de Abril*, Lisbon, 1974.

O Programa do MFA e dos Partidos Políticos, Lisbon, 1975.

Rama, Manuela de S. and Plantier, Carlos, *Melo Antunes*, Lisbon, 1976.

Rodrigues, A., Borga, C. and Cardoso, M., *O Movimento dos Capitães e o 25 de Abril*, Lisbon, 1974.

——, *Portugal depois de Abril*, Lisbon, 1976.

Rodrigues, Jose Honorio, *Brazil and Africa*, London, 1965.

Rosa, Eugénio, *Problemas Actuais da Economia Portuguesa*, Lisbon, 1974.

Ruas, H.B., *A Revoluçõ das Flores*, Lisbon, 1974.

Salazar, António de Oliveira, *Doctrine and Action: Internal and Foreign Policy of the New Portugal, 1928-1939*, London, 1939.

——, *Discursos*, 6 vols., Coimbra, 1944-67.

Sideri, S., *Trade and Power: Informal Colonialism in Anglo-Portuguese Relations*, Rotterdam, 1970.

Soares, Mário, *Portugal's Struggle for Liberty*, London, 1975.

——, *Democratização e Descolonização, Dez Meses no Governo Provisório*, Lisbon, 1975.

——, *Portugal: quelle révolution?* Paris, 1976.

Spínola, António de, *Portugal and the Future*, Johannesburg, 1974.

Os SUV em Luta, Lisbon, 1976.

Sykes, John, *Portugal and Africa, The People and the War*, London, 1971.

Trindade, Maria, *Immigrés Portugais*, Lisbon, 1973.

Valahu, Mugur, *Angola, clef de l'Afrique*, Paris, 1966.

Valles, Edgar, *Africa, Colonialismo e Socialismo*, Lisbon, 1974.

Vintras, R.E., *The Portuguese Connection*, London, 1974.

Wheeler, D.L. and Pelisser, R., *Angola*, London, 1971.

Woolf, S.J. (ed.), *European Fascism*, London, 1968.

INDEX

Alentejo 16, 38, 124, 136, 182
Almeida, Major Dinís de 77, 82, 160,
   165, 216, 228-30
Alves, Vítor 62, 71, 73, 77, 80, 81,
   94, 100, 104, 138, 162, 167,
   202-3, 207, 210-11, 223
Angola 10, 11, 12, 15, 16, 24, 33,
   41, 47, 53, 57, 76, 143, 161-2,
   215, 217-18, 223, 228;
   decolonisation 115-21
Antunes, Melo 71, 77, 86, 100, 104,
   117, 135-6, 139, 162, 164, 167,
   172, 177, 192, 200, 202-3, 207,
   210-11, 213, 215, 223-4, 230-1,
   235
Arriaga, Kaúlza de, General
   29, 38, 42, 62, 81-2, 142
Assimilado 15-16
Azevedo, Pinheiro de, Admiral
   22, 100, 104, 142, 146, 148-9,
   201, 211, 213, 215, 218-19,
   223-4, 228

Banazol, Lieutenant Colonel
   71, 73, 80
Berlin conference, 1885 11
Bligh, Captain 155

Cabral, Amílcar 34, 53-8
Caetano 9, 10, 13, 23, 29, 30, 31,
   32, 33, 36, 38, 39, 40, 43, 47,
   63, 68, 78, 81-3, 91-4, 96,
   99, 105, 111, 113, 125, 146-7,
   166, 180, 219, 234; Guinea
   53-9
Caldas de Rainha 37, 87, 89
Cardigan, Earl of 144, 156
Cardosa, General Silva 119
Carlos, Palma 98-9, 103-5, 115-16
Carmona, General Oscar 20, 24
Carvalho, Otelo de 26, 73, 74, 77,
   81, 84, 87, 89, 100, 105-7,
   113, 125-6, 137, 140, 143, 162-4,
   169, 172-3, 176-8, 181, 194-8,
   201-2, 206-7, 210, 216, 223-4,
   227, 230, 237; Guinea 55-6
Centre Democratic Party (CDS)
   98, 140, 175, 181-3, 185, 188, 195,
   207, 223

Charais, General Franco 71, 164, 201,
   207, 213, 217-18, 236
Church 186, 199-200, 234
Clemente, Captain Duran 55, 228
Combatants Congress (June 1973)
   68
commandos 105, 143, 205-7,
   212, 215, 228-9
Communist Party (PCP) 22, 25,
   95, 102, 128, 130-2, 133-5
   137, 146, 154, 166, 171-2,
   176, 181-5, 191-4, 197, 199,
   207, 210, 215, 219, 224, 228,
   230
Contreiras, Carlos 149, 191, 193,
   213, 225, 228, 230
Coordinating Committee 81, 84,
   90, 92, 94-5, 102, 104-9, 111,
   117-18, 131, 138-40, 167;
   28 September 1974 124-8
COPCON 104-7, 125-7, 162-3,
   165, 169-70, 184-5, 194-7,
   203-7, 209-10, 215-16, 224,
   227-9
Correia, General Pezarat 71,
   118, 202, 207, 213
Correia, Ramiro 149, 151, 174-5,
   185, 191, 193
Corvacho, General Eurico 201,
   204, 210, 213
council of state 93, 95, 101-1,
   103
Coutinho, Admiral Rosa 71, 100,
   104, 142, 148-9, 164, 171-2,
   176, 192, 213, 230; Governor
   General of Angola 116-19
Crespo, Vítor 71, 109, 115, 149,
   162, 167, 202-3, 207, 223
cultural dynamization 172-7, 183-9
Cunha, Silva 41, 79
Cunhal, Alvaro 96-7, 99, 102,
   112, 118, 130-2, 134, 154, 170,
   179, 182-4, 192, 223-4,
   Custer, General George 36

Decolonization 9, 13, 16, 29,
   109-21, 127; Goa 35-7
Delgado, General Humberto
   23, 24, 105, 132, 166, 185

271

272   *Index*

'Dictatorship Craze' 42-5
desertion 32, 34, 35
'Document of the Nine' 207-9,
211

Eanes, Ramalho 75, 202, 210,
230-1, 236

Fabião, Carlos 56, 75, 81-2, 114,
137, 139, 142, 162-3, 172,
174, 201, 203, 210-13, 215,
217-18, 223, 230, 237;
revolutionary discipline 155-8
Fifth Division 105, 108, 127,
140, 154, 159, 163, 168-9,
185-6, 191, 193, 212, 219,
230; internal dynamization
157; cultural dynamization
173
Flechas 53
FNLA 17, 37, 112, 115-16
Frederick the Great 155
FRELIMO 15, 53, 55, 112, 115,
120, 177

Gable, Clark 156
Goa 10, 15, 30, 35-7
Gomes, Costa General 37-8,
44, 78, 81, 84-8, 100,
106, 109, 125, 127, 162-3,
198, 200, 201, 203, 211-12,
217-20, 224, 228
Gomes, Valera 35, 36, 38,
108, 193, 227, 229
Gonçalves, Vasco 25, 45, 104,
125-6, 135, 141, 145, 154,
166-7, 171, 176, 184, Chapter 7,
223, 225, 234
Guerreiro, Captain Martins 149, 213,
230
*Guide Document of the People –
MFA Alliance* 197-8, 200
Guinea 11, 12, 15, 16, 29,
33, 37, 53-9, 62, 67, 68, 76-7,
80, 84, 94, 105, 162, 173-4,
187, 233; decolonization 112-14

High Command 42-4, 82-3, 107;
purge 142-3

Institute of Higher Military Studies
41, 65, 81
Institute of Military Sociology 175,
184, 212
Intersindical 97; unicidade 134-5

Itegralismo Lusitano 19, 21-2

Jesuino, Jorge 71, 118, 141, 149,
170, 172, 184, 191, 193
Judas, Miguel 77, 149, 151, 223
Junta of National Salvation
93, 100-1, 114, 118, 126-7

Laughton, Charles 156
Lourenço, Vasco 75, 77, 81-2,
164, Chapter 7, 236;
25 November 1975 223-7
LUAR 164

Machel, Samora 113, 115, 177
Marques, Brigadier Jaime Silverio
105-6, 126, 142
Marques, General Silvino Silverio
116, 118
Martins, Captain Costa 134-5,
141-2, 148, 171, 191, 193,
213, 213, 230
Matos, Norton de 11, 24, 29
MDP/CDE 98-9, 134, 171-2,
182, 185, 193, 199, 207,
210
Melo, General Galvão de 100-1,
126-8
MFA 31, 32, 37, 55-6, 62, 67, 71,
73; and elections 181-4; and
the provisional government
Chapter 4; links with communists
137; institutionalization 137-41,
167-9; as a movement of national
liberation 177-9; organization
77-87; 25 November 1975 230-2;
28 September 1974 124-8
Miguel, Lieutenant Colonel Firmino
71-2, 104, 141, 191, 227
miliciano 31, 32, 63-5, 87, 168, 180,
187-8, 205, 223, 228
Military Academy 22, 31, 34,
65-9, 71-4, 77, 86, 99, 146-8,
156, 185, 188, 211
Military Intervention Group (AMI)
215
Military Police 161, 163, 194, 197,
219, 228, 230
Moniz, General Júlio 24, 25, 37-8,
44
Mozambique 11, 12, 15, 16, 29,
33, 40, 47, 53, 57, 76, 111-13,
115, 162, 167, 170
MPLA 44, 55, 71, 115-19
MRPP 134, 160, 162, 170-1

Index

273

Nationalizations 135-7
NATO 37, 64, 146-7, 160, 198
Naval Academy 22, 35, 69-70,
71-4, 77, 145-8
NCOs 18, 23, 63, 69, 74, 109,
149-51, 168, 225-6, 228, 235
Neves, Colonel Jaime 105, 143,
205-7, 212, 219, 228

'Operation Stop' 125

PAIGC 53-8, 105, 112-15
paratroops 165; 25 November 1975
223-9
pay 45-7, 71, 79, 106
People's Congress 54, 116
PIDE/DGS 22, 23, 25, 58, 76, 78,
82, 84, 87, 91, 93, 95, 169-70
Plan of Political Action (PAP)
196
Popular Democratic Party (PPD)
97-8, 134, 139, 164, 171-2,
175-6, 179, 181-4, 185, 188,
195, 198, 207, 223
Portuguese Legion 22, 23
promotion 107, 147-8
psychological action 53-6, 105

Rádio Renascença 96, 197, 200,
218, 225-6; ports 195, 217
RALIS 106, 160, 165, 194, 199, 216,
225, 227-8
Rebelo Decrees 59, 65-7, 73, 79
República 98, 194-8
Republican National Guard 22,
87, 89, 90-1, 105, 126, 165, 168,
219, 223
Retornados 121, 216
Revolutionary Council 71, 73, 104,
134, 138, 140, 145, 148, 151,
158, 167-8, 171, 176, 178, 181,
184, 196, 198, 200, 202-4, 207,
211-13, 218, 223-8, 230-1, 236
Revolutionary Party of the Proletariat
(PRP) 194
Roberto, Holden 17, 37, 116-17

Salazar 9, 10, 12, 15, 20, 21, 22,
23, 24, 30, 35, 36, 37, 38, 39,
43, 61, 68, 81, 97, 107, 146,
169
Santa Maria 25, 37
Santos, Major Hugo dos
72, 108-9, 129
Savimbi, Jonas 115, 117
Serra, Manuel 132-4
Soares, Mário 22, 31, 63, 75, 77,
94, 96-9, 102-3, 128-9, 131-5,
137, 154, 166, 169, 171-2,
176, 178-9, 183-4, 186, 191,
209, 214, 219, 222-4, 229-30,
232, 234, 237; decolonization
111-21
Socialist Party (PS) 97, 128, 130,
132-3, 172, 176, 179, 182-4,
191, 195, 197-8, 219, 223-4
Soldados Unidos Vencerão (SUV)
214-17, 219, 222-3, 226-7,
235
Spínola, General António de
29, 37, 40, 42, 44, 68, 78, 81,
142, 154, 162, 174, 176-7,
187, 233; Guinea command
53-9; *Portugal and the Future*
83-7; provisional President
Chapter 4; decolonization 109-21;
28 September 1974 124-9;
11 March 164-6
staff corps 41-2, 45
Supreme Defence Council 38-9, 43,
53, 78

Tanzania 30
Tocqueville, Alexis de 69-70,
74
Tomás, Admiral 24, 56, 68
96

UNITA 115

Zaire 30, 44, 115-16